MW01028863

Michael Brown is one of the most articulate and trusted voices in the Christian community today, and that's why his new book, *The Silencing of the Lambs*, is so timely and important. Every believer should read this well-researched resource to understand the direction of woke culture and gain the knowledge to engage with it from a biblical perspective. This should be required reading for every serious Christian.

—Phil Cooke, PhD
Author; Media Producer; Cofounder,
Cooke Media Group

This book will take you from canceled to courageous! It is a well-detailed battle plan that explains and footnotes the agenda of cancel culture, gives a strategy to overcome, and emboldens us to never be silent about the good news of salvation through Jesus Christ.

—John L. Cooper
Lead Singer, Skillet; Author, *Awake and Alive to Truth*; Host, *Cooper Stuff Podcast*

The world remains a dangerous place for many followers of Christ for a variety of reasons. In the once Christian-friendly United States, religious liberty is under assault like never before. I encourage everyone to read my friend Dr. Michael Brown's latest book, *The Silencing of the Lambs*, to arm yourself, your family, and your church for what lies ahead.

—Tim Wildmon
President, American Family Association and
American Family Radio

The writing, teaching, and preaching ministry of Dr. Michael Brown has been a powerful and prophetic voice to the American church for forty years. He has consistently challenged and inspired Christians, including me, to embrace the revolutionary message of the gospel and live their faith out in the public square regardless of the cost. Dr. Brown continually reminds us that the greatest force for cultural change today is a passionate and radically obedient church. He always delivers this powerful message with deep biblical scholarship, intellectual integrity, and the clarity of the Old Testament prophets. In his compelling new book, *The Silencing of the Lambs*, Dr. Brown warns us of the dangers of cancel culture in silencing the church with chilling impact and contemporary examples. However, *The Silencing of the Lambs* offers Christians a dynamic way forward in overcoming cancel culture with solid biblical teaching and calling us to a life of absolute surrender to the lordship of Christ. This book has truly come to the church "for such a time as this" (Est. 4:14).

—Rev. Patrick Mahoney
Director, Christian Defense Coalition
Washington, DC

Michael Brown is one of the bravest people I know. He is setting the trumpet to his mouth as a modern-day prophetic voice in identifying the serious dangers we are facing of losing our freedoms as Christians today. The criminalization of Christianity is real. Persecution is already through the door of the nation. Read this book with an open heart, and wake up to the fact that you can be a voice to help stop the loss of our democracy and biblical freedom.

—Cindy Jacobs
Cofounder, Generals International

THE SILENCING ★ OF THE ★ LAMBS

MICHAEL L. BROWN, PhD

Most Charisma Media products are available at special quantity discounts for bulk purchase for sales promotions, premiums, fund-raising, and educational needs. For details, call us at (407) 333-0600 or visit our website at www.charismamedia.com.

The Silencing of the Lambs by Michael L. Brown, PhD
Published by FrontLine, an imprint of Charisma Media
600 Rinehart Road, Lake Mary, Florida 32746

Visit the author's website at https://askdrbrown.org and BooksbyDrBrown.com.

Cataloging-in-Publication Data is on file with the Library of Congress.
International Standard Book Number: 978-1-62999-984-5
E-book ISBN: 978-1-62999-985-2

22 23 24 25 26 — 987654321
Printed in the United States of America

CONTENTS

PREFACE

On March 18, 2019, I published an article titled "The Silencing of the Lambs," which began with these words: "There has always been one end-game for the radical left: the silencing of dissenting voices, in particular conservative Christian voices."[1] For years I had observed this phenomenon, often firsthand, as Christian conservatives were increasingly marginalized and muzzled, raising my voice as loudly and clearly as possible to expose and combat this growing form of censorship.

Recently, however, this silencing phenomenon has grown to new and dangerous levels, resulting in what has now become known as "cancel culture." In fact, a Google search in late September 2021 for the phrase "cancel culture" yielded 8,790,000 results. That is an incredible number, and it is growing by the day.

Wikipedia offers this definition: "Cancel culture…is a modern form of ostracism in which someone is thrust out of social or professional circles—whether it be online, on social media, or in person. Those subject to this ostracism are said to have been 'cancelled.' The expression 'cancel culture' has mostly negative connotations and is used in debates on free speech and censorship."[2]

Simply stated, the subject of the muzzling and silencing of our voices must be addressed but not in a defeated, hopeless way. Instead it must be confronted, and using biblical principles and spiritual weapons, it must be overcome. And that is the purpose of this book, the first half of which documents the depth of this very real cultural battle, and the second half of which lays out effective strategies that can be implemented.

In my 2019 article I wrote, "You might wonder how the radical left wants to silence us. How, exactly, does it want to put us in the closet?"

I answered, "By intimidation. By ridicule. By legal action. By expulsion. By exclusion.

"Anything to avoid civil, respectful debate. Anything to avoid a genuine discussion of differences. Anything to avoid true dialogue.

"Instead, those who differ with the radical left are to be demonized, stigmatized, marginalized, and silenced."[3]

We could add today: canceled.

The good news is that the church cannot be canceled, and in Jesus' name, we will not be silenced. In fact, I believe as you read the pages of this book, as sobering as the opening chapters are, you will be encouraged, inspired, and emboldened. If all of us do our part, be it little or large, the cultural tide will turn. Mark my words.

I can also say that as an author, my initial plan in writing this book was to spend even more time documenting and analyzing the attempts to silence and cancel us, reserving the last couple of chapters to talk about how we could push back. Instead I felt stirred to devote the second half of the book, with more chapters in shorter form, to help equip us to take a stand and raise our voices. I believe it was the Lord who gave me this inspiration, including the idea of a new national holiday, outlined in the last chapter. (To be candid, the idea of advocating for this new holiday seems preposterous in the natural, but I felt prompted to do so. We shall see what fruit it bears.)

So join me in this challenging and glorious journey as we stand together with our brothers and sisters around the world who face far more intense opposition than anything we have faced to date here in America—including brutal imprisonment, torture, and death—as overcomers in the Lord. To say it again, in Jesus' name, we will not be silenced and we will not be canceled!

It is my great joy to express my appreciation to Debbie Marrie, Adrienne Gaines, and the great team at Charisma, from editing to graphic design to marketing and beyond. And I am deeply thankful to the support team at AskDrBrown Ministries, as together we seek to be a voice of moral, cultural, and spiritual revolution. And to the prayer teams and individual intercessors who hold me up on a regular basis, I am deeply indebted to each of you. Finally, to Nancy, my wonderful bride since 1976, your unwavering conviction and your utter refusal to compromise truth continue to be a strength and encouragement to me. May our grandchildren's children, still to be born, grow up in a much freer, more God-honoring America than the one we know today.

One last editorial note: I was tempted to continue to update this manuscript with the latest, relevant, breaking news right until it was ready to go to press, but not only would that weigh down the reader with more illustrations than would be needed, it would also continue to expand the size of the book, taking away from its force and power in the midst of an endless sea of details. That being said, you will find the book to be filled with real-life examples and, in terms of relevance, totally up to date.

May the Lord light a fresh fire in your heart as you read!

PART I

THEY ARE TRYING TO SHUT US UP

Introduction

THERE IS A TARGET ON YOUR BACK

THE WARNING FROM investigative journalist Glenn Greenwald was loud and clear as he spoke of the very real dangers of the rising tide of cancel culture. "Unleash this monster," he tweeted, "and one day it will come for you."[1] He was referring to the firing of Will Wilkinson, a man whom Greenwald called "as mainstream and conventional a thinker as one can find," a writer who "is unfailingly civil and restrained in his rhetoric." Yet for one sarcastic tweet, for which he apologized, Wilkinson had been fired.[2]

To quote Greenwald's tweet in full, "In the prevailing climate, the rational choice is to avoid social scorn and ostracization no matter how baseless the grievances one must appease. Unleash this monster and one day it will come for you. And you'll have no principle to credibly invoke in protest when it does."[3]

Unfortunately, by the time Greenwald posted those words on January 22, 2021, that monster had already been unleashed, and no one was beyond its reach. In fact, almost two years earlier, on April 10, 2019, an almost surreal exchange took place in the halls of Congress, as Senator Ted Cruz grilled the public policy directors for Twitter and Facebook. Was it true, Cruz wanted to know, that a tweet containing *the words of Mother Teresa* constituted hate speech? Yes, Mother Teresa. Talk about the silencing of a lamb!

Addressing the subject of Big Tech's censorship of Christian conservatives, Senator Cruz said:

> It's not just political, it's also ideological....There have been multiple instances of, in particular pro-life groups, being disfavored. For example, here is a tweet that says that "abortion is profoundly anti-women" and it's a quote from Mother Teresa and this tweet was blocked. Now it's fairly remarkable that Mother Teresa is now deemed

> hate speech. Do either of you agree with the proposition that Mother Teresa is issuing hate speech?[4]

The response from Twitter's Carlos Monje Jr. was twelve seconds of silence followed by two evasive answers.

Mother Teresa's words blocked on Twitter? Seriously?

But this kind of discriminatory treatment was nothing new. Already in 2017 it was documented that "for years, Twitter has blocked the accounts of Live Action and Lila Rose [both staunchly pro-life] from purchasing ads to reach the public. Blocked ads include information on Planned Parenthood's lack of health services for women, a map directing women to comprehensive health care clinics around the nation, and a quote by Thomas Jefferson."[5]

The reality is that if you are a conservative living in America today, there is a target on your back. If you are a Christian conservative, that target is even bigger. If you are a Christian conservative who refuses to bow down to the spirit of the age, the spirit of political correctness, that target is so big that you are a marked man or woman. A person like that—like you!—must be silenced. In the words of Jennifer Roback Morse of the Ruth Institute, a conservative Christian, pro-family organization, "Cancel culture has us in the crosshairs."[6]

The mob has spoken. The cultural elites have decided. You are on the wrong side of history. You are a hater and a bigot. You are disqualified, and your views must be deleted. As Pastor Erwin Lutzer wrote, "We who are Christians have been told to stay in our corner, to pay homage to the left's revolution, and, at best, keep our mouths shut."[7]

Writing from Australia, but with a larger focus on cancel culture, researcher and cultural commentator Bill Muehlenberg asked:

> "Are you now or have you ever been a conservative or a Christian?" This is the stuff of the new witch hunt the Left is now fully engaged in....there is a full-scale purge underway by the radical secular left.
>
> They are on a search and destroy mission. Any and all recalcitrant Christians who dare to believe the Bible, who dare to stand up for God's plans for human sexuality, and who dare to offer help and prayer to others WILL be rounded up and dealt with by the Christophobic State.
>
> There will be no exceptions or exemptions. All these evil Christians MUST be properly dealt with. And that includes being banned from every form of public life in which they might have some influence. That includes anyone attempting to get into politics.[8]

This is not an overstatement, and it is not just Christian leaders who are making these observations. In August 2020, "a diverse working group of prominent thinkers, scholars, and practitioners" produced what they called the Philadelphia Statement.[9] The statement begins with this:

> Social Media mobs. Cancel culture. Campus speech policing. These are all part of life in today's America. Freedom of expression is in crisis. Truly open discourse—the debates, exchange of ideas, and arguments on which the health and flourishing of a democratic republic crucially depend—is increasingly rare. Ideologues demonize opponents to block debates on important issues and to silence people with whom they disagree.
>
> We must ask ourselves: Is this the country we want? Surely not. We want—and to be true to ourselves we *need*—to be a nation in which we and our fellow citizens of many different faiths, philosophies, and persuasions can speak their minds and honor their deepest convictions without fear of punishment and retaliation.
>
> If we seek a brighter future, we must relearn a fundamental truth: Our liberty and our happiness depend upon the maintenance of a public culture in which freedom and civility coexist—where people can disagree robustly, even fiercely, yet treat each other as human beings—and, indeed, as fellow citizens—not mortal enemies. "Liberty is meaningless where the right to utter one's thoughts and opinions has ceased to exist," Frederick Douglass declared in 1860. Indeed, our liberal democracy is rooted in and dependent upon the shared understanding that all people have inherent dignity and worth, and that they must be treated accordingly.[10]

In contrast with the philosophy that Douglass expressed, we are told today, "Oh yes, you have freedom to speak, but there are consequences to your words." Put another way, "Feel free to speak, but if you dare to speak something we deem unacceptable, you will dearly regret it." There is a price to pay for crossing the mob.

Already, in 2012, Jake Jacobs wrote this in his book *Mobocracy*:

> Wake up America, before it is too late! The mobocrats mean business. Study the mob, listen to their words and watch their ways and understand their demands to change and transform our Republic under God. Our Founders warned us that if we were to keep our Republic we would always have to remain diligent to the cause of freedom and vigilantly aware of those who would under the guise of freedom destroy life and liberty.[11]

Today, 2012 looks almost innocent. The mob was much quieter, much less threatening, much less intimidating than it is today. In fact the mob of today reminds me of the blob of movie fame. (The classic, first edition of *The Blob* came out in 1958, the remake in 1988.) The more you feed it, the bigger it gets, soon swallowing up everything in its path. And with the massive power of the internet giants today, if you challenge the system too much, you will be silenced, canceled, and swallowed up by the mob (or should I say "blob"?).

Writing on the National Association of Scholars website, David Acevedo explained how far reaching this mob rule has become:

> According to *Dictionary.com*, cancel culture "refers to the popular practice of withdrawing support for (*canceling*) public figures and companies after they have done or said something considered objectionable or offensive. *Cancel culture* is generally discussed as being performed on social media in the form of group shaming." This new form of mob rule has dominated virtually every sector of American life for the last several years: politics, journalism, music & entertainment, sports, business, and of particular interest to the National Association of Scholars, higher education.[12]

Indeed, he noted, "Those who espouse ideas considered uncontroversial even a few years ago are anathematized."[13] In fact, things have gotten to the point that within a few days' time—and as I was writing some of these very pages—Amazon removed an important, fairly written, well-researched volume on transgender identity (*When Harry Became Sally*, by Ryan Anderson, PhD),[14] a documentary on the life and legacy of Justice Clarence Thomas,[15] and six books by Dr. Seuss.[16] Yes, Dr. Seuss. Consider Anderson and Thomas and Seuss canceled![17]

Several weeks after writing this, on June 2, 2021, I received an email from Tim Wildmon of the American Family Association (AFA). He wanted all of us to know that Amazon Prime refused to carry the important, well-researched, compassionately presented documentary *In His Image: Delighting in God's Plan for Gender and Sexuality*. I know this documentary well, since I hosted it for AFA, and I can attest to what a fine production it is. As Wildmon wrote, "I am disgusted at the hypocrisy and callousness. Amazon Prime offers every kind of degrading material imaginable—including hard-core pornography and an entire LGBTQ movie collection—but refuses a fair-minded film that is well-researched, has world-class production values, and whose touchstones are truth and compassion for hurting people."[18] And Amazon allowed no appeal for the matter. Case closed! Then, on August 11,

2021, the Daily Wire reported that "the American Booksellers Association (ABA) released an update last week detailing new 'oversight' to prevent accidentally promoting conservative authors." This happened after (perish the thought!) the ABA inadvertently promoted a book by the best-selling, conservative African American author Candace Owens. They were putting measures in place to be sure this never happened again, including creating "a new Diversity, Equity, Inclusion, and Access Membership Manager position that is responsible for outreach to and support of marginalized members, as well as West Coast members in general.…This position will support BIPOC, LGBTQIA+, Two-Spirit, and Disabled members; conduct outreach to ABA members and non-ABA members of those communities…" And of course, the ABA will be aggressively "antiracist."[19]

The Hour Is Later Than We Know

Writing against the backdrop of Australia in 2021, but with clear application to America and other Western nations, Kristian Jenkins painted this vivid picture:

> Imagine a society where people, from high to low, are fired from their jobs for entering into the "wrong side" of a cultural debate, where academics are routinely sacked or sanctioned for expressing incorrect views on climate or sexuality or politics, where celebrities are stripped of accolades and authors are disinvited from award ceremonies for harbouring opinions that fail to accord with the prevailing view.
>
> Imagine a society where students inform on their professors for transgressing speech codes, where priests are brought before tribunals for teaching the [tenets] of their faith, where multiple institutions from the police to the media to the courts collude to imprison an innocent man because he holds to a purer ethic they deem dangerous and obsolete.[20]

Yet, he continued, this is not something that we have to imagine. It's happening in front of our eyes. Indeed, he wrote:

> This isn't a passage from a mid-century dystopian novel. It's not an account of conditions suffered under totalitarian regimes in the Soviet Union, China or North Korea. No…this is contemporary Australia. All the events described have occurred in Australia in recent years, yet this is but a spattering. To list all the things in this category that have occurred around the former liberal, Western, democratic nations would doubtless require volumes.[21]

Ironically, it is those who claim to be progressive and enlightened, those who call themselves tolerant, who are often leading the way in silencing all opposition. Sometimes the irony is exquisite, as in 2017, when students at University of California Berkeley—home of the Free Speech Movement in the 1960s—sought to ban Ben Shapiro from speaking on campus. So much for free speech!

Writing for the *Washington Post* on July 20, 2017, Susan Svrluga noted that "the University of California at Berkeley is again blocking a conservative speaker from coming to the flagship public campus, an advocacy group claimed, threatening the constitutional rights of students." Earlier in the year, when the intentionally provocative ex-gay conservative Milo Yiannopoulos was scheduled to speak at the school, the university police locked down the campus, canceling the event "after 150 or so 'black bloc' anarchists in masks streamed into a large crowd of peaceful student protesters, breaking windows, setting a propane tank ablaze and attacking police with rocks and firecrackers."[22] This got the attention of President Trump who tweeted, "If U.C. Berkeley does not allow free speech and practices violence on innocent people with a different point of view—NO FEDERAL FUNDS?"[23]

A few months prior, Thomas Fuller, writing for the *New York Times* on April 19, 2017, noted that Berkeley had "canceled a scheduled speech by the conservative author Ann Coulter, in the latest blow to the institution's legacy and reputation as a promoter and bastion of free speech."[24] When Coulter was invited back to Berkeley in November 2019, she did manage to speak, but the scene was quite revealing:

> More than a thousand young protesters linked arms and tried to physically block people from entering a speech by the far-right pundit Ann Coulter at the University of California, Berkeley campus on Wednesday night.
>
> Rows of students chanted "Go home Nazis!", "Shame!" and "You're not getting in", while behind them, hundreds of law enforcement officers, many in riot gear, guarded the building where Coulter was slated to speak.[25]

This was the new voice of "tolerance," expressed so ferociously at Berkeley, the seat of the Free Speech Movement. And if this was the reaction to a fearless, outside speaker like Ann Coulter, with police protection in place, what were things like for the average conservative professor on campus, let alone the average conservative student, especially if a Christian conservative?

We'll look at our university campuses in much more depth in chapter 2, but for the moment, consider this. In 2020 a Harvard University law professor actually called for homeschooling to be banned. As noted by Campus Reform:

> In a Harvard Gazette interview entitled "A warning on homeschooling," [Professor Elizabeth] Bartholet attributed rising interest in homeschooling to the "growth in the conservative evangelical movement," stating that "conservative Christians" use the practice to "escape from the secular education in public schools," after a failed effort "to have their children exempted from exposure to alternative values in schools."[26]

So, it wasn't so much homeschooling in itself that was problematic. It was Christian conservatives using homeschooling to indoctrinate their children while shielding them from the worldview of secular educators. How dare they do such a thing to their own flesh and blood? Who gave them the right to decide how to raise and educate their children? The hubris!

Now, picture yourself as an eighteen-year-old, homeschooled Christian starting your first day of classes at Harvard, quickly getting bombarded with an anti-God, anti-Christ, anti-conservative worldview, even in classes on art or math. Can you imagine the intimidation? This is nothing less than the silencing of the lambs.

As for what happens to our kids at state-run schools, they too are bombarded with ideologies that they have no idea how to resist (or even the understanding that they should resist). To give just one example out of many, Christopher F. Rufo reported on January 13, 2021, "A Cupertino elementary school forces third-graders to deconstruct their racial and sexual identities, then rank themselves according to their 'power and privilege.'"[27] Can you imagine trying to push back against this at the age of eight? And good luck being a parent who tries to take on Big Ed. (We'll revisit the question of the assault on our children in chapter 6.)

It All Exploded After the Storming of the Capitol on January 6, 2021

On January 4, 2021, two days before the storming of the Capitol, Christian thinker Tom Gilson wrote this:

> Vladimir Lenin and Josef Stalin would be so envious. Totalitarian government could be so much easier to pull off today than it was back in their days in Russia. These days it wouldn't take much; nearly all the pieces are in place here now. They had to do it the hard way: guns and gulags, KGB and secret police; black police vans carting pastors and dissidents off at midnight, to disappear where guards and fences and dogs would keep them in line and out of sight.
>
> It was all so very complicated, making dissenters disappear that way. Tyrants today need only send them to Twitter jail. Or shadowban them. Or even let algorithms do the dirty work, so they can claim a clean and respectable distance from it all. And that's only the beginning of all they can do, easily, cleanly, with a mere nod of the head and a click of the mouse.[28]

I, too, had been deeply concerned over the growing control of the Left and the attempts to silence those on the Right, tracking this important subject for more than fifteen years. And I had already completed several chapters in this book before the shocking events of January 6, 2021. Those events traumatized the nation and shocked the world. They also caused me to rewrite major portions of this book. That's how dramatically things took a dangerous turn for the worse.

That's because the horrific, inexcusable events of that day also gave those on the Left the opportunity they had been waiting for: they now claimed greater justification for silencing those on the Right, including the president himself. Yes, Twitter and other social media platforms actually banned the most powerful man on the planet, Donald Trump, the president of the United States. And they banned him for life. (We'll revisit that important topic in chapter 3.)

But that was just the tip of the iceberg. Now anyone who voted for Trump (which includes me, along with many of you reading this book) is considered part of the storming of the Capitol. In fact, if you are merely a Christian conservative (especially if you are white), you are guilty by default. You, too, are a white supremacist, a violent nationalist, a dangerous insurrectionist. You must be silenced! Your ideas are toxic and, if allowed to spread, will lead to an even greater attack on our government. That's what the Left is alleging.

A January 13, 2021, headline to an article by Prof. Victor Davis Hanson summed things up well: "The Capitol Incursion Offered the Perfect Crisis the Left Needed to Cancel Conservatives." He recounted how, after the 2020 election, Kathy Griffin had retweeted her own picture of herself holding up what "looked like the bloody head of a decapitated Donald Trump." Prior to that, Ayatollah Ali Khamenei, the supreme leader of Iran, "tweeted out a call to his followers to destroy Israel." Yet both tweets passed Twitter's censorship rules and were not removed or blocked while Facebook banned Trump indefinitely and Twitter banned him for life "due to the risk of further incitement of violence."[29]

But that was just the beginning. With devastating clarity Hanson pointed out the extreme double standards of the social media giants and even the publishing industry, noting how Sen. Josh Hawley's book on the tyranny of Big Tech was canceled after Hawley argued for an investigation into alleged voter fraud (which allegedly helped fuel the fires of the attack on the Capitol). Yet a book written in defense of looting (that was the actual title: *In Defense of Looting*!) was published during the height of the BLM-Antifa riots (which included both violence and an abundance of looting). What hypocrisy.

Hanson then asked why Raz Simone, an AK-47-toting rapper, wasn't banned from social media. He was the one who "took over a swath of downtown Seattle in June and declared it an autonomous zone," reigning over his district with the help of his armed guards, during which time there were at least four shootings and two deaths. Yet Simone "was neither prosecuted nor deplatformed from social media," apparently offering no "risk of further incitement of violence," despite the fact that "the lyrics of his song 'Shoot at Everyone' are full of allusions to violence, racial slurs and stereotypes. The song is posted on YouTube, and Simone still enjoys a large social media presence." Why then, Hanson wondered, "did Big Tech, the media, the publishing industry, a host of corporations and a growing number of campuses double down on censoring some free speech? Why now blacklist, censor and cancel thousands of people?"[30]

He answered: "With an unpopular Trump on the way out, and with control over the levers of government, members of the left abruptly settled all their old scores. Their aim was not just to humiliate opponents but to curtail opponents' ability to organize against them."[31] And what is the end result? Speaking of the "new electronic octopus," Hanson said that "its tentacles are strangling the thoughts and speech of an increasingly unfree America."[32]

As you will see in the chapters that follow, this is not an exaggeration at all, and words like *strangling* or *silencing* or *canceling* or *suffocating* will occur again and again. They aptly describe what we have been facing for some years now—all the more so today—as the attempt to silence us has been growing exponentially. The questions are, How will we respond?

What can we do to regain our voice? And how can we turn this rapidly closing door into the biggest platform we have ever known?

We'll answer those questions in the second half of the book. But first we must understand the urgency of the hour. If we don't stand our ground today, we will likely be silenced—or even canceled—tomorrow.

How bad are things right now? Just turn the page.

Chapter 1

CANCELED!

WE'RE USED TO seeing TV series canceled: when they're not popular enough, they go off the air and no new episodes are produced. Or subscriptions can be canceled. You no longer want to receive a particular magazine, so you notify the company: "I'm canceling my subscription." From then on, no more copies of that magazine are sent your way.

Today, it is people who are canceled—not just rejected or ignored or even belittled but canceled. "We will hear from you no more!" Today, it is not just dissenting views that are dismissed. It is the dissenters themselves who are dismissed, as in eliminated, snuffed out, and removed.

These dissenters may not be eliminated physically, but they are eliminated ideologically. Their influence is removed to the point that they lose their voices and their relevance. It is as if they were no more. "You are hereby canceled!"

This is the type of thing that happened in totalitarian regimes like Stalin's Russia or Mao's China, where dissenters were exiled, imprisoned, or executed. They were, quite literally, canceled. Now it is happening in America and other "free" countries.

Think back to someone like Leon Trotsky, "a leader of the Bolshevik revolution and early architect of the Soviet state."[1] He had been imprisoned as a Marxist revolutionary but then rose to prominence as one of the revolution's leaders. Stalin, however, saw him as a threat, first deporting him to a remote part of the Soviet republic, then exiling him from the country entirely. Ultimately, he was assassinated while living in Mexico. Canceled for good!

Even the memory of Stalin's perceived adversaries had to be eliminated. According to History.com,

> After consolidating his power in 1929, Stalin declared war on Soviets he considered tainted....Beginning in 1934 he wiped out an

> ever-changing group of political "enemies." An estimated 750,000 people died during the Great Purge, as it is now known, and more than a million others were banished to remote areas to do hard labor in gulags.
>
> During the purges, many of Stalin's enemies simply vanished from their homes. Others were executed in public after show trials. And since Stalin knew the value of photographs in both the historical record and his use of mass media to influence the Soviet Union, they often disappeared from photos, too.[2]

Things were not much different in Mao's China:

> After its relatively lukewarm start, the Suppression of Counter-revolutionaries campaign escalated quickly at the end of 1951. This escalation was driven by CCP cadres, government propaganda and popular action.
>
> One of the features of the Suppression campaign in 1951 were huge mass meetings, held in public spaces or stadiums and attended by thousands of people.
>
> These meetings were urban versions of rural "Speak Bitterness" hearings but tended to be deadlier for those who stood accused. Suspects were paraded, accused of counter-revolutionary activities or sympathies, intimidated into self-criticism then subjected to humiliation, beatings or execution. At some mass meetings, more than 200 people were shot.
>
> According to Mao, 700,000 "class enemies" were executed during the Suppression campaign. Some historians consider this figure a significant underestimation of the death toll.[3]

Following in the footsteps of Mao, although not yet to the same levels of evil, China's President Xi Jinping is canceling all opposition to his growing dictatorial powers, to the point that the verb *disappear* is commonly used in the active sense. In other words, someone does not simply disappear; instead, you "disappear" him.

A headline on *The Diplomat* website stated, "The People China 'Disappeared' in 2018: From a movie star to university students, no one is immune."[4] One day they were raising their voices in disagreement and protest. The next day they were gone.

The article explained:

> It's not uncommon for individuals who speak out against the government to disappear in China, but the scope of the "disappeared" has expanded since President Xi Jinping came to power in 2013.
>
> Not only dissidents and activists, but also high-level officials, Marxists, foreigners, and even a movie star—people who never publicly opposed the ruling Communist Party—have been whisked away by police to unknown destinations.
>
> The widening dragnet throws into stark relief the lengths to which Xi's administration is willing to go to maintain its control and authority.[5]

Here in America, we are not dealing with the same level of suppression and oppression, and most of it is not coming from the government. Dissenters are not being whisked away by police, never to be heard from again. They are not being deported by a government agency to a secret location, there to languish in obscurity for decades.

Rather, they are being canceled by the PC culture. They are being deemed so out of sync or offensive that not only must their views be eliminated; *they themselves must be eliminated*—not by execution or imprisonment but by social banishment. In some cases, the very record of them must be removed, with their social media accounts purged as if they had never been. They have been canceled. They have been "disappeared."

When the Liberal Left Warns Against Cancel Culture

As a former op-ed writer for the *New York Times*, Bari Weiss is anything but a flaming conservative. Rather, as described by the very liberal (and irreverent) Bill Maher, she is "a hip, millennial, Jewish bisexual girl living in San Francisco."[6] Yet she found the atmosphere at the *Times* to be so intolerant of dissenting views that she ultimately left, penning a scathing letter on her way out the door. She wrote, "My own forays into Wrongthink have made me the subject of constant bullying by colleagues who disagree with my views. They have called me a Nazi and a racist"—yes, that's how some of her *New York Times* coworkers spoke of this liberal, bisexual Jew.

She noted that "some coworkers insist I need to be rooted out if this company is to be a truly 'inclusive' one, while others post ax emojis next to my name." That is "ax" as in "ax her" or, worse still, "Off with her head!" She continued, "Still other New York Times employees publicly smear me as a liar and a bigot on Twitter with no fear that harassing me will be met with appropriate action. They never are."[7] And I repeat: this is all being said about a liberal, bisexual Jewish millennial from San Francisco.

Speaking about another open letter she coauthored with Thomas Chatterton Williams of *Harper's Magazine*, Weiss told cultural commentator Bill Maher what is happening now is different from criticism.

> We're used to criticism. Criticism is kosher in the work that we do.... Criticism is great. What cancel culture is about is not criticism. It is about punishment. It is about making a person radioactive. It is about taking away their job.[8]

She continued:

> It's not just about punishing the sinner. It's not just about punishing the person for being insufficiently pure. It's about this sort of secondary boycott of people who would deign to speak to that person or appear on a platform with that person...And we see just very obviously where that kind of politics gets us. If conversation with people that we disagree with becomes impossible, what is the way that we solve conflict? It's violence.[9]

Violence indeed, but of another kind. In the end, though, the result is the same, just as in Russia under Stalin or China under Mao or Xi. If you dissent, you become "radioactive." You lose your job. You lose your public identity. It is as if you have lost your life. That's why Weiss likened cancel culture to "social murder."

What does this look like in practice? I was speaking at a Church and State conference in Australia in March 2020, right before travel shut down because of the pandemic. At the conference I met a woman named Bindi Cole Chocka and heard her story firsthand. This is how she describes herself on Twitter: "The Cancelled Artist. Had a national platform as an award-winning Australian artist. Now #cancelled due to my conservative Christian views."[10] The national platform disappeared the moment her non-PC, conservative Christian views were known.

The new rule is "Thou shalt not dissent"—or else. The PC culture will blackball you and blacklist and virtually eliminate you from the public square. Consider yourself canceled!

In the words of a university professor who resigned his position after being falsely accused of sexual harassment and bullying, "Cancel culture is a phrase but what happens to the real people who are canceled?...Even very high-profile individuals have for the most part just up and disappeared. It's dangerous. Anyone can get canceled over anything. It's the weaponization of the Internet and it's scary."[11]

Indeed, an open letter published by *Harper's Magazine* warned:

> Editors are fired for running controversial pieces; books are withdrawn for alleged inauthenticity; journalists are barred from writing on certain topics; professors are investigated for quoting works of literature in class; a researcher is fired for circulating a peer-reviewed academic study; and the heads of organizations are ousted for what are sometimes just clumsy mistakes. Whatever the arguments around each particular incident, the result has been to steadily narrow the boundaries of what can be said without the threat of reprisal. We are already paying the price in greater risk aversion among writers, artists, and journalists who fear for their livelihoods if they depart from the consensus, or even lack sufficient zeal in agreement.
>
> This stifling atmosphere will ultimately harm the most vital causes of our time.[12]

It can be downright deadly.

More Pushback From the Left

Sarah Silverman is another unlikely critic of cancel culture. She is a liberal Jewish comedian, known in some Christian circles for her crass jokes about Jesus.[13] But she, too, has become alarmed at the unforgiving nature of cancel culture, which judges you not only for thought crimes or word crimes you commit today but also for words you spoke or things you did many years ago. She said, "Without a path to redemption,...you take someone, you found a tweet they wrote seven years ago or a thing that they said, and you expose it and you say, this person should be no more, banish them forever."[14]

In her case, Silverman had put on blackface in a skit she did in 2007, subsequently realizing that it was offensive to black Americans and seeking to make amends for her lack of sensitivity. Yet in 2020, more than twelve years later, she noted, "I recently was going to do a movie,...then at 11 p.m. the night before they fired me because they saw a picture of me in blackface from that episode. I didn't fight it."[15] Canceled!

Australian singer and songwriter Nick Cave also took aim at cancel culture—in particular, its lack of mercy, even referring to it as "mercy's antithesis." In his view, political correctness was now "the unhappiest religion in the world," describing it as "moral certainty and self-righteousness shorn even of the capacity for redemption." He even called it "bad religion run amuck."[16]

So, the Left's opposition to religion has become a religion itself, but one characterized by lack of mercy, no forgiveness, no redemption. Who would want a religion like that? According to Cave, because cancel culture refuses to engage with "uncomfortable ideas," it "has an asphyxiating effect on the creative soul of a society." It robs us of compassion, "out of which emerges the genius and generosity of the imagination." And it stifles our creativity, with disastrous results. As he noted, "A force that finds its meaning in the cancellation of these difficult ideas hampers the creative spirit of a society and strikes at the complex and diverse nature of its culture."[17]

How stifling, even suffocating, this cancel culture has become—how utterly intolerant, how "asphyxiating," to use Cave's word. Comedian Adam Carolla even claimed that irreverent comedy shows like *Saturday Night Live* avoided doing skits mocking President Biden (and others on the Left) the way they mocked President Trump for fear of being canceled.[18] Talk about oppression by fear.

Even actor Alec Baldwin, famous most recently for his mocking impersonations of President Trump on *Saturday Night Live*, has raised his concerns, stating, "Cancel culture is like a forest fire in constant need of fuel. Functioning objectively. No prejudice. No code. Just destroy. The deserving and the undeserving alike."[19] In the words of Miley Cyrus (again, coming from anything but a conservative Christian perspective), "As a proud and loyal member of the LGBTQIA+ community, much of my life has been dedicated to encouraging love, acceptance, and open mindedness. The internet can fuel a lot of hate & anger and is the nucleus of cancel culture...but I believe it can also be a place filled with education, conversation, communication & connection." She continued, "It's easier to cancel someone than to find forgiveness and compassion in ourselves or take the time to change hearts and minds. There's no more room for division if we want to keep seeing progress! Knowledge is power! I know I still have so much to learn!"[20]

Joining these unlikely voices was perhaps an even more unlikely voice: actress Sharon Stone, best known for her roles in sexually explicit movies. "I think cancel culture is the stupidest thing I have ever seen happen," she opined during a March 2021 radio interview promoting a new book. She added, "I think when people say things that they feel and mean, and it's offensive to you, it's a brilliant opportunity for everyone to learn and grow and understand each other."[21]

A Major Conservative Publisher Meets Cancel Culture

Regnery Publishing was founded in 1947, featuring in its earlier years flagship authors such as William F. Buckley Jr. and, more recently, authors like Ann Coulter, David Limbaugh, Michelle Malkin, Dinesh D'Souza, Newt Gingrich, Mark Steyn, Mark Levin, Ed Klein, David Horowitz, Laura Ingraham, and Donald Trump. It claims to be America's "leading publisher of conservative books" and boasts that it has "one of the best batting averages in the publishing business—placing more than fifty books on the New York Times bestseller list, including numerous books at #1."[22]

Regnery is clearly a heavyweight in the publishing industry, yet even this influential conservative juggernaut ran into the jaws of cancel culture. In 2020, Regnery published Abigail Shrier's important book *Irreversible Damage: The Transgender Craze Seducing Our Daughters.* The book "critically examines from a variety of angles the medical and psychological harms teenage girls and young women experience after adopting a transgender identity and pursuing a pathway of hormonal and surgical transition."[23] In other words, Shrier documented the growing phenomenon of girls and young women who, at least for a season, identify as males, making tragic, life-altering decisions in the process.

We're talking about eighteen-year-old girls who had full mastectomies, only to deeply regret their decision just a few years later. We're talking about sixteen-year-olds who can never conceive a child because of hormone-altering drugs. We're talking about twenty-two-year-old females who have had complete sex-change surgery, only to recognize that they are not men after all. These are stories that need to be told, and they are presented in the book with both accuracy and compassion.[24]

Yet when Regnery went to take out ads on Amazon, a common practice for publishers, Amazon banned the ads. Had the book *promoted* transgender ideology and advocated for sex-change surgery, Amazon would have had no problem allowing the publisher to advertise. But since it warns against the dangers of transgender activism, Amazon said no.

In response, Regnery tweeted:

> The cancel culture has made it clear that it despises diversity of opinion, and it will not tolerate science, data, facts, or anything that

> contradicts the approved narrative. If you're not on board, you'll have your head handed to you.
>
> If you go on Amazon right now and search "transgender books," you will find paid advertisements from major publishing houses promoting books on the side of this issue Amazon apparently agrees with.
>
> But if you're a college fball coach who wears a conservative tshirt, an editor at the [*New York Times*] who runs an opinion piece by a Rep senator, or a respected journalist who writes for [the *Wall Street Journal*] investigating a serious social issue affecting young women in America, you will be silenced.[25]

Thankfully, the book itself was not banned by Amazon. Other books (and authors), however, did not fare so well, such as those of Dr. Joseph Nicolosi. Amazon purged *every single one of his books*. That's right: every one of his books. Dr. Nicolosi, who passed away in 2017 and held a PhD in clinical psychology from the California School of Professional Psychology, Los Angeles, was famous for helping men deal with unwanted same-sex attraction and was licensed as a psychologist in California.[26] Yet in 2019, Amazon removed all of Nicolosi's books, siding with those who claimed that his writings were harmful to LGBT individuals. As reported on the Church Militant website:

> The world's biggest bookseller has buckled under pressure from homosexual activists and banned the works of the world's most famous Catholic clinical psychologist on reparative or conversion therapy.
>
> Amazon pulled books written by pioneering therapist Dr. Joseph Nicolosi after British homosexual activist Rojo Alan stepped up a social media campaign calling for a ban on psychological literature on reparative therapy, which helps people seeking to change their sexual orientation.
>
> Dr. Nicolosi, who died in 2017, was a devout Catholic and licensed clinical psychologist and academic, who rejected the fatalism of the premise that people are "born gay" and have no choice. Homosexuality, he believed, is an adaptation to trauma...rooted in a same-sex attachment problem that leaves the boy alienated from his true masculine nature.[27]

Despite pressure from Republican House members, Amazon did not budge.[28] Dr. Nicolosi was canceled, made to appear as if he never existed—at least on the pages of Amazon. If he had written books such as *The Joy of Gay Sex* (now in a third, expanded edition) or *How to Bottom Like a*

Porn Star, Amazon would still be selling them. But dare to help men with unwanted same-sex attraction, and your books will suddenly disappear.

And what happens when you try to document the *health risks* of homosexual sex? Your book, too, will be banned. As MassResistance reported in August 2020:

> After 3 1/2 years of publishing our groundbreaking 600-page book, *The Health Hazards of Homosexuality: What the Medical and Psychological Research Reveals*, Amazon has suddenly notified us that it has banned it from being printed or sold on its site. Amazon is also refusing to allow us to print any more copies for our own use and has even blocked us from accessing our account records. The book was printed (and also posted as an eBook) through Amazon's Kindle Direct Publishing subsidiary.[29]

And it was no lightweight, carelessly written, polemical tome. Rather, the book was several years in the making, compiling information from the Centers for Disease Control, medical groups, and LGBT advocacy organizations—"all documented in 1,800 endnotes with up-to-date links. In today's society, this is critical information everyone should know, especially given what's being pushed on young children in schools across the country."[30]

But it, too, crossed a sacred line—the line of offending LGBTQ activists. As a result, the book was canceled.

Yet Amazon's hypocrisy runs deeper. The Republican House memo on the subject cited an article from *The Federalist* pointing out that Amazon continues to sell the books of Adolf Hitler, Joseph Goebbels, Benito Mussolini, Timothy McVeigh (the Oklahoma City bomber), and David Duke (a notorious anti-Semite).[31] No problem with those. But dare to suggest that someone does not have to remain gay, and you have crossed that forbidden line.

As *The Federalist* article stated, "The gay community, a supposedly oppressed and marginalized group, wields an extravagant amount of power today, and does so without regard for the rights of anyone who chooses to not support them." That's why the author had asked, "How long until the most widely read book in the world [the Bible!] is banned because it takes a dim view of homosexuality?"[32]

But it was not only Amazon that decided to cancel ex-gay material. In 2017, Vimeo removed all 850 videos posted by Pure Passion Ministries and shut down their account. Canceled! The videos, produced by Dr. David Kyle Foster, himself an ex-gay, pointed to new life and transformation through the power of the gospel, viewing homosexuality as just another aspect of sexual brokenness. Such views were considered "demeaning" by Vimeo, and Foster's ministry was banished from their site.[33] Scrubbed!

As I wrote in 2017, "If Jesus has changed your life and set you free from homosexual practice, your testimony is not welcome on Vimeo—not now, not ever. And if you see homosexuality as another aspect of sexual brokenness, something for which Jesus died and something from which you can be healed, your opinion is not welcome on Vimeo. Case closed, door shut, end of subject."[34] (We will have much more to say about the canceling of ex-gays in chapter 5.)

At the same time, while Vimeo has shut down the accounts of other ex-gay organizations (ex-gay ministry and scientific organizations shall be utterly purged!), they, like Amazon and others on the Left, are guilty of blatant double standards.[35] As Foster noted in a March 2017 email to me:

> Put "jihad" in their search bar and you get 2,233 selections.
>
> Put "lust" + Vimeo in a Google search and one option is a porn filmmaker site among 288 other sites containing 2,872 videos.
>
> Google "rape" + Vimeo and you get 2,817 videos.
>
> Google "teen rape" + Vimeo and you get at least one rape video.
>
> They have "sugar daddy" dating sites, (one a gay video), plus all kinds of gay porn videos. You can watch some of Allen Ginsberg's speech glorifying NAMBLA [the North American Man/Boy Love Association] on Vimeo, all kinds of "sex on Vimeo" and "porn on Vimeo" videos that, from the thumbnails, are completely pornographic. Where is their concern for the girls and boys who have been sex trafficked for such videos?[36]

Such is the immoral hypocrisy of today's cancel culture. Yet the threat of being canceled paralyzes many with fear. In fact, when President Trump's legal team was challenging the 2020 election results, other legal firms balked at taking up his case. Why? As attorney James Troupis explained when testifying to the Senate, "One of the reasons I was called [was] because virtually every major law firm in the country and in this city [Washington DC] refused to represent the President....Not because of the lack of merit in his claims—we've certainly demonstrated that there's merit—but because of the cancel culture."[37] Regardless of one's view of the merits of Trump's claims of election fraud, it is sobering to realize what people will do (and not do) to avoid being blacklisted.

Cancel culture was also able to shut down Rev. Franklin Graham's evangelistic meetings scheduled in several different venues in the UK. His biblically based statements about marriage and sexuality were deemed too offensive and controversial. And what happened to the signed contracts that Graham had with these different venues? They were canceled too.[38]

Speaking of the UK, in February 2021, Matthew Hyndman, cofounder of the group Ban Conversion Therapy, took issue with Prime Minister Boris Johnson's statements that religious liberties must be protected even if "conversion therapy" was banned on a professional level. For Hyndman, that still left the door open for dangerous abuse, so he wrote, "Those who resist legislation against conversion therapy often resist the idea of a prayer or a pastoral conversation being subject to the scrutiny of law. However, if these things take place in an overwhelmingly homophobic or transphobic context the pernicious power of prayer must be dealt with."[39] Note those words carefully: "the pernicious power of prayer must be dealt with." And you thought I was exaggerating?

When the Left Cancels Itself

Most of us know the story of *Animal Farm*, George Orwell's classic allegory that brilliantly exposed the real nature of communism. In the end, the farm animals that were liberated from human tyranny became the new tyrants. The formerly oppressed became the oppressors. The system devoured itself.

We're seeing that now with cancel culture, which is why even Hollywood celebrities, well-known for their anti-conservative positions, are raising concerns about this dangerous new trend. How far, then, will this go? Who (or what) will be canceled next? As expressed by actor Ilan Srulovicz, the CEO and founder of Egard Watch Company but famous for his role in *The Walking Dead* TV series, "If you're in Hollywood and you come out with an opinion that's different than what Hollywood deems acceptable, you're vilified, you're targeted, your career is over....Hollywood actually sets trends. It sets culture. And this is really a cultural battle. We have to make it acceptable once again to disagree with each other and to have a diversity of opinion."[40]

Phyllis Chesler, now a retired psychology professor, wrote an August 2020 op-ed titled "How I Got Canceled." In it she describes herself as "a trendy feminist icon, a 'public intellectual,' garlanded not once, but twice, by front-page *New York Times* book reviews." Indeed, she says she appeared on the magazine's cover and best-seller lists and was quoted frequently. Then in 2003, she published *The New Anti-Semitism* in which, she explains,

"I dared to hold the Western 'progressive' intelligentsia responsible for collaborating with Islam's Big Lies about Israel and the Jews. I also suggested that in our time, anti-Zionism *is* anti-Semitism."[41]

Surprised that her book was not reviewed by the *Times*, she wrote to the book review editors, asking what had happened. She received a dismissive reply, and from that day until now, the *Times* has not reviewed any of her books.

But that started back in 2003. What happened next was even more disturbing. Having been rejected by the *Times*, she began to make some new acquaintances—specifically, conservative acquaintances. The nerve! Now her liberal friends cut her off entirely. She was working with the enemy.

Still, she would not back down, determined to expose some of the worst practices of Islam, including honor killing. As a result, in 2017, when it was announced that she was going to address this subject at the University of Arkansas Law School, three anti-Zionist professors threatened violence if she delivered the lecture, even via Skype. The university, in turn, caved to their demands. The cancel culture thrives on bullying.

Chesler wrote in her op-ed that she learned it was dangerous to speak critically of anything having to do with Islam or Muslim behavior, including things like polygamy, honor killing, forced marriage, pedophilia, and learning to hate the infidels. At the same time, she explained, she discovered that it was "unacceptable in the academy or in almost all mainstream media to praise anything that Israel has ever done, especially if it's true; to write that *jihad* is a religious commandment in Islam; to challenge the utter stupidity of identity politics and the consequent balkanization of reality; and to document that women, like men, have internalized sexism." In sum, you cannot challenge any part of today's "politically correct madness without risking everything."[42]

How many are willing to risk everything? How many instead take the convenient (and cowardly) way out (including Christian leaders)? How many choose to sacrifice their integrity to avoid being shunned or purged?

Other feminists have also experienced the wrath of cancel culture. About three thousand people signed a petition to cancel feminist icon Germaine Greer's 2015 lecture at Cardiff University. And who was it that didn't want her speaking there? The radical Left. Yes, they claimed, "Greer has demonstrated time and time again her misogynistic views towards trans women, including continually misgendering trans women and denying the existence of transphobia altogether."[43] Put simply, Greer had the audacity to say that "trans women"—meaning, biological males who identify as females—are not really women.

Greer was able to deliver her lecture despite the protests, but she pulled no punches in criticizing the opposition she faced: "It strikes me," she said, "as a bit of a put-up job really because I am not even going to talk about the issue that they are on about. What they are saying is that because I don't think surgery will turn a man into a woman I should not be allowed to speak anywhere."[44] Precisely.

There is actually a term for people like Greer: TERF, standing for "trans-exclusionary radical feminist." So, being a radical feminist is not enough today. You must also affirm the talking points of transgender activists; otherwise, you will be marginalized, excluded, or even canceled. There have even been attempts to cancel J. K. Rowling, the mega-best-selling author of the Harry Potter series. She objected to the idea that "people menstruate," stating correctly that it is only *women* who menstruate. The outrage against her was immediate and intense: cancel her and her books![45]

A major study has even been written on the canceling effects of transgender activism, authored by a number of leading feminists. The title is revealing: *Female Erasure: What You Need to Know About Gender Politics' War on Women, the Female Sex and Human Rights*.[46] The very meaning of *female* is being erased.

Not only so, but we are now being told that the very concept of *lesbian* is in danger of being eliminated. According to a December 26, 2020, tweet from the UK's *Telegraph*, "Lesbian[s] are facing 'extinction' because of the 'disproportionate' focus on transgenderism in schools, a controversial campaign group for gay rights has claimed."[47] After all, if a heterosexual male—who is, by definition, attracted to women—identifies as a female, doesn't that make him a lesbian? And if a lesbian can have male private parts, as the article states, then the very meaning of *lesbian* disappears. Talk about an unintended result of the radical Left.

In keeping with this, an October 7, 2020, story on the staunchly pro-LGBT Velvet Chronicle website stated, "Lesbian Playwright Canceled by Thought Police." Yes, "This tactic of 'activists'—threatening livelihoods, careers, dragging names through the mud—is used as a warning shot to others to stay in line." In this case, Carolyn Gage, a lesbian playwright, was "accused of thoughtcrime and canceled by the thought police." Specifically, the Richmond Triangle Players decided to cancel their production of *The Second Coming of Joan of Arc* despite weeks of rehearsals after scrutinizing Gage's Facebook and concluding that she was transphobic.[48]

Cancel culture has no limits—and remember that here, it is a pro-LGBT website protesting the canceling of Gage's play.

Even Prof. Richard Dawkins, one of the world's most influential atheists, has been canceled—first from a university event, and then from an atheist society. He was scheduled to address the College Historical Society at Trinity College Dublin, a famous *debating* society, well known for its free exchange of ideas. But because of his views on Islam (just one of the major world religions that he ridicules) and his alleged sexism, he was disinvited. As the Historical Society's statement explained, "The comfort of our membership is paramount."[49] Make our students uncomfortable, even in a debating society (!), and you will be disinvited. Deplatformed. Canceled.

In response, the editors of *Spiked* wrote that "a debating society, of all places, should provide an open forum for discussion and critical thinking—instead of trying to keep members comfortable by censoring 'offensive' speakers."[50] Exactly. The Free Speech Union tweeted a quote from the article that said, "No Platforming a speaker merely means that the 'correct' position has been decided in advance. Any institution genuinely committed to public debate should push back against this illiberal trend."[51] But will they?

Then, in April 2021, after Dawkins had compared Rachel Dolezal's identifying as black (she is actually white) to transgender identity, the American Humanist Association excommunicated Dawkins, finding some of his statements to be "antithetical to humanist values."[52] They even rescinded his 1996 Humanist of the Year Award. In response, Prof. Steven Pinker, another prominent atheist, along with philosopher Rebecca Goldstein, who won the same award in 2006 and 2011, respectively, commented, "To demonize a writer rather than address the writer's arguments is a confession that one has no rational response to them." Indeed, they wrote, "This illiberal response is all the more damaging to an organization that claims to repudiate the repressive practices of religion."[53] How revealing.

With regard to campus policies, Dennis Prager wisely observed that because the Left controls most of our universities, most of the media, and most of Hollywood, little or no dissent is allowed in those settings. That's just what the Left does. He wrote, "The left always suppresses speech. Since Vladimir Lenin and the Bolshevik Revolution in Russia in 1917, there has been no example of the left in control and not crushing dissent."[54] If you find an exception to this statement, it will be the exception that proves the rule.

In Prager's view, there is a difference between liberal and left, since liberals believe in free speech while leftists do not. He continued:

> (The present leftist threat to freedom in America, the greatest threat to freedom in American history, is made possible because liberals think they have more to fear from conservatives than from the left. Liberals do not understand that the left regards liberals as their useful idiots.)...That is why we have "cancel culture"—the silencing and firing of anyone who publicly dissents from the left, and even "publicly" is no longer necessary.[55]

Where Do We Go From Here?

As with much of this book, as I was writing it, a flood of new material became available, forcing me to wonder, "At what time do I stop documenting the latest incident in the silencing of the lambs? How many examples of cancel culture do we need?"

Here are just a few of the relevant headlines that were posted in a period of roughly two weeks:

- January 12, 2021: "Bryan Cranston: Cancel Culture Has Made Us 'Harder and Less Understanding, Less Tolerant, Less Forgiving'"[56]
- January 14, 2021: "Harvard Students Seek to Revoke Trump Graduates' Diplomas After Capitol Hill Violence"[57]
- January 14, 2021: "I'm Sounding the Alarm: PRC-Style Censorship Has Arrived in the United States"[58]
- January 18, 2021: "More Than 250 Authors, Agents Compare Trump to 'Son of Sam' Killer"[59] (This was an attempt to stop any publisher from publishing Trump's memoirs.)
- January 18, 2021: "Governor Ron DeSantis Vows to Put an End to the Censorship of Conservative Ideas"[60]
- January 18, 2021: "Kristy Swanson Demands Her Removal From All John Hughes Movies If Trump Gets Erased From 'Home Alone 2'"[61]
- January 19, 2021: "My Pillow CEO Says Bed Bath and Beyond, Kohl's to Stop Selling His Products"[62]
- January 21, 2021: "Five Universities Who Canceled Trump Officials and GOP Lawmakers"[63]
- January 21, 2021: "Canceling Culture"[64]

- January 24, 2021: "I Read the Book Target Banned That's Critical of Transgenderism in Girls—It's Essential Reading for This Day and Age"[65]
- January 25, 2021: "'The Walking Dead' Actor Ilan Srulovicz Talks Cancel Culture, Media Censorship: 'It Is Orwellian'"[66]
- January 28, 2021: "It's Liberals vs. Liberals in San Francisco After Schools Erase Contested Names" ("Incredulous parents and the mayor criticized the school board's decision to change the names of 44 schools that honor historical figures like Jefferson, Lincoln and Paul Revere.")[67]

And I repeat: these were just a few of the relevant headlines and articles posted during this short window of time. To document all the relevant stories would take an encyclopedia, let alone a book or even a chapter in a book. In fact, the very week I was writing these words, there was more breaking cancel-culture news: the popular actress and former MMA star Gina Carano was canceled by Disney Studios from her major role in *The Mandalorian* and dropped by her talent agency—all because of her conservative views.[68] Hasbro Toys even scrapped her *Star Wars* action figures.[69]

But she was not going down without a fight. In fact, within days of her firing, she was hired by the new media arm of the conservative *Daily Wire* group, whose best-known spokesman is Ben Shapiro. As Carano said:

> I cried out and my prayer was answered. I am sending out a direct message of hope to everyone living in fear of cancellation by the totalitarian mob. I have only just begun using my voice which is now freer than ever before, and I hope it inspires others to do the same. They can't cancel us if we don't let them.[70]

Exactly! "They" do not have power over "us" unless we concede our own rights. No one can ultimately silence us.

Unfortunately, according to a Cato poll published July 22, 2020, "62% of Americans say they have political views they're afraid to share." Specifically:

> A new Cato national survey finds that self-censorship is on the rise in the United States. Nearly two-thirds—62%—of Americans say the political climate these days prevents them from saying things they believe because others might find them offensive. The share of

> Americans who self-censor has risen several points since 2017 when 58% of Americans agreed with this statement.
>
> These fears cross partisan lines. Majorities of Democrats (52%), independents (59%) and Republicans (77%) all agree they have political opinions they are afraid to share.[71]

Note that carefully: almost two-thirds of Americans *self-censor* for fear of the consequences of expressing dissenting views. How many pastors and Christian leaders do this very same thing? "I dare not speak the truth and rock the boat. I dare not offend anyone by being honest. Best to keep my views to myself and stay with what is politically safe." People who think like this, especially Christian leaders, are serving themselves more than they are serving others or serving the Lord. Let that sink in until it stirs you to action.

Really now, it is bad enough that cancel culture is trying to put us in the closet and silence us for good. It is far worse when we go into the closet of our volition and silence ourselves. Why on earth would we do that?

A young man wrote to our ministry, saying, "Your resistance to the 'progressive' culture encourages me to do the same. I am 22 years old. By the time I am your age, what is left of my Judeo-Christian culture (I am English) may be long gone. I intend, by God's grace, to stand for the truth as you are doing."[72]

I certainly hope that his assessment of the future is wrong. That being said, if we bow to cancel culture today, he could well be right about tomorrow. That's why Phyllis Chesler's counsel is wise. Having noted that "you do not challenge any part of this politically correct madness without risking everything," she added this: "I recommend that more of us do just that. Courage is now our only alternative."[73]

That is how we overcome cancel culture: courage! It truly is our only alternative. (We'll lay out a specific plan of action in the second half of the book. For now, we'll continue to outline the very real obstacles we face.)

Chapter 2

THE CAMPUS THOUGHT POLICE

IT IS DIFFICULT to describe how far our college and university campuses have lurched to the left in recent decades. Suffice it to say that "according to a recent [2018] study on faculty party affiliation by the National Association of Scholars, the ratio of Democrats to Republicans at Williams College is 132:1; at Swarthmore it is 120:1; and at Bryn Mawr it is 72:0. At many of America's best research universities, the ratios are only moderately better."[1] For good reason, the 2018 article citing this study was titled "The Disappearing Conservative Professor." How did this happen right in front of our eyes?

In 2020, a report that focused on Harvard University found the same situation prevailing on that iconic campus: "A recent survey by the *Harvard Crimson* found that conservatives make up just over 1% of the school's faculty."[2] Chew on that one for a moment. The implications are massive.

Your child has the honor of being accepted to Harvard University, one of the most respected schools of higher learning on the planet. One day she (or he) will be a Harvard grad! But at what cost to your child's soul? To what degree will Christian students at Harvard unlearn the values and beliefs their parents have instilled in them? To what extent will they be indoctrinated into a godless (or anti-God) worldview?

After all, college and university students look up to their professors, who, in their eyes, are so brilliant and enlightened. Surely these learned teachers must be right. And so the instructors become the new role models (and almost surrogate parents) for your children. As a result, many of these kids, now young adults, will fall away. (According to Campus Renewal, 60–80 percent of professing Christian students "become disengaged with their faith" during their first year in college. Another factor, of course, is the party-filled, anything-goes atmosphere on many campuses.)[3]

Yet it is to Harvard (and similar schools) our children must go, even though the faculty will be stacked against their beliefs by as much as 100 to 1. Think about *that*. And think about the tens of thousands of other students from all kinds of backgrounds who will graduate from Harvard with their own worldviews shifted strongly to the left.

More than ten years ago, I was meeting with some Christian leaders in New York City, including some Christian educators. One of them, a woman who was teaching at Queens College (where I earned my bachelor's degree), shared an eye-opening personal story.

Upon receiving her PhD, she was hired as a faculty member at Queens, excited for this new opportunity God had given her. The first week of the fall semester, she met with the faculty members from her own department as they reviewed their experiences from the previous school year. To her shock, the professors boasted about how many students they had "deconverted." One said, "I managed to persuade ten of my students to abandon their faith." Another replied, "I got eleven!" She was absolutely mortified.

I certainly had my share of hostile professors in college and university, and in my case, it forced me to study harder and dig deeper, which ultimately helped my faith in the long term. But for many other students, when it comes to their faith, they are hurt far more than they are helped. And, more to the point here, the campus atmosphere has become far more hostile to believers today than it was back in the 1970s and 1980s, when I was in school (specifically, for me, from 1973 to 1985).

Jon Shields, author of "The Disappearing Conservative Professor" article, noted:

> By most accounts, 1969 was not a banner year for conservatism, at least not on America's college campuses. Looking back, however, it is striking just how well represented conservatives were in the ranks of the American professoriate. In that turbulent year, about one in four professors were at least moderately conservative, according to survey data collected by the Carnegie Commission on Higher Education.[4]

Frankly, having only 25 percent of the professors classified as "at least moderately conservative" was a cause for real concern. But it is a far cry from today, especially in some fields of study. Shields writes:

> Conservative representation is even worse today in the social sciences and humanities, where they have practically disappeared from many areas of inquiry. Nearly every recent survey of the university places the percentage of conservative and Republican professors in these fields in the single digits. Conservatives also tend to cluster in economics departments, leaving other disciplines with hardly any center-right thinkers....[B]y some prominent measures Republicans make up 4% of historians, 3% of sociologists, and a mere 2% of literature professors.[5]

Writing for the *Washington Post* in 2016, Christopher Ingraham observed that if you had been in college or university during the last twenty-five years, you wouldn't be "surprised to hear that professors have become strikingly more liberal." Indeed, a higher education survey indicated that while in 1990, "42 percent of professors identified as 'liberal' or 'far-left,'" by 2014, "that number had jumped to 60 percent." During that same period of time, academics who identified as moderate had dropped by 13 points, while those who identified as "conservative" or "far-right" dropped by nearly 6 points. As a result, he observed, "In the academy, liberals now outnumber conservatives by roughly 5 to 1. Among the general public, on the other hand, conservatives are considerably more prevalent than liberals and have been for some time."[6]

Things have become so unbalanced on our campuses that the title of Ingraham's article is "The Dramatic Shift Among College Professors That's Hurting Students' Education." And note this well: the article was published in the strongly left-leaning *Washington Post*. Even the *Post* recognized that this far-left shift was hurting, not helping, the students. That's how bad things have become.

When *Progressive* Really Means *Oppressive*

But our campuses have not only lurched far to the left. They have become increasingly oppressive in the process, as viewpoints that oppose the prevailing leftist ideology are actively suppressed—by the faculty, by the administration, or by fellow students. Cancel culture is having a field day in our institutions of higher learning.

As David Acevedo explained:

> Academic cancellation usually goes something like this: 1) a professor, administrator, or student says or writes something considered heretical by progressives; 2) outcry ensues among the faculty and student body, who demand institutional discipline; 3) administrators cave to the mob and punish the "culprit." In most cases, it really is that simple.
>
> For untenured professors and administrators, this discipline may take the form of suspension or firing, but always with a large dose of public humiliation. Tenured faculty have more protections, but schools often make their jobs harder through burdensome investigations and never-ending "sensitivity" and "implicit bias" trainings. Canceled students may have their professional careers ruined before they've begun.[7]

I received a call on my radio show about ten years ago from a professor at a college in Virginia. She explained that she, a committed Christian, was not allowed to say the word God in her classroom unless it related directly to the subject matter of her lecture. On the other hand, she was fully aware of other faculty members who regularly derided the concept of God in their classrooms, even though they were teaching on totally unrelated subjects. Bashing the Bible and the God of the Bible were just fine. Speaking about God (or the Bible) in a positive way was out of line. She assured me she had her facts right. Fail to conform, and you're out.

Campus Reform reported in August 2020 that an English professor at Iowa State University threatened to expel students who advocated "against abortion or the Black Lives Matter movement in any of their writing assignments." A screenshot of the professor's syllabus said this, in bold print: "GIANT WARNING: any instances of othering that you participate in intentionally (racism, sexism, ableism, homophobia, sorophobia, transphobia, classism, mocking of mental health issues, body shaming, etc) in class are grounds for dismissal from the classroom." And she made her intentions totally clear, saying, "You cannot choose any topic that takes at its base that one side doesn't deserve the same basic human rights as you do (ie: no arguments against gay marriage, abortion, Black Lives Matter, etc). I take this seriously."[8]

Cross this line and dare to differ with the professor's radical leftist ideology, and you are out. Dare to stand up for the lives of the unborn or question any of the BLM agenda, and you are gone. Dismissed. Expelled. Canceled!

But this is not something new, nor does it represent an isolated case. Already in 2011 in my book *A Queer Thing Happened to America*, I documented cases of Christian administrators, professors, and students who had lost their jobs on campus or been expelled from their programs simply because they differed with LGBTQ talking points. In one case, it was a respected administrator who penned an op-ed for her local newspaper on her own time, taking issue with a local gay activist based on her understanding of the Bible. For that, she was fired. In another case, it was a Catholic professor teaching on Catholic beliefs in a religion class in his university. For that, his class was dropped—and him with it. In still another case, it was a pastor's wife, studying counseling in graduate school, who was bounced out for adhering to her own conscience. For that, she was expelled from the counseling program, ultimately leading to two court cases, the first one standing with the university and the second standing with her. What a battle just for being a Christian on campus.[9]

Since the writing of that book, things have become much worse, making it harder and harder for believers on campus simply to be true to their faith, let alone express their faith openly. Even non-Christian faculty members are complaining about the stifling of honest academic inquiry and the exchanging of different points of view whenever the PC narrative is being challenged.

Again in 2020, the *Washington Times* documented how "a vocal minority has summoned the spirit of collective control over what can be thought and said" at many colleges and universities. These schools have "helped to shut down debate in the classroom. They have also chilled research and discouraged professors from presenting dissenting ideas to the general public. A blanket of ideological conformity now covers most campuses."[10] As the old proverb goes, "The tallest blade of grass is the first to be cut by the scythe." Better to conform and save your career than to stand out and be cut down.

A January 2020 headline of *The Guardian* (UK edition) proclaimed, "Sacked or Silenced: Academics Say They Are Blocked From Exploring Trans Issues." Reporting on the situation in the UK, the article explained that "the transgender debate cuts across many academic disciplines, including law, education, gender studies, philosophy and history. So-called gender-critical feminists, who believe that gender is a social construct rather than innate, say they want to explore trans issues within their fields, but that they, and the debate as a whole, are being stifled in British universities."[11] By all means, do not dare rock this boat.

When Language Is Policed

But it is not only ideas that are policed on campus; it is also language. There are words you cannot say as well as concepts you cannot address. What's more, there are other words you *must* say. Back in 2016, it was this concept of enforced speech that was the straw that broke the camel's back for University of Toronto psychology professor Jordan Peterson. (This was shortly before he rose to international fame as a public, conservative intellectual.)

Dr. Peterson was a long-time student of totalitarian regimes, and the moment he learned that certain speech was being required in Canada (and on his campus), he made clear that he would not conform. Specifically, he refused the order to use gender-neutral pronouns, such as referring to a so-called nonbinary individual as "they" or "ze." Aside from the fact that he recognized the absurdity of the practice—since these individuals were, in fact, either male or female—he would not allow anyone to tell him what words he must say, especially on a university campus.

When he went public with his free-speech talks, the university took a stand as well. Should he be taken to court, his school would not support him. Thankfully, in Peterson's case, his principled stand launched him into international prominence as a conservative thinker. (For more on professor Peterson, see chapter 18.) Others have not fared as well, while still others have decided it was easier to conform than to buck the system.

As for students on campus, it is incredibly difficult for them to go against the grain, since it would mean (1) disobeying or disrespecting their professors; (2) risking getting a failing grade or, worse still, being kicked out of class; and (3) alienating their fellow students, most of whom have no problem acquiescing to these demands.

A few years ago, I was asked to speak to a group of Christian college students who had gathered for a special retreat, focusing on LGBTQ issues. When I finished, I asked them what they were encountering on their own campuses. One student said, "I go to a very liberal school in California, and my major is in one of the most liberal fields within the school. The first week of the semester, in almost every single class I have, each professor goes around the room asking the students for their PGPs [preferred gender pronouns]." This is now the campus norm.

It is very difficult for a student to say, "Actually, I believe God made us male and female, so I'm going to stick with 'he' and 'she.'" To do so is to appear judgmental, to exclude yourself from the rest of the class, to dishonor the professor, and to brand yourself a bigot in the eyes of your peers. Would you be willing to do this as an eighteen-year-old freshman?

You might say, "But what's so bad about just going with the flow? After all, if that's what someone requests, I want to respect it."

The problem, again, is that this is being imposed on students and faculty. It is enforced speech. Not only so, but this practice doesn't simply contradict biblical truths. It contradicts reality. For example, an individual on the Ask a Non-Binary website posted this:

> These are all the gender neutral pronouns I've managed to hunt down but I am **ABSOLUTELY CERTAIN** there are several missing....

- They/them/their/themself
- tey/tem/ter/temself
- ey/em/eir/emself
- e/em/eir/emself
- thon/thon/thons/thonself
- fae/faer/faers/faerself
- vae/vaer/vaers/vaerself
- ae/aer/aers/aerself
- ne/nym/nis/nymself
- ne/nem/nir/nemself
- xe/xem/xyr/xemself
- xe/xim/xis/ximself
- xie/xem/xyr/xemself
- ze(or zie)/zir/zirs/zirself
- zhe/zhir/zhirs/zhirself
- ze/hir/hirs/hirself
- sie/sier/siers/sierself
- zed/zed/zeds/zedself
- zed/zed/zeir/zedself
- ce/cir/cirs/cirself
- co/cos/cos/coself
- ve/vis/vir/verself
- jee/jem/jeir/jemself
- lee/lim/lis/limself
- kye/kyr/kyne/kyrself
- per/per/pers/perself
- hu/hum/hus/humself
- bun/bun/buns/bunself
- it/it/its/itself

> I've also seen "yo" and "fey" pronouns but I have no idea how to conjugate them. And I'm off to still hunt for more! If you know of any GN pronouns feel free to reblog and add unto the list and I'll edit the original as well.
>
> OH MY GOSH!!
>
> SO IMPORTANT!![12]

College campuses now put out similar lists for their students. You must get your pronouns right—or else!

To be clear, I do not write these things to demean those who struggle with gender identity confusion or to mock the challenges they face. Nor do I fault those who feel that sensitivity and compassion lead them to address people by whatever name or pronoun they desire. Instead, I cite this to point out how far left-wing activism can go and how utterly wrong it is to *force* people, both faculty and students, to use terminology like this.

And what about those students (and faculty) who genuinely feel that it is *not* loving to depart from reality and refer to a biological male as "she"? What do we say to those who refuse to call someone "zed" (to borrow a pronoun from the list above)? The transphobia police will find you, and the consequences could be severe. A high school teacher was already fired for this very thing, in 2018. He committed the high crime of insubordination.[13]

To cite one more example, on November 22, 2020, Owen Stevens, a student at the State University of New York, posted an Instagram video in which he stated:

> Hey, everybody. I'm gonna double down on this point right now. I wanna make myself very clear, so hear what I'm saying. A man is a man. A woman is a woman. A man is not a woman, and a woman is not a man. A man cannot become a woman, and a woman cannot become a man. If I'm a man and I think I'm a woman, I'm still a man. If I'm a woman who thinks I'm a man, I'm still a woman. Regardless of what you feel on the inside, [it's] irrelevant to your biological status. It doesn't change the biology. The biology is very clear. It's very, very, very clear. And it's binary and easy. You fall into either man or woman. And if you're intersex, you either become a man or woman eventually. And that is such a small...group of people that it makes no sense to justify that as statistically significant and apply that to our definition of gender. It wouldn't make any sense.[14]

For this, he was found in violation of his university's inclusivity rules. Specifically, "The school's Dignity for All Students Act mandates that teachers foster 'a diverse campus community marked by mutual respect for the unique talents and contributions of each individual.'" As a result, he was "suspended from his field teaching programs." Not only so, but his status will remain the same "until he successfully completes a 'remediation plan.'"[15] Perhaps the school authorities should have simply sentenced him to a reeducation camp.

As for other restrictions of free speech on campuses that have nothing to do with LGBTQ issues—or even religious controversies—the Foundation for Individual Rights in Education (FIRE)[16] put out a list of "10 Worst Colleges for Free Speech: 2021" that provides one shocking example after another of the campus thought police at work. To cite one case in point, in October 2020, St. John's University in Queens, New York, removed

> adjunct professor Richard Taylor from the classroom indefinitely after finding him in violation of the school's anti-bias policy, without either showing him the evidence against him or providing him an opportunity to appeal.
>
> Why, you ask? Because he asked his history students to consider whether transatlantic trade had any positive effects on biodiversity. And how does that violate the school's bias policy? St. John's won't explain its rationale or share the evidence it used to reach that conclusion, except to say it got one complaint from an actual student in the class and 300 form letters from a student group calling for him to be fired.[17]

Taylor was accused of justifying slavery, which he quite explicitly did not. In fact, when asked that question in his class, he made plain that "no one [was] justifying slavery and asked students to consider global trade as a whole, including lives lost to disease and lives saved from famine."[18] Taylor, for his part, is fighting back with a lawsuit.

What Happened to Open Debate?

Jonathan Sacks, the late chief rabbi of the United Kingdom, remarked that "the university must be the guardian of open debate, courteous argument, civil speaking and respectful listening. It must provide space for dissenting minds and for voices that challenge our comfortable assumptions. It must teach us to distinguish truth from falsehood, cogent argument from sophistry, the presentation of evidence from mere passion and persuasion."[19] Today, this has been turned on its head.

I'm sure there are plenty of fine universities in America today where the students are challenged and stretched. But far too many schools are coddling their students rather than challenging them (at least, emotionally), thereby producing graduating classes filled with pampered young adults.

As I wrote in a 2017 article, "How bad are things on some campuses? Not only are schools offering coloring books and crayons during finals week to help students deal with stress. (I kid you not.) Not only are schools providing safe-spaces where students can go to escape from the conflicts of the real world. Not only are schools issuing guidelines for campus speech, replete with the latest trigger warnings to guard against microaggressions....But schools are now responding to student tantrums: If you threaten to throw a fit, we will back down, post haste. We do not want to get you upset!" Accordingly, as noted in the introduction, when Ann

Coulter was scheduled to give a speech at Berkeley, "Just the threat of protests was enough to shut the event down."[20]

As for trigger warnings, schools now alert students to events or lectures that might disturb them. And somehow it is almost always the conservative perspective that the students find troubling. This begs the question "Why isn't the Right triggered by the Left in the same way that the Left is triggered by the Right?" As noted by crisis PR representative Juda Engelmayer, with reference to Hollywood, "Anything that's going to offend the left is a problem...I have clients who are making an extraordinary effort to post what the social left wants to see."[21]

In 2016, at California State University San Marcos, "a 'trigger warning' was sent out notifying all students and faculty that there would be a pro-life display on campus" the following week. "An email from the university's Office of Communications, obtained by *CampusReform.org*, pointed out that the 'presentation is not a university sponsored presentation,' that it could be 'disturbing and offensive,' but that presentations like this on campus were 'protected under the First Amendment.' Oh, the evils of free speech." Try as they might to squelch it, this time they could not. But at least they could protect their students from being triggered by the pro-life presentation.[22] (And how ironic that these students would be triggered by a pro-life presentation, telling the truth about abortion, but not triggered by the act of abortion itself.)

Then there are the dreaded microaggressions. What, exactly, are these? To cite some examples, in 2016, in Worcester, Massachusetts, Clark University's new chief diversity officer issued guidelines for incoming students, including these: Don't say "you guys," since that could be interpreted as excluding women. Don't ask an Asian student for help in math or ask a black student if he plays basketball, since to do so would be to stereotype and thereby commit a microaggression. These must be avoided at all costs.[23]

And because men are so sexist and, by their very maleness, inherently guilty, any words with *man* or *men* in them must be removed. As Tom Ciccotta reported (once more, in 2016), "In an increased effort to be politically correct, a new inclusive language policy from administrators at Princeton University is seeking to end the usage of gender-specific words like 'man' on campus."[24]

Yes, students must "refrain from the use of gendered language," since the gender binary of male and female "does not take into consideration individuals who identify as otherwise, including and not limited to transgender, genderqueer, gender non-conforming, and/or intersex."[25]

What, exactly, does this look like in practice? Instead of saying "average man," students are urged to say "average person" or "ordinary person." And rather than saying "best man for the job," they should say "best person for the job," while "layman" should be replaced with "layperson" or "non-specialist."[26]

Of course, "man and wife" must go, being replaced by the far superior "spouses" or "partners," while "man-hours" is to be replaced by "person hours" or "work hours."[27] (I can hear someone ask, "So, how many person hours will it take to complete this job?")

Naturally "manpower" is out, to be replaced by "personnel" or "staff" or "workers" or "workforce," while even "man-made" is off limits, to be replaced by "artificial, handmade, manufactured, or synthetic." And God forbid you use the word "workmanlike," since that nasty *m* word is hidden right there in plain sight. Instead, students should say "skillful."[28]

Yet it gets more absurd still. In an effort to not offend or commit microaggressions or trigger students, more sensitivities need to be developed. As reported in August 2020 on Campus Reform, "The Mount Holyoke College Office of Diversity, Equity, and Inclusion shared a guide on social media called 'Phrases You Didn't Know Were Fatphobic.'" These allegedly "fatphobic" phrases included seemingly innocuous lines such as "that's so flattering on you," "you have such a pretty face," "you carry yourself well," and "I'm so bad for eating this." Also, the college pointed out, to call a fat person "brave" for wearing a non-flattering outfit was to imply that "overweight people 'shouldn't show off [their] bodies or be proud of them' and that 'no one should be considered "brave" for simply existing in their fat body.'" Even to call an outfit "flattering" was to imply that dressing oneself is about appearing "smaller" and fitting into "society's outdated thin ideal."[29]

You do *not* want to be fatphobic.

In all seriousness and by all means, we should walk in love toward others and be sensitive to their needs. How is it ever good to body-shame someone? And we certainly have our blind spots, not knowing how our words can hurt and wound. Let's all learn and grow and be gracious in our communication. But the current campus craze with microaggressions and trigger warnings and safe spaces and required speech and forbidden speech represents a sensitivity gone too far, especially when, in some cases, there are penalties for nonconformity. It was for good reason that I titled this chapter "The Campus Thought Police."

When Christian Groups Are Targeted

Ultimately, one group in particular has been singled out on college campuses: Christian conservatives—to the point of schools banning their organizations from campus. I documented this already in *A Queer Thing Happened to America* (which was published in 2011), citing examples from the years before that, and it continues to happen to this day. In fact when that book was released, I sent word to Christian friends in different states who had strong connections to local campus ministries, offering to have a respectful and civil debate with a qualified representative on any topic in my book. What were the results? In state after state I was told, "Not a chance. There's no way the campus ministries will host something like that. It's way too controversial and could threaten our standing with the school." In fact some of them told us that if we tried to bring the event to the campus, they would oppose it.

Yes, some campus ministries actually threatened to oppose my engaging in a public debate (or even delivering a lecture) on a subject such as "The Bible and Homosexual Practice" or "Should Same-Sex Marriage Be Legal?" Some of these campus leaders were concerned that my presence would disrupt the good relationships they were building with the LGBTQ community, not realizing that my style of presentation would actually build bridges, not burn them. But others admitted their concern that they would be banned from campus if they hosted me. That was a risk they were not willing to take.

Unfortunately you can run, but you can't hide, and the campus thought police were not waiting for open lectures and debates representing a biblical viewpoint on sexuality. Instead, on campus after campus, they were coming after Christian groups simply for being Christian, ordering these groups to change their standards and allow non-Christians to be part of their leadership teams. In response to this, all the way back in 2013, I wrote an article titled "Can a Muslim Lead the Christian Campus Club?" Here's the article in full:

> If we follow the logic of the Supreme Court, a Muslim could lead the Intervarsity Christian Fellowship club on your local campus. As absurd as this sounds, it is the very real, potential outcome of some recent Court rulings, and it is in keeping with the decisions made independently by a number of colleges and universities.
>
> In June 2010, the Supreme Court ruled 5-4 that the "University of California's Hastings College of the Law acted reasonably, and in a

viewpoint-neutral manner, in refusing to officially recognize and give funds to a campus chapter of the Christian Legal Society because the group refused to abide by the school's requirement that student groups open their membership to all" (as reported by Peter Schmidt for *The Chronicle of Higher Education*).[30]

The university had been sued by the Alliance Defense Fund when "the school refused to recognize the campus Christian Legal Society chapter, Hastings Christian Fellowship (HCF), because it [would] not agree to a non-discrimination policy that would require the group to admit non-Christians as members and officers."[31]

In expressing the majority opinion, Justice Ruth Bader Ginsburg wrote that it is "hard to imagine a more viewpoint-neutral policy than one requiring *all* student groups to accept *all* comers," noting that, "Hastings, caught in the crossfire between a group's desire to exclude and students' demand for equal access, may reasonably draw a line in the sand permitting *all* organizations to express what they wish but *no* group to discriminate in membership."[32]

In a strongly worded dissenting view for the minority, Justice Samuel Alito claimed that the majority opinion rested on the principle of "no freedom for expression that offends prevailing standards of political correctness in our country's institutions of higher learning," warning that "the Court's treatment of this case is deeply disappointing" and its decision "arms public educational institutions with a handy weapon for suppressing the speech of unpopular groups."[33]

The court's decision also opens the door for campus lunacy. What if a bunch of ardent Republicans decided to take over the campus's Democratic club? Or atheists decided to take over the Hindu club? Or Jews for Jesus decided to take over the Hillel club? Or Greenpeace devotees decided to take over the hunting club? Or meat-lovers decided to take over the PETA club? Or gay activists decided to take over the Intervarsity Christian Fellowship club? Or evangelical Christians decided to take over the LGBT club? (Oh wait. I'm sure someone would find a way to stop that.)

Is it unreasonable that campus groups would require members—let alone officers—to adhere to their values and beliefs? Isn't that the purpose of the club?

Yesterday, the *Washington Post* reported on the decision by Vanderbilt Catholic (a campus group with 500 members) to leave Vanderbilt University "in a dispute over the school's non-discrimination policy that bars student groups from requiring their leaders to hold specific beliefs." (All students are allowed to attend meetings but the leaders must adhere to specific beliefs.) As P. J. Jedlovec, the group's president, stated, "If we were open to having non-Catholics lead the organization, we wouldn't be Catholic anymore."[34] This is not exactly rocket science.

While Vanderbilt Catholic has simply chosen to buck the system, other Christian groups still trying to work within the system at Vanderbilt have been suspended. (For the record, Vanderbilt was founded as a Methodist institution.)

The *Post* article noted that "similar disputes have taken place in California, New York and North Carolina. The University of Buffalo suspended the InterVarsity Christian Fellowship in December after a dispute over a gay student member. The University of North Carolina-Greensboro refused to recognize a Christian group called Make Up Your Own Mind because it discriminated on the basis of faith for leaders. The school relented after being sued."

Note carefully the words "discriminated on the basis of faith for leaders." How can it be called "discrimination" when a Christian group requires its leaders to hold to Christian values and beliefs? Rather, it is "discrimination" when the university refuses to allow a Christian group to be Christian.

Last month, the Supreme Court turned down an appeal brought by the Alliance Defense Fund on behalf of Christian groups challenging the policy at California state universities which did not allow them to restrict "membership in their groups to people who agree with their Christian values and beliefs." Yet every other campus group is allowed to require their officers to agree with their beliefs and even to restrict membership to those who agree. Just not the Christians![35]

So, according to the court's decision, it is not discriminatory for the College Democrats to require that its leaders be Democrats, but it is discriminatory for a Christian group to require that its leaders be Christian. How remarkable.

It appears, then, that a PETA campus group might not be overrun (or run) by cheeseburger-munching students but a Christian group just might be overrun (or run) by Muslim students. I can hear Justice Alito (and the other dissenting justices) saying, "I told you so!"

Since 2013 the same scenario has repeated itself time and again: If you want to keep your status on campus, you must rewrite the Bible and compromise your convictions. If you want to do ministry here, you will have to embrace practicing lesbians into your leadership. If you want to stay, you must mix Christian and gay. And there is no sign of this outright discrimination against Christians letting up.

Todd Starnes reported in February 2018 that "a well-respected Christian student organization at Harvard University has been placed on probation after they allegedly forced a bisexual woman to resign from a leadership position for dating a woman....Harvard College Faith and Action was put on 'administrative probation' for a year. The group is [the] largest Christian fellowship on campus."[36]

In March 2018, the *Federalist* reported that "InterVarsity Christian Fellowship, a student group, was recently kicked off the Michigan-based Wayne State University's campus, solely for asking it be allowed to choose leaders who share its faith. Until this trouble with the school, the student group had been on campus for over 75 years. Incidents like this have been occurring on college campuses recently at an alarming rate."[37]

In September 2019, "Duke University's student government denied official status to a religious organization [the campus ministry Young Life] because it excludes LGBTQ people from holding leadership positions."[38] When the ministry applied for status on the campus, "the Duke Student Government Senate unanimously declined to recognize Young Life as an official Duke student group."[39] Consider that door slammed shut. And yet there is more.

When a Christian University Is Targeted for Being Christian

Trinity Western University (TWU) is a major Christian school in Canada featuring forty-eight undergraduate programs and nineteen graduate programs (as of this writing). From 2009 on, it required its students and faculty to commit to live by basic Christian standards while in the university's environment. This meant that to be a student or faculty member in good standing, you could not commit fornication or adultery, nor could you engage in same-sex relationships.

These standards were part of TWU's mandatory Community Covenant Agreement for a decade, requiring "that all students and faculty pursue a holy life 'characterized by humility, self-sacrifice, mercy and justice, and mutual submission for the good of others.'" Members were required "to abstain from using vulgar language, lying or cheating, stealing, using degrading materials such as pornography, and 'sexual intimacy that violates the sacredness of marriage between a man and a woman.'"[40]

Unfortunately, when TWU sought to open its law school—potentially the only Christian law school in Canada—it fell afoul of Canada's LGBT activists and their allies. They argued that TWU was discriminating against LGBT students, and the Canadian Bar Association sided against TWU. Consequently, if you graduated from TWU with a bona fide law degree, you would not be allowed to practice law in Canada. So the matter was taken to court, with ups and downs along the way.

Still, there was a ray of hope for TWU when a regional court ruled in its favor. And so, in 2018, when the case arrived at Canada's Supreme Court, many were expecting a positive outcome for freedom of religion. Instead, "in a pair of 7-2 rulings, the majority of justices found the law societies of British Columbia and Ontario have the power to refuse accreditation based on Trinity Western University's so-called community covenant."[41] Or, to paraphrase, the Supreme Court ruled that if a Christian law school wants accreditation, it must abandon its biblical values. How else can this be interpreted?

When the Supreme Court ruling came down, I wrote:

> Honestly, I don't know where TWU goes from here. And I don't know how the believers in Canada will respond.
>
> But I can say this to my friends and colleagues and fellow-educators and communicators here in America: We either use our liberties or lose them. We either stand fast and stand tall and stand strong, or we cower in a corner. We either do what's right today, or we apologize to our children tomorrow.
>
> It's time to push back.
>
> What will you do?[42]

What *did* the leadership of TWU decide? They caved. They capitulated. They sold their Christian soul, at least to a very significant degree. Better to compromise with LGBT activists and revise their covenant, they reasoned, than to forfeit the ability to have a law school. "The Community Covenant will no longer be mandatory as of the 2018–19 Academic year with respect to admission of students to, or continuation of students at, the University," the board resolution stated.[43] The Christian covenant was now optional. What a terrible shame.[44]

Back here in the States, Azusa Pacific University (APU) caved as well, bowing to the demands of LGBTQ activists. This is all the more striking given that APU calls itself "a community of disciples and scholars preparing to impact the world for Christ"[45] and its motto is "God first."[46] But when it came to taking a stand for biblical values, the cost was too high. So much for the school's motto.

For several years, behind the scenes, I worked with Azusa board member

Raleigh Washington to help shape biblically based statements regarding sexuality and gender, and for a time, the board held its ground, even under pressure.[47] But then, in 2018, the school leaders reversed their position on same-sex relationships,[48] only to reverse their position again and reaffirm their biblical values within weeks,[49] only to capitulate in the end.[50]

A colleague of mine, Walt Heyer, himself ex-transgender (meaning that he had sex-change surgery and lived as a woman for years before being transformed by the Lord),[51] had delivered lectures at APU several times and was well received. But a few years back, he contacted me, concerned that something had shifted. (Things had been escalating since 2013, when a theology professor came out as transgender, as a result of which she was asked to leave.)[52] When I reached out to school leadership, they assured me that nothing had changed. But it had.

I recognize, of course, that schools want to be as "inclusive" as possible. And I understand that a truly Christian campus does not want to make others feel inferior. At the same time, there are thousands of campuses to choose from, and if a student is not comfortable with a school's standards and values, he or she can go elsewhere. More importantly, when a Christian school is told that it cannot operate according to Christian principles, then the atmosphere has changed from inclusive to exclusive: it is now Christian values and Christian believers that are being excluded.

In 1958, President Dwight Eisenhower responded to a letter written by Robert Biggs, a terminally ill World War II veteran who had wished for a greater sense of certainty in Eisenhower's speeches. Biggs wrote, "We wait for someone to speak for us and back him completely if the statement is made in truth." In the midst of a gracious and wise response, Eisenhower noted that "in a democracy debate is the breath of life."[53] Sadly, on campuses throughout America and abroad, that "breath of life" is being extinguished.

But all hope is not lost. Not by a long shot. As the *Daily Signal* reported in October 2019, "In a significant win for religious liberty, a federal court last month ruled that a state university in Iowa can't require a Christian student organization to have non-Christian leaders." According to the court, the university was guilty of discrimination against the Christian group, InterVarsity, when it kicked the group off campus for requiring that the leaders of this Christian group be Christian. Really! Other religious groups were kicked off campus too, including a number of non-Christian groups, all for requiring their leaders—not members—to adhere to their particular religious beliefs. As the court ruled, the university's actions were so blatantly discriminatory that "top university officers, including the vice president, must pay out of their own pockets to cover the group's legal fees."[54] The court actually told the school administrators that it was "'hard-pressed to find a clearer example of viewpoint discrimination' than the actions they took against the InterVarsity Christian Fellowship."[55]

Plenty of Christian campuses (and ministries) have not caved, while others are pushing back. So on with the godly resistance. With hearts of compassion and backbones of steel, with the Word of truth and the Spirit's empowerment, we cannot be defeated.

Chapter 3

BIG TECH TAKES CONTROL

IT WAS JANUARY 8, 2021, and the wave of headlines was absolutely shocking: Twitter Bans President Donald Trump. Twitter Bans Trump for Life.[1] Seriously? Twitter banned the most powerful man on the planet? Twitter shut him out from his 88.7 million followers? Twitter blocked Donald Trump? For life? I never thought I would see the day.

Barely twenty-four hours earlier, former First Lady Michelle Obama posted this on her social media accounts: "Now is the time for Silicon Valley companies to stop enabling this monstrous behavior—and go even further than they have already by permanently banning this man from their platforms and putting in place policies to prevent their technology from being used by the nation's leaders to fuel insurrection."[2] And soon enough, it was done. The president of the United States of America was banned by social media. Big Tech was flexing its muscles, and other major social media platforms joined the ban, either permanently or indefinitely.

All this happened, of course, in the immediate aftermath of the appalling and outrageous storming of the Capitol on January 6 in conjunction with the Stop the Steal rally in Washington, DC. In light of this, Trump was temporarily suspended from Twitter, Facebook, and Instagram for fear that he would further incite the crowds to violence. But after he issued an important and conciliatory statement the night of January 7,[3] on what basis was he now being banned, especially *for life*? Was this not a shocking act of overreach by the so-called Masters of the Universe?[4]

In the words of former UN ambassador Nikki Haley, posted on Twitter, "Silencing people, not to mention the President of the US, is what happens in China not our country. #Unbelievable."[5] She was absolutely right. (Remember what we wrote in chapter 1 about people being "disappeared" in countries like China.)

At the same time this was happening, both the Apple App Store and Google Play cracked down on the Parler app, which had become the new choice for many conservatives leaving Twitter. Apple ordered Parler to remove certain content or be banned, while Google actually banned it.[6] Shortly after that, Apple decided to ban Parler entirely. Then, within hours, Amazon, which hosted the Parler app, shut it down, crippling this rapidly growing social media site overnight. Big Tech had spoken. The Masters of the Universe said, "Silence!" And it was done.[7]

So much for the constant liberal retort to conservatives, "If you don't like our platforms, go and build your own." Not so. Parler built its own, and Big Tech shut it down.[8]

Not long before this, YouTube shut down Steve Bannon's *War Room* podcast, while attorney Sidney Powell and General Michael Flynn had their Twitter accounts shut down as well.[9] The Big Purge was at hand. Even if you don't agree with many or even most of their positions, on what basis were these accounts shut down? That's the important question.

Fox News commentator Greg Gutfeld was so fed up with what was happening that he decided to leave Twitter himself (he had roughly 1.5 million followers at the time), tweeting this final message:

> okay, this IS my last tweet:
> CNN tries to get FNC banned.
> Apple targets Parler.
> Publishers dump writers.
> music labels drop artists.
> twitter bans/removes thousands.
> tech companies join hands.
> this redefines who the true rebels are.
> if you like the purge, you're the servant.[10]

Of course, many of us took strong exception to President Trump's tweets for years, and many indefensible statements were made by some of the people who were banned. Still, it is shocking to watch a crackdown like this happen in front of your eyes. In fact, I wrote the opening paragraphs to this chapter as all this was happening in real time, capturing the shock and emotion of the moment—and the word that comes to mind right now is *eerie*. It's like watching a news report about a communist takeover of your country, but you can hear the soldiers marching closer to your home as you watch.

Of course, these social media platforms have to draw the line somewhere, and some speech should be forbidden. It's just that virtually all the major platforms lean dangerously left, so when the crackdowns come, it is conservatives who are disproportionately singled out. As some Republican congressmen wrote to Facebook (regarding Trump being banned), "The debate about how to effectively deal with these and other individuals is necessary and important....However, we remain concerned that the deplatforming standards are not applied in a fair and neutral manner."[11] Yet it wasn't always like this.

The So-Called Masters of the Universe

Some of us are old enough to remember a world without internet, cell phones, and wireless communication. Some of us remember when the only way to get a letter to someone was by mail, not by fax and surely not by email. Some of us still remember getting online for the first time and learning the basics of the World Wide Web. Now it is almost impossible to imagine a world without internet, email, texting, instant communication, and immediate access to an almost infinite amount of information.

The scary thing is that a few giant companies virtually rule the web, hence the nickname the Masters of the Universe. They can affect the outcome of elections. They can affect the news that you see (or don't see). They can affect what information you receive. And they can affect what information you disseminate. They can also affect the flow of commerce and monetary exchange. It is here that cancel culture finds an all-powerful ally. The end result is chilling.

Consider what Twitter did to the *New York Post* in the weeks leading up to the 2020 presidential election. According to the *New York Times*, the *Post* is "the oldest daily newspaper published continuously in the United States," dating back to 1801 when it was named the *New York Evening Post*.[12] To this day it remains one of the most influential papers in America, ranked number four in terms of readership as of 2017.[13] Yet when Twitter did not approve of the *Post*'s exposé of a major scandal involving Hunter Biden, the son of then presidential candidate Joe Biden, it simply shut the *Post* down—and I mean that literally—on Twitter.

It was not just that Twitter included a disclaimer to the story, alleging that it was disputed. It was not even that Twitter deleted the relevant tweet. Instead, Twitter actually shut down the *Post*'s entire account, saying they would not reinstate it until the *Post* removed the tweet in question. Not only was this gross overreach by Twitter, but it may also have influenced the outcome of the election in Biden's favor, especially when we realize that Twitter suppressed the Hunter Biden story in its entirety, blocking others from sharing the *Post*'s article. (I'll return to the question of whether this affected the outcome of the election shortly.)

Of course, Twitter had no problem with allowing every kind of allegation against President Trump to be posted by all kinds of media outlets. Go ahead and sling the mud! But when it was a story from a major news outlet that challenged Twitter's leftist, PC sensitivities, that story had to be silenced. And if Twitter could do that to an entity as powerful as the *New York Post*, Twitter could do that to you or me. In the case of the *Post*, the paper's Twitter account was frozen for sixteen days, an eternity on social media, after which it was finally reinstated (thankfully, without the *Post* having to capitulate, although it was obviously quite a battle).[14]

Not long after that, once the elections had taken place, we learned that the Department of Justice had been looking into corruption charges involving Hunter Biden for quite some time. As reported by CNN on December 10, 2020:

> After going quiet in the months before the election, federal authorities are now actively investigating the business dealings of Hunter Biden, a person with knowledge of the probe said. His father, President-elect Joe Biden, is not implicated.
>
> Now that the election is over, the investigation is entering a new phase. Federal prosecutors in Delaware, working with the IRS Criminal Investigation agency and the FBI, are taking overt steps such as issuing subpoenas and seeking interviews, the person with knowledge said.[15]

Why, then, did Twitter suppress a related story involving Hunter Biden's laptop? Twitter claimed that private email addresses were being shared, but that was not the case, nor were other reasons that were offered accurate. In the end Jack Dorsey, Twitter's embattled CEO, tweeted, "Our communication around our actions on the [*New York Post*] article was not great. And blocking URL sharing via tweet or [direct message] with zero context as to why we're blocking: unacceptable."[16] Conservative journalist Mollie Hemingway was none too subtle when she responded, "YOU SHOULD NOT BE INTERFERING IN ELECTIONS ON BEHALF OF YOUR PREFERRED CANDIDATE PERIOD."[17]

Things actually intensified to the point that the Senate called Dorsey in for a hearing via Zoom, during which Sen. Ted Cruz asked him with evident anger, "Mr. Dorsey, who the h—— elected you and put you in charge of what the media are allowed to report and what the American people are allowed to hear, and why do you persist in behaving as a Democratic super PAC silencing views to the contrary of your political beliefs?"[18]

Commenting on all this several weeks leader, former presidential candidate and Speaker of the House Newt Gingrich wrote:

> When Twitter and Facebook censored the oldest and fourth largest newspaper (founded by Alexander Hamilton) because it accurately reported news that could hurt Biden's chances—where were *The New York Times* and *The Washington Post*?
>
> The truth of the Hunter Biden story is now becoming impossible to avoid or conceal. The family of the Democrat nominee for president received at least $5 million from an entity controlled by our greatest adversary [meaning China]. It was a blatant payoff, and most Americans who voted for Biden never heard of it—or were told before the election it was Russian disinformation. Once they did hear of it, 17 percent said they would have switched their votes, according to a poll by the Media Research Center. That's the entire election. The censorship worked exactly as intended.
>
> Typically, newspapers and media outlets band together when press freedom is threatened by censorship. Where was the sanctimonious "democracy dies in darkness?" Tragically, *The Washington Post* is now part of the darkness.
>
> But this is just a start. When Twitter censors four of five Rush Limbaugh tweets in one day, I fear for the country.
>
> When these monolithic internet giants censor the President of the United States, I fear for the country.[19]

Gingrich had far more to say, all of it raising serious concerns about the current (and potentially future) state of our country. All-out censorship could be coming, at least from social media giants and the mainstream media, meaning that multiplied tens of millions of Americans will be hindered from sharing their points of view, while multiplied tens of millions of other Americans will be hindered from hearing those points of view, which, to be candid, they may not even know exist.

As for how this censorship affected the elections, the Media Research Center, a conservative organization, conducted a poll shortly after the elections. According to the poll, about 17 percent of those who voted for Biden stated that they would *not* have voted for him had they known the truth about his record along with the truth about Trump's record (since many of them were not aware of Trump's many positive accomplishments, which the mainstream media rarely reported). "The biggest movement away from Mr. Biden was among his voters who only after the election learned about shady business deals involving Mr. Biden's son, Hunter. Forty-five percent of Biden voters said they didn't know about Hunter Biden's deals, and 9.4% said they would not have voted for the former vice president had they known."[20] To repeat the words of Gingrich, "That's the entire election."

You might say, "Facebook and Twitter and Google and YouTube and the like are all private companies, and they can do whatever they choose to do. It's our choice as to whether we participate. As for the mainstream media, the same holds true. They can be as biased or unbiased as they desire. We choose whether or not to watch."

There are two problems with this line of reasoning: (1) These social media giants serve as platforms rather than publishers, and they gained their massive following by allowing anyone to post anything within certain guidelines (such as prohibiting nudity or blocking posts calling for violence against others). So, we all joined in and signed on, some of us spending many years building our social media audiences, only to have the rules change midstream with a decided lurch to the left. This is unethical and unfair. (2) The mainstream media outlets, from ABC to NBC and from CNN to MSNBC, all claim to be reporting the news, in contrast, say, with a conservative radio host who is giving his or her take on the news. This is deceptive and misleading.

Interestingly, in July 2018, when Facebook was in the midst of a major lawsuit, *The Guardian*, a leading British publication, ran a headline that read, "Is Facebook a Publisher? In Public It Says No, but in Court It Says Yes." According to the story, whenever Facebook has been questioned about its alleged "disruption of the news industry," its response has been the same: it is neither a publisher nor a media company. Rather, it is a tech platform. But the story continues, "in a small courtroom in California's Redwood City on Monday, attorneys for the social media company presented a different message from the one executives have made to Congress, in interviews and in speeches: Facebook, they repeatedly argued, is a publisher, and a company that makes editorial decisions, which are protected by the first amendment."[21]

This new claim, then, which contradicts Facebook's longstanding position, "is Facebook's latest tactic against a high-profile lawsuit, exposing a growing tension for the Silicon Valley corporation, which has long presented itself as neutral platform that does not have traditional journalistic responsibilities."[22]

The lawsuit was based on issues other than censorship, but the case itself is quite relevant to the issue of censorship, since it presses the question of whether or not Facebook is a neutral platform. And when you realize that, as of this writing, a staggering 2.91 billion people are listed as active Facebook users, you realize how powerful these social media giants can be.[23] (That number represents about half of all human beings on the planet over fifteen years old.)[24] And they are on Facebook because they understand it to be a neutral platform, sharing their viewpoints freely and entrusting some of their personal information with Facebook privately. But can Facebook be trusted?

As reported by *The Intercept* on October 15, 2020, with reference to the Hunter Biden story in the *New York Post*:

> Just two hours after the story was online, Facebook intervened. The company dispatched a life-long Democratic Party operative who now works for Facebook—Andy Stone, previously a communications operative for Democratic Sen. Barbara Boxer and the Democratic Congressional Campaign Committee, among other D.C. Democratic jobs—to announce that Facebook was "reducing [the article's] distribution on our platform": in other words, tinkering with its own algorithms to suppress the ability of users to discuss or share the news article. The long-time Democratic Party official did not try to hide his contempt for the article, beginning his censorship announcement by snidely noting: "I will intentionally not link to the New York Post."[25]

Shall I quote Newt Gingrich once again? Perhaps this really did influence the election results, which is a frightening possibility given that Facebook and Twitter built their empires on our shoulders, gaining our trust as a neutral platform only to use that very platform, it appears, for partisan, leftist purposes. And when you add in the power of Google, which receives millions of queries *per minute*, the prospects become more frightening still, since there are now well-documented claims that Google decides which search results you see—in particular, which results you see first.[26] So much for its alleged neutrality.

In the very strong words of Sen. Ted Cruz, "I think hands down Google is the most dangerous company on the face of the planet. Google is the most dangerous because it's the biggest by far. It is the most powerful by far. It controls the vast majority of searches people do."[27]

Fox News' Tucker Carlson was even more blunt:

> Apart from Fox News, pretty much every major media outlet in the United States is beholden to Silicon Valley. Referrals from search engines and social media sites generate revenue that news organizations need to survive. So if you mess with Big Tech, you die. Those are the new rules, and they are unsustainable. You can't have a democracy in a system like that because people can't get the information they need to make informed decisions. You bypass the First Amendment.[28]

Even the British comedic actor Rowan Atkinson had something to say about all this, noting that "the problem we have online is that an algorithm decides what we want to see, which ends up creating a simplistic, binary view of society. It becomes a case of either you're with us or against us. And if you're against us, you deserve to be 'canceled.'" So said the man famous for playing Mr. Bean.

He added, "It's important that we're exposed to a wide spectrum of opinion, but what we have now is the digital equivalent of the medieval mob roaming the streets, looking for someone to burn. So it is scary for anyone who's a victim of that mob, and it fills me with fear about the future."[29] Let's call it the digital mobocracy.

Even Roger Daltrey, famed as the lead singer of The Who, weighed in with his concerns on the power of artificial intelligence (AI), especially when combined with woke culture. He said, "We should just go back to print and read books again. I don't know, we might get somewhere because it's becoming so absurd now with AI, all the tricks it can do, and the Woke generation....It's terrifying, the miserable world they're going to create for themselves. I mean, anyone who's lived a life and you see what they're doing, you just know that it's a route to nowhere."[30]

To be sure, some of us have been calling out these social media giants for years, with my first relevant article on the subject dating back to 2012. (I was hardly the first to do this, and even in 2012, this was not the first time I encountered social media censorship, as indicated by the article's title: "The Facebook Censor Strikes.")[31] By 2019, I had written twenty more articles documenting double standards, especially on Facebook and YouTube.[32]

This is best illustrated by the fascinating story of what happened to our animated, six-minute video "Can You Be Gay and Christian?" which was first posted in May 2018.[33] At this moment it remains on YouTube, with more than 197,000 views, over 4,400 comments, and 7,100 thumbs up compared to 5,200 thumbs down. But we have been banned from advertising the video on YouTube, where it has also been demonetized (meaning, it can be watched ten million times, and we would receive no income from the views).

Initially, YouTube approved our advertising campaign, which was quite modest, amounting to perhaps one or two thousand dollars. But the ads began appearing on gay and transgender YouTube channels—meaning that if you went to get an update on a teenager's sex transition on his or her YouTube channel, you might see our ad pop up first, featuring the opening seconds of my video with me asking, "Can you be gay and Christian?"

This was actually not our intent, since, in my mind, a person's channel is his or her space and, if possible, YouTube should not be running ads that are directly hostile to that channel's point of view. But what happened is what happened, creating a massive uproar that reached to high-level management within Google. Gay and trans YouTubers were up in arms, playing clips of our video (that they then mocked, of course), which then led to gay news outlets bashing our video, which then led to news outlets such as *Forbes*, *Business Insider*, and *The Independent* (UK) reporting the story.[34] (Ads for the conservative Christian law firm the Alliance Defending Freedom were also being aired on some of these LGBTQ channels, which added to the uproar.)

Soon enough, YouTube informed us that we could no longer advertise our video and that it had been permanently demonetized. Not long after that, every single video on the AskDrBrown YouTube channel was demonetized—at that point, more than 1,600 videos—with YouTube providing no explanation to us other than pointing to vague community guidelines that did not apply to the vast majority of our videos. Over time, most of these videos were remonetized. But to this day, no matter what content is found in our videos, the moment they are posted on YouTube, most of them are instantly flagged, which then requires us to ask YouTube to do a manual review, after which most of them are accepted. But why are they being flagged in the first place? It looks like we made it onto their list.

We actually produced a video one day in which I smiled at the camera and said, "Have a nice day. Have a really nice day. I hope you have a great day." That was about it, for less than a minute. We did it just to see if it would get flagged. Somehow, in that case, it didn't. But we have had other videos, almost as generic, that did get flagged. Why? As for other individuals or organizations with YouTube channels, their videos have been demonetized or restricted or removed entirely; in some cases, their whole channels have been removed for very sketchy reasons.[35] And while YouTube reviewers have, for the most part, been fair to us, we still can't tell why one video is approved for monetization and another is not, and there is certainly no basis for the vast majority of our videos being flagged at all. Why us?

Here, too, you have a situation where you can work for years to gain a YouTube following, abiding by the guidelines they have posted, only to see the goalposts move again and again. This is hardly a neutral platform. Worse still, many who post on YouTube use that as their place of video storage, not having the ability to store so many video files on their own. At YouTube's discretion, those videos could one day be removed without warning—and that means wiped from memory for good.

Getting back to our video "Can You Be Gay and Christian?," we learned through a Google software engineer name Mike Wacker what happened behind the scenes.[36] It turns out that Google employees who saw our video began to complain about it, leading to an outcry within the company. "How can you allow such a bigoted video to be promoted on our platform?" (That's my paraphrase of the complaint.)

More specifically, the video was flagged in June 2018 in the "Yes at Google" internal listserv, an e-list "run by Google's human resources department, according to those communications and other internal documents" (this, according to an anonymous source sharing information with the *Daily Caller*). "The listserv has more than 30,000 members and is devoted to policing 'microaggressions' and 'micro-corrections' within the company, according to its official internal description."[37]

In the end, "Google's vice president for product management and ads, Vishal Sharma, agreed that the video was too offensive to air as an advertisement."[38] And that's how the decision was made to ban our video from being advertised—meaning, we were banned from paying YouTube/ Google money to promote more views on our video. So much for neutrality. So much for impartiality. So much for being a platform rather than a publisher.

Some of my colleagues are regularly banned on Facebook, including one of the top Christian cultural commentators I know: Bill Muehlenberg, an American who has lived in Australia for many years. His columns, which are posted to his own website,[39] are always well thought out and carefully documented. Yet when he posts links to his articles on Facebook, he is sometimes banned for thirty days at a stretch, being banished to what he calls "Facebook prison."

One of his posts, dated April 18, 2019, was titled "Facebook Prisoner #9473782," in which he wrote:

> It seems that I am a recidivist. I appear to be a repeat offender. Evidently I am an evil person who must be locked away for the good of society. My humble thoughts are so damaging and threatening that in order to maintain the secular left status quo, I must be made an example of.
>
> I must be locked up. I must NOT be allowed to share truth on the social media. There is nothing worse it seems than to be an independent thinker who dares to offer contrarian points of view. In the name of diversity, all diverse posts will be pulled, and all diverse thinkers will be banned. Thanks FB.[40]

Check out his columns for yourself, and ask yourself if he is exaggerating at all. Having read many of his articles, having written the foreword to one of his books, and having spoken together with him at a conference in Australia, I can assure you that absolutely nothing he has written merits his being banished from Facebook, not for a single minute, let alone for weeks on end. And yet, at the very same time, as I and others have documented, Facebook will allow the vilest imaginable pages to go unchecked, including pages devoted to vulgar and graphic assaults on religious faith, especially Christianity. So much for being a neutral platform. (As if to underscore the gravity of the situation, on May 27, shortly before this book was submitted for editing, the same Bill Muehlenberg I just quoted sent out an urgent message, stating that he had been terminated by Facebook with no reason given. Canceled! Eliminated! As he explained, "Over 15 years' worth of work with hundreds of thousands of posts, comments and articles completely erased—in an instant! Nearly 5,000 contacts all stolen away from me! Stalin would be so very envious! Hitler would be jealous!")[41]

The bias of these social media giants is also seen in more subtle ways, such as Amazon's refusal to allow the Alliance Defending Freedom (ADF) to be part of its Smile program, which donates 0.5 percent of your Amazon purchases to a charity of your choice. This can include ministries and other nonprofits as well as formal charities. My own ministry fits under this program, which means that if you wanted us to receive 0.5 percent of your Amazon purchases, you would designate us on Amazon Smile and that amount would be donated to our nonprofit organization every time you purchased something there.

But when the ADF applied to the program, Amazon rejected them, since they had been designated a hate group by the notoriously left-leaning Southern Policy Law Center (SPLC), an organization once known for its exposing of legitimate hate groups, like neo-Nazis, but now better known for being an ideological hate group itself, with a focus on attacking Christian conservatives in particular.[42] The same thing happened to the Family Research Council (FRC), another highly respected Christian organization. Amazon excluded them from their Smile program, based on the SPLC listing.[43]

What makes this especially shocking, though, is that the ADF and FRC are not some obscure little Christian nonprofits. The ADF has argued numerous cases before the Supreme Court, winning some notable victories along the way. As even Wikipedia acknowledges:

> Alliance Defending Freedom (ADF) has been involved in several landmark United States Supreme Court cases, including *Rosenberger v. University of Virginia*, *Good News Club v. Milford Central School* and *Town of Greece v. Galloway*. *Rosenberger* was ADF's first landmark case, described by law professor Marci Hamilton as a "fork in the road" with respect to judicial review of the Establishment Clause of the First Amendment. *Good News Club* and *Town of Greece* established important precedents relating to Free Speech and the Establishment Clauses of the First Amendment respectively. But its most notable legal victory involved a 2014 case challenging the Affordable Care Act, or Obamacare. In *Burwell v. Hobby Lobby Stores, Inc.*, the Court ruled that the birth control mandate in employee funded health plans was unconstitutional. The case set a precedent for evaluating legal questions relating to religious liberty. Since 2015, ADF has played a role in five victories at the Supreme Court.[44]

Yet Amazon refused to allow this Christian nonprofit organization to be listed under its Smile program. Is this anything less than outright anti-Christian bigotry and bias?

As for the FRC, led by Tony Perkins, it is one of the nation's largest pro-family, pro-life, conservative Christian organizations, often with access to the highest echelons of the government. Speakers at the FRC's Values Voter Summits have included presidents, most recently Donald Trump, and prime ministers, including Israel's Benjamin Netanyahu. Yet the FRC, because it has been blacklisted by the SPLC, is banned from receiving funds through Amazon Smile. Once again, this is outright anti-Christian bias. It cannot be ignored.[45]

Exposing Radical Islam Can Get You in Trouble Too

On a very different front, activist Pamela Geller explained in February 2018:

> Google...has scrubbed all internet searches of anything critical of jihad and Sharia. So, if you google jihad and you google Sharia and you google Islam, you're going to get Islamic apologetics, you're going to get "religion of peace." Whereas my site used to come up top, page one for jihad and Sharia or Islam [or JihadWatch did], you can't find it now. They scrubbed 40,000 Geller posts of Google.[46]

She continued, "You know what? It's Stalinesque."[47] She wasn't exaggerating, and her example is just one of many. These days, all you have to do is label something as "hate speech," and you can get it removed from social media in a hurry.

Even Joe Rogan, hardly a conservative activist, noted how squirrelly things have become with hate-speech labeling on social media. (The context of his comment was his interview with Douglas Murray, himself anything but a conservative activist, noting how Murray's discussion with atheist Sam Harris was somehow labeled hate speech, thereby in violation of Twitter's community guidelines.)[48]

Yet Geller and Rogan made their comments during the years of the Trump administration, when he and the Department of Justice fought aggressively for our religious rights. Speaking in late 2020, the influential YouTube commenter Dave Rubin, who is gay yet somewhat conservative ideologically, raised some strong concerns about where Big Tech and censorship were going. He said:

> The ship has sailed with Big Tech....If Biden gets in, and especially if [Democrats] have the Senate—Trump was the last thing that was stopping Big Tech from lowering the boom—but I think 2021 will be the year of the bannings. It'll be soft bannings at first. It'll be more algorithmic depressions, deboosting, shadowbanning, that sort of thing, but then they'll start picking people off.[49]

Even Vice President Pence weighed in on this internet bias in 2020, saying, "I think we got to call them out. We got to hold them accountable every time there is an indication of censorship."[50] What happens when those in the White House or Congress or courts actually *support* such censorship? And what happens when the president of the United States, the most powerful leader on the planet, is banned by Twitter and Facebook and other social media platforms? What does that say about how powerless the rest of us are when these internet giants turn against *us*?

Over in Scotland, former Parliament member Brian Monteith, who first got involved in politics in the mid-1970s, noted that at that time, competing groups sought to have others "no-platformed," lest their views would gain a foothold and become popular. For example, the Anti-Nazi League attempted to get the National Front group "no-plaformed." He realized that "the smart way to deal with them was to challenge them to debate and beat them with facts, truth and appeals to community solidarity. Banning such people would only have made them victims that would in turn generate sympathy towards them and their cause."[51]

It was open debate, Monteith argued, that exposed these groups for who they really were. "History shows," he writes, "that by trusting in open debate they were repudiated overwhelmingly in election after election at both national and local level....My own experience of cancel culture demonstrates it threatens our ability to establish the truth or debate and develop the best social or economic policies. Only the enemies of an open and harmonious society can benefit—which makes it imperative Facebook reforms its protocols."[52]

These internet giants have the power to become the ultimate silencers. And they have targeted many conservative Christian lambs for silencing. It is a threat we must take very seriously.[53] That's why on May 24, 2021, Florida Governor Ron DeSantis signed Senate Bill 7072 into law, holding "Big Tech accountable by driving transparency and safeguarding Floridians' ability to access and participate in online platforms."[54]

Said DeSantis, "Many in our state have experienced censorship and other tyrannical behavior firsthand in Cuba and Venezuela. If Big Tech censors enforce rules inconsistently, to discriminate in favor of the dominant Silicon Valley ideology, they will now be held accountable."[55]

Lieutenant Governor Jeanette Nuñez added, "What we've been seeing across the U.S. is an effort to silence, intimidate, and wipe out dissenting voices by the leftist media and big corporations. Today, by signing SB 7072 into law, Florida is taking back the virtual public square as a place where information and ideas can flow freely."[56]

In short, if Big Tech is guilty of censorship, Big Tech will pay a price. The resistance continues to rise. The lambs are taking a stand.

Chapter 4

THE BLM-JEZEBEL CONNECTION

I WAS ABOUT TO go on a radio station to do an interview during the height of the Black Lives Matter protests in 2020—protests that had quickly turned into bloody riots, with buildings on fire, police cars smashed, and broken bodies lying in the streets. The elections were only a few months away, and the interview was supposed to focus on the relationship between Evangelicals and Donald Trump. But the interviewer had a different plan. First, he wanted to talk about my 2019 book *Jezebel's War With America*.[1] What, he wondered, was the connection between Jezebel and the riots shaking our cities?

In *Jezebel's War With America*, I outlined the spiritual connection between idolatry, baby killing, pornography, radical feminism, the war on gender, the rise in witchcraft, the emasculating of men, and the silencing of prophetic voices. The handwriting was on the wall. The message was undeniable. The same demonic spirits that worked through Queen Jezebel in the Bible three thousand years ago were at work again in America in a major, concerted way, seducing and destroying and intimidating and silencing. In that sense, once again, we were at war with "the spirit of Jezebel," in many ways the archetypical silencer of the lambs.

When writing *Jezebel's War With America*, I felt supernaturally gripped by God, being moved on to complete 70 percent of the core of the book in an intensive six-day period. During those days, the words came pouring into my heart and mind as quickly as I could write them, almost around the clock. Months later, once the book was released, many readers were gripped with that same intensity, unable to put it down. In fact, the first printing sold out the first week it was released.

Something was going on, and it was clear that the book brought a timely message to America. But what on earth did Jezebel have to do with the Black Lives Matter protests? The civil rights movement was hardly demonic, and this, we were told, was just today's version of that movement. It was a wake-up call to the nation. It was the coming together of young and old to protest police brutality against black Americans. It was a mandate to take the message of racial equality even deeper. It was time for lasting reforms. Surely black Americans have suffered more than their share of injustices and insults and incriminations. And surely every person of conscience should agree with this. I, for one, want to stand with my black brothers and sisters across the nation wherever they experience unequal and unfair treatment, and I want to do so loudly and clearly.

But there was more to the story than just civil rights. There was more to the story than a battle against racial injustice and a protest against police brutality. Instead, we quickly learned that the mantra "Black lives matter" (something that should be affirmed by every American) was not the same as the actual BLM organization.[2]

We quickly learned that the BLM organization wasn't concerned about many other black lives, such as the lives of black children killed in random inner-city shootings, the lives of black babies aborted in the womb, or the lives of black youths snuffed out in gang violence. We also learned quickly that something else was fueling the fires of the BLM organization, especially among its founding leaders. It was quite reminiscent of the spirit of Jezebel!

This Jezebelic influence becomes apparent the moment you begin to dig deeper into the origins of the movement. That's when you learn that BLM was founded by three black women, Patrisse Cullors, Alicia Garza, and Opal Tometi. Tometi is described as "a transnational feminist" and "a student of liberation theology,"[3] which goes hand in hand with the widely circulated quote from Cullors that she and Garza "are trained Marxists."[4] As for the connection between liberation theology and Marxism, especially in this context, Professor Anthony Bradley, himself black, has pointed out that "black liberation is Marxist liberation."[5]

A website celebrating "lesbians who tech" states that Cullors came out as queer at sixteen years old and moved out of her home.[6] Garza describes herself as a "Black queer woman" and states that "we must view this epidemic [of racial inequality] through a lens of race, gender, sexual orientation and gender identity."[7] That's why a June 21, 2020, ABC News article declared, "From the start, the founders of Black Lives Matter have always put LGBTQ voices at the center of the conversation."[8]

Reading through the official BLM statement (which was scrubbed from their website after a number of us drew attention to it), it seems as if being queer is as much of an issue for the movement as being black. Accordingly, there are several references to "trans," along with attacks on heterosexuality as the norm, as highlighted here: "We make space for *transgender* brothers and sisters to participate and lead. We are self-reflexive and do the work required to *dismantle cisgender privilege* and uplift Black *trans* folk, especially Black *trans* women who continue to be disproportionately impacted by *trans*-antagonistic violence."[9]

Even more forthrightly, the statement reads, "We foster a *queer-affirming* network. When we gather, we do so with the intention of freeing ourselves from the tight grip of *heteronormative thinking*, or rather, the belief that all in the world are heterosexual (unless s/he or they disclose otherwise)."[10]

The only references to heterosexuality are negative, as in "cisgender privilege" and "heteronormative thinking." So, BLM is fighting not just against "white privilege" but also against "heterosexual privilege." Make no mistake about it. That's why the statement also goes out of its way to include people of "actual or perceived sexual identity, gender identity, gender expression."[11] The leaders have made themselves abundantly clear.

But there's more, and this has often been missed in commentary on BLM beliefs. While their statement includes references to "mothers" and "parents," *there is not one single reference to fathers*. Not one. (Contrast this with the multiple references to queer and trans and gender identity.)

As for any mention of "men" or any reference to a male-led household, these are found only in totally negative contexts. Specifically, "we build a space that affirms Black women and is free from sexism, misogyny, and environments in which *men are centered*" (emphasis mine). Oh, those terrible, evil men. And this: "We make our spaces family-friendly and enable parents to fully participate with their children. We dismantle the *patriarchal practice* that requires mothers to work 'double shifts' so that they can mother in private even as they participate in public justice work."[12]

Yes, that oppressive, husband-wife, male-female union—that outdated, outmoded patriarchal dinosaur—must be dismantled. (And note the assumption that if something is "patriarchal," it is unfair to women. A truly fair relationship would have the husband home with the kids while the wife is out doing "public justice work.") This is the language of radical feminism in unabashed, undisguised form. This, too, is part of the queer, trans-affirming spirit. This, too, is the spirit of Jezebel. In sum, one of the main BLM goals stated, "We disrupt the Western-prescribed nuclear family structure requirement by supporting each other as extended families and 'villages' that collectively care for one another."[13] Is that clear enough?

So, without question, the official BLM movement, in contrast with the larger stand for racial justice, is Marxist-based, queer-affirming, trans-activist, traditional-marriage degrading, radical-feminist promoting, and more. In a certain sense, it is fatherless as well. It is certainly Jezebelic.

Yet there is still more. Patrisse Cullors has described how she and her colleagues called on the spirits of the dead at their BLM rallies and how these events had religious connotations for them, based on ancient African practices. She shared this openly in an interview with Professor Melina Abdullah, former chair of the department of Pan-African Studies at California State University, Los Angeles, and a cofounder of the Los Angeles chapter of Black Lives Matter.[14]

Their relevant video discussion on Facebook was posted on June 13, 2020.[15] Four days before that, Hebah Farrag posted an article on the Berkley Center website titled "The Fight for Black Lives Is a Spiritual Movement." Farrag explained how Professor Abdullah met with a BLM group in front of the house of Los Angeles mayor Eric Garcetti:

> She led the group in a ritual: the reciting of names of those taken by state violence before their time—ancestors now being called back to animate their own justice:
>
> "George Floyd. *Asé.* Philandro Castille. *Asé.* Andrew Joseph. *Asé.* Michael Brown.[16] *Asé.* Erika Garner. *Asé.* Harriet Tubman. *Asé.* Malcom X. *Asé.* Martin Luther King. *Asé.*"
>
> As each name is recited, Dr. Abdullah poured libations on the ground as the group of over 100 chanted "*Asé*," a Yoruba term often used by practitioners of Ifa, a faith and divination system that originated in West Africa, in return. This ritual, Dr. Abdullah explained, is a form of worship.[17]

Yes, this helps fuel the fires of the BLM movement: worship of the dead, calling on the dead, asking the spirits of the dead to empower the living today.

Abdullah and Cullors discussed this openly on their Facebook video, which Abraham Hamilton III brought to national attention on his daily radio show on August 13 by playing relevant clips in context.[18] In the video Abdullah stated that "we become very intimate with the spirits that we call on regularly. Right, like, each of them seems to have a different presence and personality. You know, I laugh a lot with Wakiesha, you know, and I didn't meet her in her body. Right, I met her through this work." Yes, the spirits of the dead even have names, like Wakiesha, with whom Abdullah exchanges some laughs.

Cullors, in response, explained how she has been empowered by these spirits and how the mantra to "say his (or her) name" was more than a slogan. It was an appeal to the spirits of the deceased to rise up and work through her and others. As summed up by Cullors, "The fight to save your life is a spiritual fight."[19] Ah, but it is the wrong spirit that is being invoked. Spell it out with me: J-E-Z-E-B-E-L.

And what happens to those who would dare stand up to this radical movement? The response is swift and clear: not only will you be marginalized as a racist and a bigot, but your business might be burned down or you yourself might suffer violence. Do not mess with the BLM movement!

After I discussed the Jezebel-witchcraft-BLM connection on a YouTube platform carefully watched by its critics,[20] the video was posted on an ultra-left website.[21] The responses were predictable, including comments like these: "Yeah pal, keep it up and they will be calling your name" (in other words, "you'll be dead soon"). And "Time to bring the lions back to the collisium [sic] for a buffet." Yes, bring back those lions to kill the Christians!

Of course, these were just irresponsible internet comments with no substance or force behind them. But they do reflect the hostilities we face and the battle we are in, and they do remind us of some of the demonic power fueling the BLM movement (which, to say once more, I separate from the fact that every black life matters).

We are dealing again with the spirit of Jezebel, the spirit of fear and intimidation. It is the spirit behind the war on gender and the emasculating of men, the spirit behind sexual perversion. It is the spirit of witchcraft. And it is absolute confirmation of the message of *Jezebel's War With America*, since what was very clear in 2019 became even clearer in 2020, flooding into our neighborhoods and communities and schools and, from there, leaping onto the screens of our TVs and smartphones and tablets.

Jezebel was on the march, out and proud, fierce and defiant, spreading in numbers and influence and power by the day. And this was not just a violent, bullying movement. It was a movement of indoctrination. All Americans must be trained in this new reality, or else. Jezebel smelled blood and was ready to take over.

From the Streets to the Classroom

But this was not simply a movement taking place on the streets and in the world of politics. It was a movement to indoctrinate the young as well, with major BLM talking points being adopted in school districts across

America. To give one case in point, an internet announcement posted November 16, 2020, urged New York City educators to "Vote YES on the Black Lives Matter at Schools Resolution at the UFT Delegates Assembly."[22]

The resolution was drafted "in collaboration with union leadership and educators within the Movement of Rank and File Educators and Black Lives Matter at Schools NYC Group," with a link to the latter.[23] That website, in turn, linked to the thirteen guiding principles of Black Lives Matter, which included queer affirming, transgender affirming, and "black villages."[24]

Queer affirming was defined as "working towards a queer-affirming network where heteronormative thinking no longer exists." *Transgender affirming* was defined as "the commitment to continue to make space for our trans siblings by encouraging leadership and recognizing trans-antagonistic violence, while doing the work required to dismantle cisgender privilege and uplift Black trans folk." The definition was followed by this value statement: "Everybody has the right to choose their own gender by listening to their own heart and mind. Everyone gets to choose if they are a girl or a boy or both or neither or something else, and no one else gets to choose for them." As for *Black villages*, it was defined as "the disruption of Western nuclear family dynamics and a return to the 'collective village' that takes care of each other."[25]

On November 19, 2020, the New York City teachers union passed the resolution, voting to incorporate these radical leftist guiding principles into their school curriculum.[26] And note this: 90 percent of the delegates voted yes.[27]

Interestingly, it was on November 18, 2020, that the *New York Post* reported that Megyn Kelly was pulling her kids from the private school they attended in New York City. It had become just too "woke" and "far-left" for Kelly, who cited a letter circulated by the school's diversity group. It stated, "There is a killer cop sitting in every school where white children learn. They gleefully soak in their whitewashed history that downplays the holocaust of indigenous native peoples and Africans in the Americas. They happily believe their all-white spaces exist as a matter of personal effort and willingly use violence against black bodies to keep those spaces white."[28]

But not even this was woke enough for these New York City educators. The public schools needed to adapt all thirteen of the guiding principles of the BLM movement, and woe to the educator who tried to resist.

There Is a Real Connection Between Cancel Culture and BLM

In his July 4, 2020, speech at Mount Rushmore, President Trump called cancel culture "one of [the woke mob's] political weapons" that is "driving people from their jobs, shaming dissenters, and demanding total submission from anyone who disagrees."[29] Critics dismissed his warning, claiming that cancel culture was "something that does not exist."[30] In response, William A. Jacobson posted an article titled "Cancel Culture Is Real."[31]

He wrote that cancel culture is not only real, "it's getting worse with the increased power of the Black Lives Matter movement." People are "being investigated or losing their jobs for criticizing BLM's origins or tactics." He continued, "This cancel culture has nothing to do with criticism or debate, and everything to do with silencing opposition so there is no debate. I know. I'm going through it now over my criticisms of BLM."[32]

In 2008, Jacobson, a clinical professor of law at Cornell Law School, started the Legal Insurrection website, which he describes as "a conservative law and politics website," resulting in a stream of threats and attacks, including calls for his firing, from people outside the school. But things got much worse in June 2020 when he wrote two blog posts critical of BLM, the first focusing on the myth of "Hands up! Don't shoot!"[33] and the second speaking against the rampant rioting and looting.

As a result, Cornell alumni launched an email and petition drive calling for his ouster, while twenty-one of his colleagues denounced him in a letter to the student newspaper, the *Cornell Daily Sun*. He was also denounced by the dean of the Cornell Law School, who did not give Jacobson the opportunity to rebut his charges, and a coalition of roughly twelve clubs are now boycotting his courses, calling on others to do the same.

Because of Jacobson's academic status, he cannot be fired for expressing these views. But, he writes, "I offered to publicly debate a student representative and a faculty member of their choice, but that offer was rejected. They don't want to criticize me. They want to silence criticism of BLM. While I refuse to be silenced, others are not able to risk such career pressure."[34]

As of June 6, 2020, the Free Speech Union listed the following as casualties of differing with the BLM movement:

- Grant Napear, who was fired from his radio station and forced to resign as play-by-play announcer for the

Sacramento Kings NBA basketball team for daring to tweet "All Lives Matter"

- Gordon Klein, a UCLA professor put on a leave of absence for refusing to cancel a final exam after the death of George Floyd
- Stu Peters, a radio host who was suspended for challenging the idea of "white privilege" while debating with a caller
- Martin Shipton, chief reporter of the *Western Mail*, who was "forced to step down as a Wales Book of the Year Judge after he complained that the Black Lives Matter protest in Cardiff broke the Welsh Government's social distancing rules"[35]

In the days that followed, these entries were added (among others):

- June 9, 2020: "The editor-in-chief of Bon Appetit, Adam Rapoport, has stood down after a piece he wrote genuflecting to BLM was judged to be insufficiently pious by his staff (and he wore an inappropriate Halloween costume 13 years ago)."[36]
- June 10, 2020: "LA Galaxy player Aleksandar Katai has been 'released' by the club following critical posts made by his wife Tea Katai about BLM protestors on Instagram."[37]
- June 10, 2020: "Leading economists, including Paul Krugman, are calling for Harald Uhlig, a professor of economics at the University of Chicago, to be fired as editor of the Journal of Political Economy because he criticised the BLM movement."[38]
- June 10, 2020: "BLM activists are demanding that Paw Patrol, the popular children's cartoon on the Nick Jr. channel, should be cancelled because it shows a positive view of police. This, in spite of the show muting its content on June 7th to show solidarity with BLM."[39]
- June 11, 2020: "David Shore, a 28-year-old data scientist, has been fired for tweeting an article by a biracial Princeton African-American studies scholar suggesting that rioting is politically counterproductive."[40]

- June 11, 2020: "Disney, T-Mobile, Papa John's, SmileDirectClub and Vari have pulled their ads from Tucker Carlson Tonight because of the Fox host's criticisms of the Black Lives Matter movement."[41]
- June 12, 2020: "Jessica Mulroney, has been fired from Canadian reality show I Do, Redo and Meghan Markle's best friend, after getting into an argument about BLM with a black influencer on Instagram."[42]
- June 14, 2020: "Lego has suspended advertising building sets and products including police stations, city police vests and the White House in solidarity with the BLM movement."[43]
- June 17, 2020: "Tiffany Riley, the headmistress of a high school in Windsor, Vermont, has been forced to take 'administrative leave' after writing a Facebook post in which she said, 'Just because I don't walk around with a BLM sign should not mean I am a racist.'"[44]
- June 26, 2020: "The Chair of the Board of Governors at British Columbia University, Michael Korenberg, has resigned after liking tweets criticising Antifa and Black Lives Matter protestors."[45]

And on and on it goes. Talk about silencing in the extreme.

The issue is not whether one agrees with all the actions and statements of these men and women. Instead the issue is that, for all practical purposes, they were denied the right to hold to an opposing viewpoint, however nuanced or fair or accurate or well stated that viewpoint might be. You either embrace BLM, with all its talking points and emphases, or you are out. In short, it is a matter of conform or be gone, of fall into place or be banished, of do obeisance or be labeled a racist. That is how cancel culture works.[46]

Punished for the Sins of Your Past

This reminds us of another aspect of cancel culture: you can be condemned today for something you did years ago, and I don't mean breaking the law or committing adultery. I mean you can be punished today, as an adult, for something stupid you said as a teenager, in particular, when it comes to race. There is no mercy, no forgiveness, no restoration, and no rehabilitation within this ruthless culture.

Consider the case of Mimi Groves, a championship-winning cheerleader in high school who was accepted by the University of Tennessee, her dream school, and by their cheerleading squad, which is one of the top squads in the nation. When she was fifteen, she posted a *three-second* video on Snapchat while she sat in her car in traffic, saying, "I can drive, [N-word]." That was it. Three years later, in the aftermath of the death of George Floyd, and while a senior in high school, she used her Instagram account to encourage people to "'protest, donate, sign a petition, rally, and do something' to help support the Black Lives Matter movement."[47]

So, whatever her intent was when she was fifteen, it was clear now that racial justice was important to her and that she wanted to stand with black Americans. And how many of us did not say or do something stupid and insensitive at the age of fifteen? What if those of us who are older today had social media when we were teens? How many of our idiotic moments would come back to haunt us years later?

Unfortunately for Mimi, one of her high school classmates, Jimmy Galligan, whose mother is black and whose father is white, decided to make an example of her after a friend sent him a text message with her three-second video. He sent it to the school faculty and administrators, but they did nothing about it, leaving him frustrated and angry.

So he waited for an opportune moment, and when he saw Mimi's post in support of Black Lives Matter, which he should have cheered, he decided instead to strike again, posting her three-second, offensive video on Instagram once he learned which college she planned to attend. From there, the video spread to other social media platforms, including TikTok, as a result of which the University of Tennessee received a flood of emails and letters, protesting Mimi's presence on the campus. And so, "within two days, she was kicked off the university's cheer team and forced to withdraw from UT under pressure from admission officials, citing hundreds of emails and phone calls from outraged former and current students. 'They're angry, and they want to see some action,' an administration official told Groves and her family, as reported by the *New York Times*."[48]

As for Jimmy Galligan, he says he has no regrets about what he did, feeling that he taught Mimi a lesson. As for Mimi, even though she issued a heartfelt apology for her earlier video, cancel culture demonstrated that it does not know how to forgive.[49] What a terrible and unfortunate shame.

I certainly hope that as Jimmy grows and matures, he will regret the damage that he did. And I hope that Mimi's story will have a very happy ending.

What is clear, though, is this: the nation has become so "woke" to social injustice and racial slurs that there is virtually no path of redemption for those who previously sinned—even for three seconds at the age of fifteen. How different this is from the example of Dr. Martin Luther King Jr., who said, "We must develop and maintain the capacity to forgive. He who is devoid of the power to forgive is devoid of the power to love....There is some good in the worst of us and some evil in the best of us. When we discover this, we are less prone to hate our enemies."[50] (We will return to this principle in chapters 14 and 15.)

Right now, hatred is consuming our society, with cancel culture helping to lead the way. And once again, even some within Hollywood are upset with it. The latest incident (meaning, as I write; once you read this book, there will doubtless be other examples) involves the long-time host of the TV show *The Bachelor*, Chris Harrison. Although I've never watched the show, I do know it is quite popular, and I've read that Harrison has hosted the show for years.

That ended in 2021, when photos surfaced of a contestant who had attended an Old South–themed party three years before. Harrison initially wanted to offer the contestant, Rachael Kirkconnell, some grace, saying in an interview that this happened in 2018 rather than 2021, at which time not everyone was as conscious of the racial insensitivity involved in these parties. After the interview, Harrison then issued this statement, which said, in part:

> What I now realize I have done is cause harm by wrongly speaking in a manner that perpetuates racism, and for that I am so deeply sorry. I also apologize to my friend Rachel Lindsay for not listening to her better on a topic she has a first-hand understanding of, and humbly thank the members of Bachelor Nation who have reached out to me to hold me accountable....I promise to do better.[51]

But that was not enough, leading to his resignation from the show. (Ironically, the current show involved a Black bachelor for whom the women were competing, with Kirkconnell being a lead contestant.) Not everyone was happy with that. As reported by Fox News, "Political satirist Tim Young said Harrison's temporary removal is 'ridiculous' given that Harrison's verbiage 'wasn't even offensive. He made the point that what this contestant did attending that party in 2018 was still OK, and now in 2021 it's not because everybody is being offended by cancel culture."[52]

According to Young, Harrison was being canceled because he noted "the nuance of cancel culture," claiming that "he's being canceled for pointing out that cancel culture has shifted in three years." This view was shared by Dan Gainor, vice president of the Media Research Center. In his view, Harrison's firing was "insanity." He said, "This is the kind of thing that we saw during the Chinese cultural revolution. This isn't something that happens in a free country." And Gainor placed the blame for today's cancel culture squarely on the left, who, he said, "replaced the Bible with their own new bible of sin."[53]

Well said!

The challenge for those who love the Lord and love their neighbor is to stand up for justice and to build bridges of reconciliation, while at the same time standing against the radical BLM movement, especially in its attempts to silence all dissenting views. It is to say that every black life matters and that we are committed to exposing racial inequality wherever it exists in our society without being intimidated by the BLM mobocracy or by a politically correct, leftist-driven, even Marxist-influenced agenda. It is to bow the knee to God alone, doing what is right in His sight regardless of cost or consequences. The question is, Will we?

Chapter 5

WHY ARE THESE LAMBS SO DANGEROUS?

LAMBS, IN THEMSELVES, are not threatening in the least. To the contrary, lambs are thought of as innocent, as those that go silently to slaughter. Why, then, should lambs, spiritually speaking, be viewed as such a threat to the world? Why would lambs be considered so dangerous, speaking here obviously of Christian "lambs"?

I could understand if Christians were forming armed militias and marching down the streets, threatening to subdue or kill those who stood in their way. But that is not what is happening among true followers of Jesus. Instead, we are seeking to live out our faith, to make Jesus known to a dying world, and to advocate for godly standards in our society—standards that we believe are in the best interest of our nation. Yet the very stands that we take are viewed as dangerous. The darkness does not like it when the light is turned on.

But there is another group of lambs that seems even less threatening. I'm talking about people who are just trying to live their lives. I'm talking about people who are not aggressively pushing an agenda on the society. I'm talking about people who have experienced great personal rejection and pain. In fact, in many cases they have lived through double rejection and pain. Yes, I'm speaking here about those who identify as ex-gay or ex-trans.

First they were rejected when they came out and announced that they were gay (or lesbian or bisexual or transgender or queer). Then, after having a life-changing experience with the Lord, they were rejected again for leaving behind their gay (or lesbian or bisexual or transgender or queer) lifestyle.

Why are these lambs so dangerous? Why is their very existence strenuously denied? Why are they considered such a threat?

To be sure, we have seen the silencing tactics of LGBTQ activists for many years now. We have seen their efforts to stifle opposing viewpoints, to suppress scientific claims that challenge their positions, to marginalize and demonize those who do not support their agenda. As I've been saying since 2004, those who came out of the closet (from their perspective, fighting for equality and freedom) want to put us in the closet. Those who were once marginalized and rejected now want to marginalize and reject those who differ with them, especially those whose differences are scripturally based. And you can be assured that these activists will be relentless in their efforts. As I've also said for years, the unspoken mantra of radical LGBTQ leaders is "We will intimidate and we will manipulate until you capitulate."

On a certain level, though, that is understandable. Those who were once bullied often become the bullies. And from an LGBTQ perspective, this is not some secondary agenda. This is about *their* lives, about being able to live freely, about having their relationships and identities recognized, just as heterosexual individuals and couples have done for millennia.

Still, the question remains, How could such a small percentage of the population wield so much power and influence? How could roughly 5.6 percent[1] of the nation intimidate multiplied tens of millions of others? The answer is that "gay rights" (or "LGBTQ rights" or even "transgender rights") have been embraced as the civil rights issue of our day. As then presidential candidate Joe Biden tweeted on January 25, 2020, "Let's be clear: Transgender equality is the civil rights issue of our time. There is no room for compromise when it comes to basic human rights."[2] Or, in the words of then secretary of state Hillary Clinton in 2011, "Like being a woman, like being a racial, religious, tribal, or ethnic minority, being LGBT does not make you less human. And that is why gay rights are human rights, and human rights are gay rights."[3]

In response to this way of thinking, Big Business, Hollywood and the media, Big Tech, and the educational system have all embraced the goals of LGBT activism, openly coming against those who do not conform. That is how the intimidation has become so powerful. And from a spiritual perspective, we could also say that this represents the spirit of the age, the spirit of the world, and therefore it is fundamentally anti-God and antichrist.

Of course, as followers of Jesus, we believe that every human being is created in the image of God and should be treated with dignity and respect. And when God calls us to love our neighbor as ourselves, that includes our gay or lesbian or transgender neighbor. In that sense, I can agree with what Hillary Clinton and Joe Biden were saying. Absolutely and categorically. But to the extent they mean that we are called to redefine marriage, that we are required to let transgender preferences trump the everyday needs of other people, that we are expected to negate biological reality, or that our biblically based views are being silenced, then I absolutely and categorically reject their words without equivocation or apology.

So, What Is the Issue With Ex-Gay and Ex-Trans Lambs?

But we still have not answered the question asked in the title of this chapter. Why are these activists so threatened by those who once identified as LGBTQ but no longer do? What is so dangerous about ex-gays? Why must they be silenced as well? Why are these lambs so dangerous? We'll return to that question shortly. First we need to look more closely at some of the silencing tactics of LGBTQ activists in recent years.

In 2012, GLAAD, which originally stood for the Gay and Lesbian Alliance Against Defamation, launched its so-called Commentator Accountability Project[4] (now known as the GLAAD Accountability Project). It started with a list of thirty-six "anti-gay" commentators—people whom GLAAD urged the mainstream media to keep off the air. Why? The views of these commentators were considered dangerous and could hurt people. Plus, GLAAD alleged, they really weren't experts in their fields. Among the first names listed were Chuck Colson, Tony Perkins, and Jim Daly, all of them highly respected national Christian leaders. Blacklist them![5]

As GLAAD explained, the

> Commentator Accountability Project (CAP) aims to put critical information about frequent anti-gay interviewees into the hands of newsrooms, editors, hosts and reporters. Journalists or producers who are on deadline often don't have the time to dig into the histories of a commentator. Audiences need to be aware that when they're not talking to the mainstream media, these voices are comparing LGBTQ people to Nazi Germany, predicting that equal treatment of LGBTQ people will lead to the total collapse of society, and even making accusations of satanic influence.[6]

So, these conservative leaders, presented in the most demeaning light possible, should be kept off the major networks. Their ideas—actually, our ideas, since I am on that list as well—are too toxic to be entertained. Only the pro-gay side should be presented. In light of that, I suggest that GLAAD really stands for the Gay and Lesbian Alliance Against Disagreement. Dissenting positions must be banned.

Another major player in censorship is the Southern Poverty Law Center, commonly known as the SPLC. As noted in chapter 3, this organization was once well known for exposing groups like the KKK. In more recent years it has become known as an extreme leftist organization, actively opposing conservative Christian groups and even organizations or individuals that seek to expose radical Islam.[7] Among those targeted by the SPLC are groups like the Family Research Council, led by the just-mentioned Tony Perkins and highly respected in Washington, DC, politics, to the point that presidents have spoken for their summit meetings. The SPLC also targeted the highly influential American Family Association, led by Tim Wildmon, as well as the Alliance Defending Freedom, one of the leading Christian legal organizations in America and one that has successfully argued several major cases before the Supreme Court.

Yet the SPLC had the audacity to label all of them as hate groups, just like neo-Nazis and the KKK. And lest you think that the SPLC is just a marginal fringe group, in years past, law enforcement—even up to the FBI—often relied on their data. They are also massively funded, to the point of allegedly having several hundred million dollars in the bank.[8]

In 2012, I made it onto a special SPLC list titled "30 New Activists Heading Up the Radical Right."[9] As I wrote in response:

> I never expected to be on the same list with the leader of the New Black Panthers (Malik Zulu Shabbaz), a former Grand Wizard of the Knights of the Ku Klux Klan (David Duke), a Jew-bashing White Supremacist (Don Black), and a Neo-Nazi (Morris Gullet), but thanks to the investigative genius of the Southern Poverty Law Center (the SPLC), I have made it into the big time.
>
> Yes, according to the SPLC's latest "Intelligence Report" (Summer 2012, Issue Number: 146), I am now on the illustrious list of "30 New Activists Heading Up the Radical Right." (You may want to think twice about reading the rest of this article. It's possible that your computer or digital device will be tracked by anti-radical-right cybermoles.)
>
> Also on the list were Pamela Geller (anti-Muslim!), Joseph Farah of World Net Daily (Patriot movement!), and David Barton (anti-gay historical revisionist!), among others. Yes, these are just some of the "new activists heading up the radical right." How ominous.[10]

And what, exactly, was my crime? I, too, was "anti-gay" (this subsequently was changed to "anti-LGBT"). I was put in the same category as white supremacists, neo-Nazis, and the New Black Panthers.

To be candid, as I stated in that same article, this was a real badge of honor for me, a sign that I was standing for righteousness. I was being slandered and maligned because of my biblical beliefs. But make no mistake about it: many others saw this attack from the SPLC as evidence that I was an evil and dangerous person, to the point that protests have been held outside university campuses before I spoke, with specific reference to the SPLC list. (One flyer attacking me in 2018 featured this caption: "Southern Poverty Law Center officially labels him as a hate group member.")[11]

Not only so, but the SPLC has been consulted by Big Tech for guidance on which organizations and individuals they should censor. That's why, as mentioned previously, Amazon has banned groups like the ADF or FRC from being listed as charities on their website, meaning that buyers cannot designate them to receive a portion of the sales. That is downright discriminatory, but it is part and parcel of LGBTQ activist efforts to silence those who differ with them. The SPLC has also counseled YouTube regarding which channels should be banned. This, too, is a very dangerous trend.[12]

Facebook has also relied on groups like the SPLC and GLAAD.[13] That's why it cracks down so hard on Christian conservatives. That's why our posts are often the first to be removed and our pages the first to be shut down. Twitter has also looked to some of these leftist activist organizations for guidance. That is why their community guidelines and rules are so skewed against people like us. And while I am not complaining or speaking in unbelief when I say these things, I *am* being a realist. That's why I've been sounding the alarm on this since 2004. It was clear that this censorship and suppression was coming, and I (along with others) tried to alert us so that we could catch it before it got to where it is today. Unfortunately, this is now where we currently stand. The question is, What are we going to do about it moving forward?

On January 24, 2021, I discovered that I had been temporarily locked out of my Twitter account, but there was no further explanation or way to appeal. I was simply informed that I had violated the Twitter rules and I was banned from using the account for the next twelve hours. I searched online for a way to appeal and found a way to submit my request. Not long after that, I received my answer from Twitter: I was being punished for a tweet that I had posted four days earlier. The tweet read, "Will I get punished by Twitter for saying that, in God's sight, 'Rachel' Levine (nominated by Biden to be his assistant secretary for HHS) is a man?" It looks like I got my answer!

As I wrote later that day:

> Yes, that was the offending tweet. It looks like Twitter answered my question!
>
> When biological truth conflicts with transgender activism, biological truth is banned.
>
> When biblical truth conflicts with transgender activism, biblical truth is banned.
>
> There was nothing hateful in the tweet.
>
> There was nothing that would incite violence.
>
> I didn't even "deadname" Levine, referring to him as "Richard."
>
> I simply stated the truth. In the sight of God, President Biden's nominee for assistant secretary for Health and Human Services is a man.
>
> Someone might challenge the statement, asking what gives me the right to speak for God.
>
> Someone else might claim to have a different perspective on God's point of view.
>
> And, of course, an atheist would dispute the whole notion of God.
>
> Fair enough. We can have those debates.
>
> But to block me for this tweet? Really?[14]

Ironically, on the very "rules" website to which I was directed, Twitter made this statement: "Twitter's purpose is to serve the public conversation. Violence, harassment and other similar types of behavior discourage people from expressing themselves, and ultimately diminish the value of global public conversation. Our rules are to ensure all people can participate in the public conversation freely and safely."[15] These days, it appears that "public conversation" goes only one way. Other colleagues of mine have been banned from social media platforms or had their pages or accounts removed. They crossed the forbidden line. They poked the LGBTQ bear.

As expressed by the Catholic author John Zmirak shortly after he was banished by Twitter:

> Remember the rules, people. It's okay to argue that every young person on earth should have his or her puberty blocked, using dangerous hormones. It's fine to promote, in all seriousness, hunting down every last unborn baby with Down Syndrome, and killing him in the womb. Or to defend China's massive use of Uyghur slave labor

to make Nike sneakers, Apple products, or just plain pick cotton in the fields. It's also acceptable to promote a global totalitarian religious state that persecutes homosexuals—as long as that state is Muslim.[16]

It's Worse Than You Think

Whole books could be written on this subject, documenting case after case after case of LGBT discrimination against others. But rather than make this abstract, let me give you a very personal illustration. I was speaking in Canada in 2019 when I was introduced to a man whose story I had referenced in my talk. I had read about his situation but didn't know him firsthand. It appeared that he and his wife were separated, and there was contention over the direction their fourteen-year-old daughter was taking. She wanted hormone treatment to start transitioning to male, and her father opposed it. So the case was taken to court, and the court sided with the daughter. But it gets worse.

Not only did the court tell the father that he did not have the right to stop his fourteen-year-old daughter from getting these potentially dangerous hormone treatments, but the court also ruled that he could not refer to his own daughter as "she" or call her by her real name. In fact, the court banned him from not only doing it in public but also speaking about (or to) his daughter in that way in private. In other words, in the privacy of his own home, if he referred to his daughter by her real name or referenced her as "her" or "she," he could be arrested and put in jail.[17]

I am not exaggerating this story in the least. I read about it and researched it online, I met other Christian leaders who knew the story firsthand, and then I met the father and spoke to him face to face. Can you imagine a situation like this? But it gets worse still—much worse.

When this father defied the court order not to speak publicly about his daughter's case, he was arrested and put in jail. Then, after serving one month in prison, his attorney made preliminary arrangements for a plea bargain with the court, allowing for his immediate release. Instead, when he got to court, the judge sentenced him to a total of six months in jail, along with a $30,000 fine.[18] And did I mention that he was placed in a high-security prison filled with violent offenders for what amounts to solitary confinement for up to twenty-three hours a day?[19]

And shall I tell you about workplace laws in New York City, where you could get a fine of $250,000 for refusing to refer to a transgender-identified person by the name of his or her choice or refusing to allow the person to use the bathroom of his or her choice?[20] Or shall I point to Norway, where making a private comment deemed hateful to an LGBT person or persons could get you a one-year jail sentence? If you dare to make the comment in public, you're looking at three years in jail, the same penalty for third-degree murder (meaning, by neglect) in Norway. You heard that right.[21]

And speaking of Norway, how about Norway's near-neighbor Finland? As of May 2021, "a Christian member of the Finnish Parliament [was] facing six years imprisonment for allegedly committing three crimes, including 'hate speech,' for sharing her opinion on marriage and human sexuality on social media, on television and in a pamphlet."[22] Does this sound crazy and impossible? Does it seem that there must be more to the story that we're not being told? Here is all you need to know. The parliamentary member in question is Päivi Räsänen, former Minister of the Interior. She is a member of the Evangelical Lutheran Church of Finland, former chair of the Christian Democrats, and a medical doctor with five children and six grandchildren. Yet she "has been under police investigation since June 2019 for publicly voicing her opinion on marriage and human sexuality in a 2004 pamphlet, for comments made on a 2018 TV show, and a tweet directed at her church leadership." Remarkably, she now faces two years in prison for each of the three criminal charges brought against her.[23]

So, for publicly questioning her church's teaching on the Bible and sexuality via Twitter, she is potentially facing six years behind bars. In response, Räsänen said fearlessly:

> I cannot accept that voicing my religious beliefs could mean imprisonment. I do not consider myself guilty of threatening, slandering or insulting anyone. My statements were all based on the Bible's teachings on marriage and sexuality....I will defend my right to confess my faith, so that no one else would be deprived of their right to freedom of religion and speech. I hold on to the view that my expressions are legal and they should not be censored. I will not back down from my views. I will not be intimidated into hiding my faith. The more Christians keep silent on controversial themes, the narrower the space for freedom of speech gets.[24]

Her warning is totally accurate and very timely. In fact, a Finnish pastor has been under investigation for comments he made about homosexual practice back in 2004![25] But will we wake up and speak up, or will America soon be like Norway or Finland or Canada—or England? Over in the UK, not only have a number of street preachers been arrested over the years for simply sharing what the Bible says about marriage and family and sexuality,[26] but on May 9, 2021, Christian Concern, a major legal organization in the UK, reported, "A Christian chaplain has launched legal action after being reported to the government's terrorist watchdog and losing his job for delivering a sermon in a school chapel that encouraged respect and debate on 'identity ideologies.'"[27] He preached this sermon in a chapel service for a school that claims to have a "'protestant and evangelical' Church of England ethos"—and for this, *he was reported as a terrorist to the government.*

Prior to his sermon, which was preached in response to questions from the students about LGBTQ issues, the school had brought in Elly Barnes, CEO and founder of Educate & Celebrate, whose mission statement reads, "We equip you and your communities with the knowledge, skills and confidence to embed gender, gender identity and sexual orientation into the fabric of your organisation."[28] But the school chaplain, Rev. Dr Bernard Randall, became concerned when, during the training of the school staff, Barnes instructed them to chant "Smash heteronormativity." And now, for preaching a fair-minded sermon that encouraged open dialogue and debate, the school reported him "to the government's counterterrorism watchdog, Prevent, as a potentially violent religious extremist." He was even reported "to the Local Authority Designated Officer (LADO) as a danger to children, which is the same point of contact for reporting concerns over paedophilia."[29] I am not making this up.

And what about Marion Millar, a Scottish feminist activist and the mother of two autistic children who has been charged under the Malicious Communications Act for allegedly transphobic tweets posted in 2019 and 2020? She is facing a potential two-year sentence (!) for the tweets, one of which simply "included a picture of a ribbon in the purple, white and green of the suffragette movement." Said Millar after a two-hour meeting at the police station, "I have been charged, I am absolutely gutted, I can't describe in words the stress this is causing me."[30] And all this for posting pro-feminist, anti-trans activist tweets.

The Pressure Is Mounting by the Day

For many years now, the Human Rights Campaign, better known as the HRC, has been monitoring businesses for their LGBTQ-related policies. And this organization carries tremendous weight, even to the point of hosting presidential debates and having past presidents speak at their fundraising events. Partly because of their influence, an overwhelming number of big businesses in America conform to their radical recommendations.[31] (For the record, I'm on their hate list as well.)[32]

More recently, however, they have been pushing their agenda aggressively in our children's schools and on our college campuses. As Dr. Albert Mohler explained on November 18, 2020:

> The accreditation of Christian colleges and schools has just been directly targeted by the nation's most influential LGBTQ organization. The Human Rights Campaign has recently issued a document directed at the incoming administration entitled *Blueprint for Positive Change 2020*. The *Blueprint* demands that President-elect Biden adopt a legislative agenda and enact specific executive orders that are in line with the LGBTQ movement—a movement that Biden pledged to champion.
>
> Contained within its pages are perhaps some of the most alarming demands that threaten religious liberty, and the mainstream media has given little to no attention to this dimension of the report.[33]

And what, exactly, does this mean? Mohler spells things out:

> In clear text, for all the world to see, the Human Rights Campaign summons the Biden administration to deny accreditation—or, at the very least, to facilitate the denial of accreditation—to Christian institutions, Christian colleges and universities, and, for that matter, *any* other religious institution or school that does not meet the demands of the LGBTQ orthodoxy. This would mean abandoning biblical standards for teaching, hiring, admissions, housing, and student life. It would mean that Christian schools are no longer Christian.
>
> This is insidious from top to bottom. Schools that will not get in line with the moral revolution, if the Biden Administration acts as demanded, will be denied their accreditation. We must not miss the language: Accreditation should be revoked for those who do not meet the LGBT "non-discrimination" standards or "science-based curricula standards."[34]

As Mohler rightly states, "In terms of accreditation, that is an atomic bomb."[35]

A few years ago, after speaking at a church in Florida, I was taken to lunch by two young couples. Both of the wives taught in elementary schools, one of them teaching first graders. Both of the women told me that the LGBTQ agenda was pervasive in their schools. They both said that if they raised any issue with the curriculum, it would cost them their jobs. Even the first-grade teacher said that this was the case in her classes. And this was completely without the new, discriminatory, silencing agenda proposed by the HRC.

That's why cancel culture is especially hard at work within LGBTQ activism, which includes a large array of powerful and influential LGBTQ allies. To give one case in point, in 2013, Pastor Louie Giglio was scheduled to pray at the second inauguration of President Barack Obama. Pastor Giglio is a well-known evangelical leader who is actively involved in fighting human trafficking, and it was in that context that he was invited to pray at the inauguration.

However, word surfaced that fifteen to twenty years earlier, in one of his sermons, Giglio affirmed biblical teaching about homosexual practice. That was it. One sermon. One time. And nothing that could be remotely called homophobic. Yet the outcry was so great that Pastor Giglio was basically disinvited, because of which he willingly withdrew from the event.[36] There was no way he would be allowed to speak having committed such a terrible sin some years earlier. Oh, the horror!

From a Christian perspective, I honestly wonder how it is that he mentioned the subject only once in all those years of public preaching. After all, as a pastor this is included in teaching about human sexuality and holiness, and the subject of homosexual relations is certainly quite relevant in our society today, coming up in almost any discussion with young people about Christian values. But the fact is that this was not his focus in preaching, to the point that only one reference was found in one single message. But that was more than enough for cancel culture, even in 2013.

To quote Dr. Mohler again:

> The imbroglio over Louie Giglio is the clearest evidence of the new Moral McCarthyism of our sexually "tolerant" age. During the infamous McCarthy hearings, witnesses would be asked, "Are you now or have you ever been a member of the Communist Party?"
>
> In the version now to be employed by the Presidential Inaugural Committee, the question will be: "Are you now or have you ever been one who believes that homosexuality (or bisexuality, or transsexualism, etc.) is anything less than morally acceptable and worthy of celebration?"[37]

As for Giglio's specific sermon, Mohler notes that it was,

> as we would expect and hope, filled with grace and the promise of the Gospel. Giglio did not just state that homosexuals are sinners—he made clear that every single human being is a sinner, in need of the redemption that is found only in Jesus Christ. "We've got to say to the homosexuals, the same thing that I say to you and that you would say to me...It's not easy to change, but it's possible to change," he preached. He pointed his congregation, gay and straight, to "the healing power of Jesus." He called his entire congregation to repent and come to Christ by faith.
>
> That is the quintessential Christian Gospel. That is undiluted biblical truth. Those words are the consensus of the Church for over 2,000 years, and the firm belief held by the vast majority of Christians around the world today.[38]

Yet it was for this very content that Pastor Giglio was found unfit to participate in a presidential inauguration—and remember the sermon was preached fifteen to twenty years earlier.

The War Against Ex-Gay and Ex-Trans Christians

Again, I could go on and on with examples like this, but by now the picture is clear. So let's turn our focus to the specific subject of this chapter: Why are ex-gay and ex-trans individuals considered so dangerous? Why must these lambs be silenced? I personally know quite a few ex-gay Christians, along with an increasing number of ex-trans Christians. Most of them are extremely kindhearted people—people who do not strike me as nasty and mean-spirited and aggressive. They have already been through a lot, and they tend to be very compassionate and caring. Not only so, but many of them have suffered tremendous rejection over the years, because of which most are not looking for another battle.[39]

Think about it for a moment. At one point in their lives, these people came out as gay or transgender. They may have been bullied in school. They may have lost friends over the years. Their families may have rejected them. Their churches may have spoken against them. This was the first trauma they had to survive, a trauma that could have lasted for many years.

Then they found a new community. They found new relationships. They found others who affirmed and accepted them. They were embraced as gay or transgender. But then something else happened. They became convinced that God had a better plan. They realized that they were not living according to His will. They cried out for forgiveness and transformation.

And whether their attractions changed or their identity issues disappeared, one thing was clear to them: God did not want them to live as gay or trans.

Because of this, they had to come out again. They had to suffer rejection for a second time. They had to be criticized and vilified and even demonized for the choices they were making. And all this happened to them despite the fact that they were not being hostile or confrontational or angry or hateful. There were simply saying, "This is what the Lord has for me."[40]

What, then, makes them so dangerous, to the point of society seeking to deny their very existence? Why are others in the LGBTQ community so hostile to them, even saying, "You do not exist! You are lying! You know inside who you really are. You are just putting on an act." Why this reaction? Why does their existence pose such a threat?

The answer is simply this: If there is such a thing as ex-gay or ex-trans, then the whole idea that you are born that way and cannot change goes out the window. If it is true that being homosexual or bisexual or transgender is not innate and immutable, then these things cannot rightly be compared to skin color, in which case LGBTQ rights cannot rightly be compared to the civil rights movement. Yet that concept has undergirded LGBTQ activism for decades. "This is who we are! We were born this way, and we cannot change, and it is cruel and human to suggest otherwise."

Therefore, the very existence of ex-gay and ex-trans individuals challenges this foundational assumption. It also says, "Even if you were born gay or trans, the fact is that all of us are born broken and flawed and fallen as human beings. And to all of us Jesus says, 'You must be born again!' Plus, the bottom line is that there is no reputable scientific evidence that we were born this way, and our own lives prove that change is possible." This is why the very existence of ex-gay and ex-trans individuals must be so strenuously denied. They completely undermine one of the main pillars of LGBTQ activism. That is why they are considered such dangerous lambs.

From "Gays Cannot Change" to "You Must Stay Gay"

But it doesn't stop there. It is now illegal in many states in America,[41] along with some foreign countries,[42] for minors to receive professional counseling to help them with unwanted same-sex attractions or gender-identity confusion. You heard that right. Illegal. The UN is even trying to ban it internationally.[43]

As I explained in April 2018:

> For the last few years, a growing number of states and cities have embraced legislation making it illegal for *minors* struggling with unwanted same-sex attractions or gender confusion to receive professional help, even with the full support of their parents.
>
> This would apply to a 14-year-old girl who was raped by her uncle at the age of 8 and now repulsed by men and attracted to women. If her parents stood with her and she wanted to meet with a trained counselor to help to get to the root of her attractions, in some states, that would be illegal. No professional counselor or therapist or psychologist would be allowed to help her.
>
> Yet in these same states, if an 8-year-old girl believed she was really a boy and wanted to receive professional help to affirm her male identity, that would be perfectly legal. A counselor could tell her parents to encourage her to dress and identify as a boy. That counselor could also recommend that, at age 10, she start taking hormone blockers, then prepare to "transition" fully to male at age 16, then has sex-change surgery at 18, with hormones prescribed for life.
>
> That would be perfectly legal. But for that same 8-year-old girl to say, "I want to be at home in the body God gave me. I don't want hormones and surgery. Can anyone help me?" The answer would be, "No. Such help is illegal."[44]

As outrageous as this is, it gets worse still. In 2018, California strongly considered passing a bill that would make it illegal for *all people of all ages* to get professional counseling for unwanted same-sex attraction or gender-identity confusion. That's right. All people of all ages. It was only with great effort that the bill was pulled before it was presented for a likely positive vote. You can be assured that it will raise its head again in the days ahead. (I dubbed this the "You Must Stay Gay" bill.)

Outside America, the state of Victoria in Australia has now made this into law. It doesn't matter what your life experience was. It doesn't matter if you were sexually abused. It doesn't matter if you are convinced by the Bible that God has a better way. It doesn't matter what your social or moral or familial convictions might be. If you have unwanted same-sex attraction or are suffering from gender-identity confusion, you cannot receive professional counseling to help you deal with the roots of these issues and explore ways to change.

Lest you think that I'm exaggerating in the least, let me give you the specifics of the legislation in Australia:

> The Change or Suppression (Conversion) Practices Prohibition bill makes it illegal to try to change or suppress a person's sexual orientation or gender identity in Victoria.
>
> It also gives the Victorian Equal Opportunity and Human Rights Commission (VEOHRC) the power to investigate reports of conversion practices and refer matters to police.[45]
>
> The law includes prison terms of up to 10 years or hefty fines for anyone caught trying to suppress or change someone's sexuality by conducting suppression practices.[46]

Yes, you read that correctly. As a professional counselor, you could go to jail for ten years for helping someone deal with his or her unwanted same-sex attraction. Ten years! This goes beyond silencing the lambs. This goes beyond cancel culture. This is now a matter of imprisoning people who simply want to help the lambs. This is why I and others have been raising our voices so loudly for so many years. These are the kinds of things we warned against. It is well past wake-up time.

This also helps explain why Amazon purged all the books of psychologist Dr. Joseph Nicolosi, a pioneer in ex-gay counseling, as we mentioned in chapter 1, as well as other ex-gay-related books. To that list we can also add books by authors Anne Paulk and Joe Dallas, who are prominent in ex-gay ministry. Dallas' *Desires in Conflict: Hope for Men Who Struggle With Sexual Identity* and Paulk's *Restoring Sexual Identity: Hope for Women Who Struggle With Same-Sex Attraction* were sold on Amazon for years, but "are now no longer available for purchase," according to the *Christian Post.*

As Dallas rightly stated, "Amazon's decision is no surprise since today's culture is caving to the goals of the LGBTQ political movement, which have always included the silencing [of] any disapproval of homosexuality."[47]

That's why Dr. Kenneth Zucker, considered by many to be the leading authority on transgender-identified children—and not a Christian, let alone a fundamentalist Christian by any stretch of the imagination—was forced out of the clinic he led for many years in Canada, simply because he would not bow down to radical trans-activist ideologies.[48]

That's also why social media sites have shut down the pages of ex-gay networks. It's why I wondered in 2018 if California would be banning the Bible, since the Bible clearly teaches that change is possible for everyone, including those with same-sex attraction.[49] And what would happen to pastors who offer counseling to congregants, including minors, with unwanted same-sex attraction or gender-identity confusion? In countries like Australia, pastors are openly saying that they will not submit to this draconian bill.[50]

The Argument Against "Conversion Therapy"

You might be wondering if any other argument is raised by those who oppose professional counseling for people with unwanted attractions or identity issues. The answer is absolutely yes. We are told that so-called conversion therapy is terribly dangerous and abusive. That's because many of those who identify as LGBTQ did try to change at different times in their lives, some of them under parental coercion. Those who underwent "conversion therapy" claim that the efforts were deeply traumatizing, and some have raised charges of ugly and abusive practices.

In some cases, it seems clear that those who have brought these charges are lying.[51] In other cases, they are referring to outmoded psychological and psychiatric practices, including shock treatment. These practices were widespread in the past for many different conditions and behaviors, and they have rightly been dropped or even outlawed.

Yet there is no question that many sincere people have been hurt in their efforts to change their sexuality or gender identity, and there is no question that children have been deeply hurt when their parents forced them to try to change. Think of a black person being told, "You must become white." Or think of a left-handed adult athlete being told he or she must become right-handed. I am sensitive to these issues, having read enough stories and interacted with enough individuals, and I always counsel parents to have an extremely loving approach to their kids who come out as gay or trans.

But that is not the real issue here. First, despite popular perceptions, there are no major studies indicating that this type of counseling is more harmful than any other type of counseling that tries to help people bring about lifestyle or emotional or psychological change. As with all types of counseling and therapy, there are good outcomes and bad outcomes.[52]

As noted in a decision made by the Eleventh Circuit Court regarding a proposed ban on sexual orientation change efforts (SOCE) in Boca Raton, Florida:

> Defendants say that the ordinances "safeguard the physical and psychological well-being of minors." Together with their amici, they present a series of reports and studies setting out harms. But when examined closely, these documents offer assertions rather than evidence,

> at least regarding the effects of purely speech-based SOCE. Indeed, a report from the American Psychological Association, relied on by the defendants, concedes that "nonaversive and recent approaches to SOCE have not been rigorously evaluated." In fact, it found a "complete lack" of "rigorous recent prospective research" on SOCE. As for speech-based SOCE, the report notes that recent research indicates that those who have participated have mixed views: "there are individuals who perceive they have been harmed and others who perceive they have benefited from nonaversive SOCE." What's more, because of this "complete lack" of rigorous recent research, the report concludes that it has "no clear indication of the prevalence of harmful outcomes among people who have undergone" SOCE. We fail to see how, even completely crediting the report, such equivocal conclusions can satisfy strict scrutiny and overcome the strong presumption against content-based limitations on speech.[53]

Not only so, but no one is talking about coercing minors to do anything. And no one is talking about carrying out barbaric practices on children or adults. To the contrary, we are talking about the government refusing counseling—in other words, sitting and talking with someone—to those who want it. This is a matter of saying to someone, "You must stay gay!" or "You must stay trans!" Governments are saying, "You are not even allowed to consider the possibility of change!" Who on earth gave them that right?

What a cruel position for a state or country to adapt. What an egregious example of governmental overreach. What an insult to personal freedom, not to mention religious liberty. What an invasion of doctor-client privacy (or, in some cases, religious leader and parishioner privacy). Could you imagine laws like this in any other similar situation? Could you imagine telling someone, "You have an obese gene, so you must stay fat." Or "You will always be angry. You were born that way. You can't even try to change." Or "You will always be addicted to pornography. You have had sexually unclean thoughts as long as you can remember. You just have to accept it." Who can imagine such a thing?

Of course, to those who celebrate their gay or transgender identity, such comparisons are terribly offensive. But to a man who desperately wants to be attracted to his wife rather than to other men, to the young lady who really wants to marry a man and have biological children rather than have a lesbian relationship, or to the ten-year-old child who is tormented, feeling that he is trapped in the wrong body, all these feelings and perceptions are very negative. Why shouldn't they be allowed to explore the possibility of change, especially if they are people of faith and believe that all things are possible with God? Or, at the least, why shouldn't they be allowed to get professional help in discovering the roots of their feelings and perceptions, with the goal of starting a new life? To ask again, who gives the government the right to intrude into such personal decisions?

That is why we must go back to the first point I made. The reason for the all-out attack on any type of efforts to bring about change is because *the very existence of ex-gay and ex-trans individuals threatens to undermine the entire LGBTQ movement.* Because of that and because of the intense attack coming against these precious people, with all my heart I urge Christian leaders around the world to stand with these brothers and sisters, and I urge Christian individuals and families to help shield them from the onslaught and attack and from the lies and the pressure. You can do that by learning to be sensitive to their stories, to their history, and to their current challenges. You can do that by not shunning them due to the controversies involved. You can do that by demonstrating true love.

With the loudest voice possible, then, let us join together with our ex-gay and ex-trans friends in shouting to the world, "In Jesus, change is possible—wonderful, lasting, glorious change. All things are possible with the Lord!"[54] And let us go preach liberty to all in the power of the Spirit and in the name of the Lord.

These lambs will not be silenced—not on our watch.

Chapter 6

THE ALL-OUT ASSAULT ON OUR CHILDREN

SATAN IS NOT just trying to silence the next generation. He is seeking to wipe it out, declaring an all-out war on our children. They are being slaughtered in the womb. They are being kidnapped and sold into sex slavery.[1] They are being raped and abused and neglected and used. They are being brainwashed by their teachers and bullied by their peers. They are lost and lonely, depressed and suicidal. They cut themselves and kill themselves. Their innocence is being robbed, and their security is being stolen.

Without exaggeration, we can say that no generation in American history has been subject to such a concerted demonic attack. Just put yourself in the place of a child today, starting your dangerous journey to adulthood from within the womb. From the moment of conception, your life is at risk. Will you make it out of the womb, or will you be like the multiplied millions who have been cut down before they could breathe their first official breath?

The demonic attack against you is especially acute if you are a black baby. You have less than a 75 percent chance of making it out of the womb alive because of abortion.[2] If you are a black baby conceived in New York City, you have less than a 50 percent chance of making it out of the womb alive.[3] As a result, "According to the Centers of Disease Control and Prevention, abortion kills more black people than HIV, homicide, diabetes, accident, cancer, and heart disease…combined."[4] Can anyone spare some tears?

In your case, thankfully, you survive your mother's pregnancy and emerge from the womb to take that first breath, a beautiful little girl. But are you born into a broken home? Will you know your biological mother and father? Or will your mother's boyfriend abuse you physically or even sexually? Perhaps your father is an anonymous sperm donor. Who are you, really? Will you ever know for sure?

Once again, though, you are among the fortunate ones. You have a mommy and a daddy, and they love to do special things with you, like take you to the library, even as a toddler. One of the highlights is an event called Drag Queen Story Hour. Those drag queens are so fun!

A couple of years later, in your pre-K class, the teacher reads storybooks to you, pretty books with colorful pictures. Some feature boys wearing dresses; others depict a little girl with her two daddies. And your teacher refers to all of you as "friends," since calling you "boys and girls" makes unnecessary gender distinctions—whatever those are. Once you're in kindergarten and first grade, you'll learn more about gender, and you'll find out that some boys are really girls and some girls are really boys. Maybe that applies to you!

Soon enough, you've discovered the wonderful world of the internet. So many games to play, and so many movies to watch. But one day, when you're just eight, you ask your mommy, "Why don't those people have any clothes on?" You have now been introduced to porn.

When you reach the age of twelve, the boy you like at school pressures you to text him a picture of yourself—naked. Soon enough, the other kids are giggling as you walk by, whispering things to each other. Your picture has now spread throughout the school.

Before you know it, you're cutting yourself to deal with the pain. But when that doesn't work, you attempt suicide for the first time. You just turned thirteen.

Lucky for you, your parents have a lot of money, so they're able to send you to a brand-new school where you meet a whole group of great new friends. And they are so cool. Two of the boys just came out as gay. They are really popular now.

As for your best girlfriend, within a year she'll get pregnant and have an abortion. (Of course, her parents won't know anything about it.) She'll also get an STD. How will she keep that a secret? But the two of you can keep your minds clear by putting on your headphones and dancing along to songs like "WAP."[5] Now you have some role models to follow.

Your kid brother, though, isn't into music. Instead he plays violent, gory, sexually explicit video games six hours a day. As for your loving parents, they're just glad both of you are staying out of trouble. And did I say you're barely fourteen?

Whatever happened to innocence? Whatever happened to purity? Whatever happened to childhood?

But there's a problem with your new school. All the girls are prettier than you and have perfect bodies, not like yours. "How I hate myself!" you say every time you look in the mirror. But no matter how little you eat, that fat is still there. It's back to cutting again.

At last, though, you find a way to ease your pain. Drugs! You already toyed with marijuana, since it's legal in your state and your parents don't mind sharing a little with you every so often. But now that you discovered uppers—how wonderful! You haven't felt this good in years. You're happy. The world is a better place. You even feel good about yourself. That is, until you can't get enough stimulants into your body and the lows become far worse than the highs. You barely survive your second suicide attempt.

Somehow, you manage to graduate from high school, enrolling in one of the top colleges in the nation. There you will learn that America is an evil country, that all whites are guilty, that belief in the Judeo-Christian God is a joke, and that there is no such thing as absolute morality. Or absolute truth. Or absolute reality. Things are what you perceive them to be. You define reality. And truth. And morality. As for subjects like history and geography, what matters is how you feel about ancient events and places on the map. That's what you're getting for more than $40,000 a year.

To be fair, though, you *will* learn some very helpful skills, like remembering everyone's preferred gender pronouns, such as *xe* and *zer* and *hir*. On the other hand, should you question anything you're being taught, you'll learn something else very quickly: dissent is not permitted. Now you're ready to be an adult.[6]

Some Jarring and Painful Stats

Obviously not every child in America shares the experiences of this child we have just described. But quite a few do, going through at least one or two of these difficult, negative, even destructive experiences. And so, having looked at the journey of an individual child in America today, let's look at some nationwide trends affecting tens of millions of young people.

We'll start with suicide. One website explains:

- Suicide is the **SECOND** leading cause of death for ages 10–24.
- Suicide is the **SECOND** leading cause of death for college-age youth and ages 12–18.
- More teenagers and young adults die from suicide than from cancer, heart disease, AIDS, birth defects,

stroke, pneumonia, influenza, and chronic lung disease **COMBINED.**

- Each day in our nation, there are an average of over 3,703 attempts by young people grades 9–12. If these percentages are additionally applied to grades 7 and 8, the numbers would be higher.[7]

A 2019 story in the *Washington Post* reports, after many years of fairly stable rates of youth suicide, from 2007 to 2017, suicides among those aged 10–24 jumped dramatically, "from 6.8 deaths per 100,000 people to 10.6." As a result, the second-most-common cause of death among young people today, meaning, among young adults and teenagers, is now suicide, passing homicides as the previous second-most-common cause of death and surpassed only by accidents.

"Just looking at these numbers, it's hard not to find them completely disturbing. It should be a call to action," said Lisa M. Horowitz, a pediatric psychologist at the National Institute of Mental Health. "If you had kids suddenly dying at these rates from a new disease or infection, there would be a huge outcry. But most people don't even know this is happening. It's not recognized for the public health crisis it has become."[8]

Going back to 2001, when teen suicide rates were much lower than today, three professors sounded the alarm:

> Between 1950 and 1990, youth-suicide rates tripled (particularly among young men), while suicide rates for adults fell by 7 percent, and suicide rates for the elderly fell by 30 percent....
>
> If youth suicide is an epidemic, attempted suicide is even more so. For every teen who commits suicide (0.01 percent each year), four hundred teens report attempting suicide (4 percent each year), one hundred report requiring medical attention for a suicide attempt (1 percent each year), and thirty are hospitalized for a suicide attempt (0.3 percent each year).[9]

Yes,

> between 1970 and 1980, 49,496 of the nation's youth (15–24 years of age) committed suicide. The suicide rate for this age group increased 40% (from 8.8 deaths per 100,000 population in 1970 to 12.3/100,000 in 1980), while the rate for the remainder of the population remained

> stable. Young adults (20–24 years of age) had approximately twice the number and rate of suicides as teenagers (15–19 years old).[10]

Along with issues like suicide, another website explains that in the next twenty-four hours, in the United States:

- 2,795 teenage girls will become pregnant.
- 15,006 teens will use drugs for the first time.
- 3,506 teens will run away.
- 2 teens will be murdered.[11]

What about children being sexually abused?

- During a one-year period in the US, 16 percent of youth ages 14 to 17 had been sexually victimized;
- Over the course of their lifetime, 28 percent of US youth ages 14 to 17 had been sexually victimized;
- Children are most vulnerable to CSA [child sexual abuse] between the ages of 7 and 13.[12]

Even more shockingly, "according to a 2003 National Institute of Justice report, 3 out of 4 adolescents who have been sexually assaulted were victimized by someone they knew well."[13] And in a major, government-sponsored 2016 report, "among the eye-opening statistics shared" was the fact that "one website on Tor hosted 1.3 million images depicting children subjected to violent sexual abuse."[14]

Focusing on the incalculable damage done by porn:

- Sixty-four percent of young people ages 13–24 actively seek out pornography weekly or more often.[15]
- Porn sites received more website traffic in 2020 than Twitter, Instagram, Netflix, Zoom, Pinterest, and LinkedIn combined.[16]
- Recorded child sexual exploitation (known as "child porn") is one of the fastest-growing online businesses.[17]

- More than 624,000 child porn traders have been discovered online in the US.[18]

Is your heart bursting yet?

In his major exposé in the *New York Times*, Nicholas Kristof put names and faces to this horrific sexploitation of children. He wrote:

> After a 15-year-old girl went missing in Florida, her mother found her on Pornhub—in 58 sex videos. Sexual assaults on a 14-year-old California girl were posted on Pornhub and were reported to the authorities not by the company but by a classmate who saw the videos. In each case, offenders were arrested for the assaults, but Pornhub escaped responsibility for sharing the videos and profiting from them.[19]

But there's more:

> That supposedly "wholesome Pornhub" attracts 3.5 billion visits a month, more than Netflix, Yahoo or Amazon. Pornhub rakes in money from almost three billion ad impressions a day. One ranking lists Pornhub as the 10th-most-visited website in the world.[20]

In this October 2020 ranking, the thirteen most-visited websites were Google, YouTube, Facebook, Twitter, Instagram, Baidu (the Chinese equivalent of Google), Wikipedia, XVideos, Yandex (Russian), Pornhub, XNXX, Yahoo, and Amazon.[21]

> Pornhub is owned by Mindgeek, a private pornography conglomerate with more than 100 websites, production companies and brands. Its sites include Redtube, Youporn, XTube, SpankWire, ExtremeTube, Men.com, My Dirty Hobby, Thumbzilla, PornMD, Brazzers and GayTube. There are other major players in porn outside the Mindgeek umbrella, most notably XHamster and XVideos, but Mindgeek is a porn titan. If it operated in another industry, the Justice Department could be discussing an antitrust case against it.
>
> Pornhub and Mindgeek also stand out because of their influence. One study this year by a digital marketing company concluded that Pornhub was the technology company with the third greatest-impact on society in the 21st century, after Facebook and Google but ahead of Microsoft, Apple and Amazon.[22]

As for kids cutting themselves (as a way to distract themselves from their emotional pain or to enable them to feel something, since they are so emotionally numb):

> Self-injury, particularly among adolescent girls, has become so prevalent so quickly that scientists and therapists are struggling to catch up. About 1 in 5 adolescents report having harmed themselves to soothe emotional pain at least once, according to a review of three dozen surveys in nearly a dozen countries, including the United States, Canada and Britain. Habitual self harm, over time, is a predictor for higher suicide risk in many individuals, studies suggest.[23]

Is your holy blood boiling now? To every parent reading these words, to every educator, to every coach or mentor, to every big brother or sister, to every responsible adult or older teen, I ask, Isn't it time to say, "Enough is enough!"? Isn't it time to shout from the rooftops, "Not on my watch!"?

Even the effects of social media can be devastating for young people, as they literally become addicted to digital stimuli. Some of the negative side effects include depression, anxiety, sleep deprivation, and communication issues.[24] The Mayo Clinic reported in December 2019 on the many negative effects of social media on teens, ranging from distraction to disruption of sleep and from exposure to bullying, peer pressure, and rumor spreading to "unrealistic views of other people's lives." Not surprisingly, the report indicated that the more time these teens spent on social media, the more likely they were to be negatively impacted, to the point that, "Another 2019 study of more than 12,000 13- to 16-year-olds in England found that using social media more than three times a day predicted poor mental health and well-being in teens." This has been confirmed by other studies which "also have observed links between high levels of social media use and depression or anxiety symptoms."[25]

So, kids today have more "friends" than ever before, thanks to social media, but are lonelier and more isolated than ever before, also thanks to social media. And whatever cruelty and bullying they may experience face to face in normal, everyday life situations is now multiplied exponentially through social media. Yet there is so much more they face in this age in which we live.

The Sexualizing of Our Children

I'm holding in my hands a book written by Catholic author Randy Engel, titled *Sex Education: The Final Plague*. Chapter titles in this confrontational, strongly worded book include "The Evolution of the Plague," "The Reactivation of the Plague," "The Collapse of the Opposition" (referring specifically to Catholic opposition), "The Production of Perverts," and "Sex Education in Catholic Drag—An Analysis of *Love and Life*." But what is most striking is that this book was first published in 1989.[26]

Yes, more than three decades ago, Engel could already point to the disastrous effects of this government-sponsored sex-education curricula on our kids. In fact, her chapter on "The Evolution of the Plague" focuses on the years 1945–1964, while her chapter on "The Reactivation of the Plague" traces things into the early 1970s. And she notes, "When the late Alan Guttmacher, M.D., former president of Planned Parenthood and a signatory of the Humanist Manifesto II, was asked how the Supreme Court abortion decision of January 22, 1973 [meaning Roe v. Wade] could be made absolutely secure—once and for all—he responded with two words: 'sex education.'"[27]

Engel cited Dr. Melvin Anchell, who argued in 1981 that

> when sex educators devalue parental influence...they in effect devalue the student's conscience. At the *same* time they are instrumental in "removing societal inhibitions," they intensify their efforts for "sexual openness" and they teach the students "to rely entirely on their own inexperienced and immature judgments and those of their peers."
>
> One of the results of this indoctrination process, charges Anchell, is the formation of a "horde culture," which is characterized by "sexual indulgences...devoid of love." The indoctrinated show no "guilt, nor do they display concern for morality." They are in effect the new barbarians![28]

Do you think Dr. Anchell was exaggerating?

But the attack on our children's innocence goes far beyond the classroom, as I noted in a two-part 2011 article titled "Please Stop Sexualizing Our Children." The article began:

> The recent cover of the French edition of Vogue magazine caused considerable controversy, and it was not because of the all too typical, female model featured in a sensual pose. Instead, it was the fact that the model this time was a 10 year-old girl.

> The headline of an article appearing on JewishJournal.com announced that, "Vogue Blurs the Line between Fashion & Pedophilia with 10 Year Old Model," and the article's author, Ilana Angel, rightly noted that, "A 10 year old is not able to distinguish between playing dress up in mommy's make-up and high heels, and proving a sexual aid to pedophiles." How true!
>
> But this is only one, extreme example of the way our kids are being sexualized. How many children watch MTV and VH1, mimicking the moves and memorizing the lyrics of the latest song by Britney Spears or Lady Gaga, having no clue that the moves they are making and the words they are mouthing are sexually charged. These kids are too young to have any understanding of sexuality, and yet it is no secret to the TV execs that these same children are a major part of the viewing audience.
>
> And was anyone really surprised when Miley Cyrus outgrew Hannah Montana and discovered pole dancing instead? What are her youthful followers to make of her now? Perhaps they'll follow her lead? Perhaps they'll ask mom and dad for a pole of their own at home?[29]

Fast-forward to 2020, when Netflix came under attack for distributing (and aggressively promoting) the French film *Cuties*. This prompted me to write four articles. The first, called "Outrage for the Children," was published August 21, 2020, and began with these words (and with each point documented):

> At what point does this stop? At what point does our society say, "Enough is enough" when it comes to the assault on our children? At what point do we stand up as a nation and put a stop to this attack on innocence?
>
> There was a time when our kids were not bombarded with "pornographic" sex-ed curricula in middle school.
>
> There was a time when condoms were not given out to elementary school students.
>
> There was a time when first graders were not taught LGBTQ terminology.
>
> There was a time when we did not celebrate 8-year-old drag queens (and when drag queens did not twerk for our toddlers in libraries).
>
> There was a time when movies were not made about 11-year-old girls joining sensual dance teams.
>
> But that time is not now, and the assault on our children's innocence is at an all time high. Should we not be concerned? Should we not be grieved? Should we not be outraged?[30]

I then pointed to the outrageous content of the new sex-ed curriculum for California children before noting, "Now, Netflix has come under attack for its new documentary called *Cuties*. Yes, 'The streaming giant is facing backlash for its promotional poster for the French film, whose young stars are 11-years-old. The promo image in question shows the children wearing revealing dance attire of shorts and crop tops and striking various dance poses, like kneeling on the floor and squatting.'"[31]

I followed that up with a September 11, 2020, article titled "The Depravity of a Culture That Celebrates the Sexploitation of Young Girls." It began:

> Now that the new Netflix movie *Cuties* is available for viewing, we know that it is far worse than we imagined. Yet there are movie critics and movie stars who are celebrating this trash rather than denouncing it. What has happened to our culture? Have we lost all vestige of a conscience?
>
> In the words of Kyle Hooten on Twitter, "*Cuties* just released and it's WAY worse than anybody expected. Netflix just published soft-core child pornography, and they'll probably get away with it."
>
> Jason Howerton's tweet was even more emphatic: "I'm dead serious, people should go to prison for this. 'Lawfully defines as pedophilia' and look at the media ratings. All of you are going to hell. #Cuties."
>
> As my wife Nancy asked when I sent her some links, "How can this even be legal????" How indeed.[32]

The third article was published September 18, 2020, titled "You Do Not Exploit Children to Teach That Exploiting Children Is Wrong."[33] I wrote this because Netflix, along with movie critics who defended *Cuties*, claimed that the film's ultimate lesson was a good one, since the young girl involved ends up breaking away from the gyrating dance group of her peers. The fatal flaw with this logic is that these little girls were sexually exploited in making the dance scenes in the movie, along with posing in sensual ways for still shots. Worse still, I read that 650 girls tried out for the parts, obviously with parental approval.[34] What were these parents thinking?

The final article, published October 15, 2020, was titled "Sorry Netflix, but You Don't Get to Lecture Americans on Moral Understanding." The article began:

> Rather than apologize for the scandal caused by the Netflix movie *Cuties*, the company's CEO, Ted Sarandos has dug in his heels, blaming American viewers rather than taking responsibility for the content.

> As reported by *Deadline*, Sarandos said, "It's a little surprising in 2020 America that we're having a discussion about censoring storytelling. It's a film that is very misunderstood with some audiences, uniquely within the United States."
>
> He continued, "The film speaks for itself. It's a very personal coming-of-age film. It's the director's story, and the film has obviously played very well at Sundance without any of this controversy and played in theaters throughout Europe without any of this controversy."
>
> What a telling statement.[35]

The article ended with this: "Sarandos actually paid us Americans an unintended compliment. We still know how to blush. That's a badge of honor that we should wear proudly."[36]

Would that more Americans would learn to blush again, and would that those of us who do blush would blush even more—at the overt, rampant, unashamed sexualizing of our children. Better still, would that we would not only blush but also take action. Outside our very own souls, is there anything more precious that God has committed to our keeping than our children?

We're not just talking about cancel culture or mobocracy or the assault on our freedoms. We're talking about a frontal assault on our offspring, on the next generation, on our posterity. This is a demonic attack on the most innocent of the lambs. What will we do?

It's Time to Take a Stand

What, then, must we do to protect the most vulnerable ones in our society? How do we save them from a demonically planned destiny and send them out to fulfill their God-given future? How do we defeat the spirit of Jezebel (and whatever other demonic powers are at work)? It starts right here, with each of us. It starts with holy indignation. With broken hearts. With godly determination. With Holy Spirit resolve. It starts right here with every one of us doing what we can to turn this sickeningly destructive tide. Satan must take his hands off our children!

How this, too, smacks of the influence of Jezebel. Jezebel represents the spirit of baby killing—in past generations, inspiring parents to burn their babies on idol altars, and today, inspiring them to snuff out their little ones in the womb. She represents the spirit of radical feminism: hating men, mocking motherhood, and despising the traditional family structure. And Jezebel represents the spirit of seduction, drawing youngsters into sexual activity and selling them into slavery. She is out to annihilate our kids.

So, to every demonic spirit who is dead set on destroying our children we say, "Take your hands off our kids! They belong to us, not to you, and you will not destroy their lives. We declare this together in Jesus' name!" Then in the sight of God pledge yourself afresh to be the guardians of your children. Your words must be backed by your actions.

We'll speak to parents directly in chapter 12, but for the moment, let me say this: We must not downplay the urgency of the hour. The matter is grave, and we cannot underestimate the intensity of the battle. We must be tenacious in God if we are to win the war for our children.

Chapter 7

OFF WITH THEIR HEADS!

WHEN YOU THINK of the atrocities committed during the French Revolution, one word immediately comes to mind: guillotine. The grisly practice of beheading political opponents reached epidemic levels during the Reign of Terror, with estimates ranging from just a few thousand to as many as seventeen thousand who lost their heads.[1] To this day, the image of this tool of execution, which was last used in France in 1977, sends a clear message: your head could be next!

That's why it was quite striking when protesters in the so-called autonomous zone in Seattle, first called CHAZ (Capitol Hill Autonomous Zone), then CHOP (Capitol Hill Organized [or Occupied] Protest), brought out a guillotine to send their own message. As Al Perrotta explained on *The Stream* on June 24, 2020:

> Last week, leftists from CHAZ…uh, CHOP…migrated over to Seattle Police Department's West District.
>
> According to the *Seattle Times*, a speaker said "It is not CHAZ, it is CHOP," then gave the gathered hordes a history quiz.
>
> "Has anybody here ever heard of the French Revolution before? That is another revolution (that happened) because people started putting property over lives! They started putting money over people! Does anyone here know what happened to the people who did not get on board with the French Revolution?"
>
> "Chopped!" the crowd replied. Again. And again.
>
> "That is the message we need to send! We are serious! This is not a joke!"[2]

Did you get the message?

A few days later, on June 30, 2020, I wrote an article titled "What Are You Going to Do When They Come for You?" It began with these words:

> To all the wealthy, liberal elites who are cheering on the protests and riots, a word of warning is in order. The same holds true for the conservative Christians who are lining up to show their support for the BLM movement. To each of you I say: Do not be deceived. The cancel culture will soon be coming for you.
>
> A few weeks ago, I read about a TV sports journalist who tweeted his support for rioters in a nearby city. "Burn that [expletive] down. Burn it all down," he tweeted with glee.
>
> Later that same day, as the mob marched towards his private neighborhood, his tone had changed. He called them animals and—get this—noted how the crowds scattered when the police arrived. How ironic! The cry to defund the police lasts only so long.
>
> Amazon's Jeff Bezos is the latest to face the wrath of the mob.
>
> As Breitbart reported, "According to a number of videos posted to social media, protesters in DC placed a model guillotine in front of Amazon CEO Jeff Bezos' Washington complex. A flyer for the event stated 'End the abuse and profiteering. Abolish the police, the prisons, and Amazon.'"
>
> And note that, "Alongside the guillotine [was] a sign reading 'support our poor communities, not our wealthy men.'"
>
> Oh, yes the guillotine once again. As in off with your head. As in CHOP....
>
> Conservative web host Drew Hernandez posted another video in which a DC protester said, "when they become threatened, and we have no voice, the knives come out." And the protester delivered these comments while standing in front of the guillotine.[3]

The article ended with "You have been forewarned."[4]

Barely one month later, on August 4, 2020, I wrote another article titled "Then They Burned the Bibles," beginning with this: "It's no surprise that rioters in Portland burned Bibles this past weekend. As we've said for weeks now, the spirit behind the riots is the spirit of lawlessness. It is anti-God and anti-Christ. That's why synagogues and churches have also been targets."[5]

I also noted the words of Ian Miles Cheong, managing editor of *Human Events*, which were widely quoted after the Bible-burning incident. He tweeted, "I don't know what burning the Bible has to do with protesting against police brutality. Do not be under the illusion that these protests and riots are anything but an attempt to dismantle all of Western Civilization and upend centuries of tradition and freedom of religion."[6]

Yes, I explained,

> What we are seeing, then, in these riots, is ultimately an attempt to cast off the rulership of God. In the words of the rebellious kings in Psalms 2 (speaking against the Lord and the Davidic monarch who ruled over them): "Let us break their chains and throw off their shackles" (Psalm 2:3). We will not have God rule over us!
>
> That's why Bibles are being burned. It is an open expression of hostility to the Judeo-Christian God and Judeo-Christian values. It is the thumbing of the nose to divine authority. And it is overt rebellion.[7]

As noted in the fourth point of Krystina Skurk's July 31, 2020, *The Federalist* article, "4 French Revolution Trends That Have Started in The United States":

> To say the French Revolution was hostile towards religion is an understatement. Church property was nationalized, tithing was outlawed, church authorities were made employees of the state, and 30,000 priests were exiled....
>
> Traditional religion in the United States has also come under attack by the modern radical left. And, while things haven't yet got to the level of the French Revolution, the current anti-Christian climate does not bode well for the future.[8]

That's why I tweeted on August 1, 2020, "First they burned the federal buildings, then they burned the churches, now they're burning Bibles. Rather than asking 'What is next?' we should ask, 'Who is next?'"[9] Yes, the real question was not "What are they coming after next?" but "*Who* are they coming after next?"

Just a few days later, these same Portland protesters set fire to the police precinct, with policemen still inside. In response Mayor Wheeler said, "You are attempting to commit murder."[10] Murder indeed. It was for good reason that I referred back to my August 1 tweet in the August 4 article "Then They Burned the Bibles." That's also why I ended the article with these words: "Let the reader be warned."[11] I was doing my best to sound the alarm.

To be sure, no one was attempting to behead Christians (or others) during these riots, and there were even brave gospel preachers who waded into the riot zones in different cities, sharing hope and life through the gospel.[12] We also know that much of the anger in these cities was directed at the police in particular, not at religious conservatives. But, as I stated, there was a reason that Bibles were burned in Portland. And there was a reason that guillotines were put on public display. The message was loud and clear: "We hate your God, we hate your Book, we hate you, and we are not playing games."

Cultural commentator Kristian Jenkins, looking at past bloody, revolutionary movements, expressed:

> And here we are back where we started at the Great Terror, the Great Purge, the Cultural Revolution, all elegantly illustrated by George Orwell's metaphoric *Animal Farm*; what begins as a utopian ideal inevitably ends up enforcing even greater oppression and loss of freedom.
>
> The ambitious young Robespierres of the world won't be hindered. History has already determined the outcome and any delay in its realisation is blamed on the forces of reaction. Therefore, they must be silenced or die...and the blood keeps flowing.[13]

Speaking more broadly of the spirit of cancel culture, Dr. Keith Ablow stated, "Canceling people taps into the most primitive and destructive of human impulses—dark, destructive, murderous psychological forces." And, he added, canceling people "is the modern-day equivalent of a stoning in the public square and—no exaggeration—if the people who celebrate this cancel culture could get away with pushing a button anonymously to vote to kill their targets for real, they would."[14]

A View From the Front Lines of the Persecuted Church Worldwide

I'm quite aware, of course, that our brothers and sisters in other parts of the world are *literally* being beheaded. I'm aware that they are dying all kinds of horrific deaths and being exposed to unimaginable torture simply because they believe in Jesus. Others have had their children taken from them, others have been imprisoned, and others have lost their jobs and all their income. Yet they stand strong in their faith despite this horrific persecution, be it in Nigeria or Afghanistan or India or China or North Korea.[15]

Some of my dearest friends outside the US are on the front lines of this very real battle, facing death threats on a regular basis. Yet they continue to preach and proclaim, and all the while here in America we compromise our convictions and water down our message because we don't want to be unfriended on social media. What a scandal! Our brothers and sisters overseas are willing to lose their lives for Jesus, while we are not willing to lose our "likes" for Him here. Something is terribly wrong.

With an attitude like this, there's no way we could stand strong if major, sustained, physical persecution hit our country in the days to come. As the Lord said to Jeremiah after the prophet buckled in the face of persecution from his own family, "If racing against mere men makes you tired, how will you race against horses? If you stumble and fall on open ground, what will you do in the thickets near the Jordan?" (Jer. 12:5, NLT). In other words, if threats from your own family cause you to cower and complain (see Jeremiah 11:18–23), what will you do when the establishment comes against you—including priests and princes and other prophets? And if you're struggling in your little hometown of Anathoth, how are you going to make it in a big city like Jerusalem?

Now is the time for each of us to gain some courage and backbone, proving faithful in the little things before the real tests come. Now is the time for us to stand up and speak up before the day comes when it may actually cost us our lives to obey the Lord. Now is the time to come to God with all our frailty and fear and say, "Lord, make Your strength perfect through my weakness!" (See 2 Corinthians 12:8–10 and Ephesians 6:10.)

One day, "Off with their heads!" could be more than an anti-Christian battle cry here in America. One day it could be literal. For those who doubt me, where is it written in the Bible that what happened in Rome almost two thousand years ago or what is happening in Nigeria today could not happen in America? Where is the chapter and the verse?

Special note: no sooner did I write these words then I received this urgent email from one on our missionaries, a single woman serving the poorest of the poor in Nigeria:

> Hi, Mike. I don't recall ever making such a request but, please, let your listening audience know what is going on with these kids and 15 staff members of the boarding school. The kidnappings and killings are occurring on a daily basis and it no longer appears to be news. Boko Haram now has engaged in a rocket attack in Maidiguri, these boys have been held captive for almost two weeks now, 17 women were kidnapped on their way to a wedding, villages are being terrorized and burned to the ground by herdsmen. When interviewing a new teacher and asking her why she came to Jebba, an impoverished town with little opportunity for employment, her answer is "There is peace in Jebba." She moved from the north with practically nothing to live in a tiny room with no toileting facilities nearby and a [salary] of less

> than $15 per month just to live without fear. I pray that Jebba remains peaceful. Many herdsmen, driven out of neighboring states, are settling here. Lots of new faces. Only Jesus.[16]

That's why the words of Joseph Parker, an older contemporary of Charles Spurgeon, will always be relevant for the people of God. He said, "The man whose little sermon is 'Repent' sets himself against his age, and will for the time being be battered mercilessly by the age whose moral tone he challenges. There is but one end for such a man—'off with his head!' You had better not try to preach repentance until you have pledged your head to Heaven."[17]

It was in response to this quote, which was made famous when Leonard Ravenhill cited it in his classic book *Why Revival Tarries*, that Keith Green wrote his song "Pledge My Head to Heaven." It ended with a powerful refrain, in which he pledged his entire life for the sake of the gospel.[18]

That is what every one of us should do with our lives and the lives of those for whom we are responsible: "Here we are, Lord. Send us and use us, regardless of cost or consequence." After all, isn't this what Jesus requires? Isn't this Gospel 101? As He said:

> If anyone would come after me, let him deny himself and take up his cross and follow me. For whoever would save his life will lose it, but whoever loses his life for my sake will find it. For what will it profit a man if he gains the whole world and forfeits his soul? Or what shall a man give in return for his soul? For the Son of Man is going to come with his angels in the glory of his Father, and then he will repay each person according to what he has done.
>
> —Matthew 16:24–27, esv

It is in this same spirit that one of my closest ministry colleagues baptizes new believers in India. After they have confessed their faith, he asks them, "Are you willing to give your last drop of blood for Jesus, your last breath?" I have witnessed hundreds of such baptisms, and in every case, without hesitation, they all answered yes. Some of them have had the sacred privilege of living out the words they spoke.

Once, while speaking to about two hundred pastors and church planters in India, I asked them, "How many of you have been physically attacked for preaching—not just verbally attacked or threatened, but physically attacked?" About three-quarters of them raised their hands, but they did so in the most nonchalant way, as if I had asked them, "How many of you had breakfast today?" No big deal. Nothing unusual. Of course we have been beaten for our faith.

Another brother working in the Middle East told me on the radio that before he baptizes former Muslims, he asks them two questions: "Are you willing to suffer for Jesus?" and "Are you willing to die for Jesus?" If they don't answer yes to both questions, they are not baptized.[19] As this leader said to me, "Can you imagine what would happen to our church memberships in America if we asked these questions before taking in new members?" Really!

I imagine the interview would sound something like this:

> So, we understand that you and your family want to become members of our congregation and that these are your main reasons: (1) you love the children's program; (2) the service is short and to the point; (3) you find it easy to listen to the pastor; (4) you love our coffee bar in the lobby; and (5) there is always adequate parking.
>
> We also see that you have all been baptized and that you agree with our doctrinal statement and are already tithing to the church. Great! We just have two final questions to ask. First, are you willing to suffer for Jesus? Second, are you willing to die for Jesus?

Can you imagine what the response would be, let alone the looks on these prospective new members' faces?

Years ago, I heard a very moving story but wasn't sure it was completely true until I asked Pastor Richard Wurmbrand face to face in October 1993. (If you're not familiar with his name, by all means read his world-famous book *Tortured for Christ* or watch the movie with the same title.)[20] He told me he knew the pastor personally and that the story was entirely true.

It took place during the Communist takeover of Romania in the 1940s, when believers came under heavy persecution. During one weeknight service, two Communist soldiers barged into a church building with guns in hand. Then they stopped the meeting and made an announcement: "If you are willing to deny Jesus, you can leave now. If you stay, we will kill you. Think about it."

A few of the Christians got up and left, but the rest stayed. The soldiers then proceeded to lock the doors so no one else could come or go. Then they put down their guns and said to the shocked congregants, "Praise God. We are Christians too. But we dare not worship with anyone who is not willing to die for Jesus."

This really happened, my friend, and it reflects a reality worldwide today: following Jesus could cost you your life, so don't plan on following Him unless you're willing to die for Him.

How different this is from the American version of the gospel—often a superficial, fleshly prosperity "gospel" that bypasses the cross, repentance, obedience, and sacrifice, offering boatloads of blessings in return for your little prayer of faith, starting right here and now.

No wonder we have so much complacency in the body of Christ today. No wonder we have so much carnality. No wonder we have so much compromise.

But no more! The stakes are getting higher, and the opposition is getting stiffer. Now, like never before in our nation's history, it is our time to stand strong. And I believe we will! The spirit of the overcomer is inside us.

A University Professor Paints a Sobering Picture

George Yancey (PhD, University of Texas) is a professor of sociology at Baylor University and the author of a number of books on racial reconciliation, as well as books on the increasingly hostile, anti-Christian environment in America, especially in academia. And he is a fair-minded scholar, basing his views on hard data, and not afraid to criticize his own evangelical side. Yet he, too, is sounding the alarm, with one volume actually titled *So Many Christians, So Few Lions: Is There Christianophobia in the United States?* (He defines *Christianophobia* as "an unreasonable hatred toward and fear of conservative Christians.")[21]

Prof. Yancey begins his 2015 book *Hostile Environment: Understanding and Responding to Anti-Christian Bias*, with a striking personal illustration. He wrote:

> I remember vividly a disturbing conversation that I once had with a good Christian friend who taught in a high school. He told me that he mentioned one day in class that some Christians around the world were being killed for their faith. To his amazement, some students approved of these murders. In their minds, it was time for Christians to face the same death that Christians had inflicted on others.
>
> I was struck by the ahistorical nature of this line of thought. Although Christians in the United States do not face jail or death for their faith, there is a long history of Christians around the world being punished for their faith. I also wondered how so much hatred had developed against Christians. This conversation took place almost

> two decades ago, and I see little evidence that this type of hatred has abated.
>
> In fact, my recent research has confirmed that such hatred is still very powerful. David Williamson and I conducted a survey of culturally progressive activists using open-ended questions. The survey questions elicited a variety of hostile statements aimed at conservative Christians. One statement in particular (from a male, age 36–45) caught my attention: "The only good Christian is a dead Christian."[22]

In short, "when one is in a war, one should offer no mercy to the enemy. The respondent made it clear that he sees Christians as the enemy and believes that no mercy should be given to them."[23]

Other respondents had comments like this:

> The only difference I see between [a] Christian fundamentalist and [an] Islamic fundamentalist is terrorism. At their heart both movements are attempts to replace their country's government with theocracies. Religion in the political arena is dangerous to freedom and should be not allowed. Even minor intrusions such as allowing religious groups to distribute public funds to the poor should not be allowed. (male, age 46–55)
>
> The Christian Right's influence in our government is as dangerous as the Taliban in Afghanistan or the ayatollahs in Iran. We cannot allow them to get a solid foothold in our government. The only way to do this without infringing on rights is to be especially vigilant and point out their bigotry and hypocrisy often and loudly so as to discredit them in the eyes of their followers and, more importantly, the eyes of the voting populace. (female, age 66–75)[24]

As Yancey explains, in many cases, what lies behind this hatred is the fear that Christian conservatives want to take over the country and impose their values on it, from outlawing abortion to discriminating against gays. And so, whatever we say or do is part of that not-so-secret plot. Yancey writes:

> For example, a female age 56–65 stated that "it's pretty troubling to me what they're doing, how sneaky they are, how they project their negativity onto others, mostly how they are trying to…and succeeding… take over our public education system." Another female age 66–75 stated that Christians are "dangerous—attending law school so they can infiltrate government and take over our country."[25]

From our perspective, of course, we are trying to save the lives of babies and to preserve God's order for the family, which we are convinced is also in the best interest of our country. We are simply pushing back against the increasing radicalism of our society, noting that abortion was illegal in most of America until 1973 and that same-sex "marriage" was not recognized until 2015. We also believe that the vision of our Founding Fathers has been violated, and we are simply fighting for what is right—even more, these days, we are simply fighting for our rights, since the so-called "progressives" would like nothing more than to silence us in the public square and take away our rights. "Stay out of the schools, stay out of the media, stay out of politics—just stay out of our way. That's why you have churches. Go and worship your God there." This is the silencing of the lambs.

That's why it was no surprise in 2008 when opponents of Proposition 8, the bill designed to uphold marriage in California, lashed out angrily against Christian supporters of the bill, carrying signs like these:

- Prop 8 = American Taliban
- Ban Bigots
- Majority Vote Doesn't Matter
- 52% = Nazi (This referred to the 52 to 48 percent vote in favor of Prop 8.)
- Don't Silence the Christians, Feed Them 2 the Lions
- Your Rights Are Next[26]

This was the response to those who said, "Marriage is the union of one man and one woman, not the union of any two people." Yes, you hateful, bigoted Christians, your rights are next. And as you can see from one of the signs, silencing the Christians was not enough. "You deserve to die! Bring back the Colosseum! Feed them to the lions!" (Remember: this was back in 2008.)

But if Christians are equated with the Nazis and the Taliban, don't they deserve to die? At the very least, people like Kim Davis, the Kentucky county clerk who refused to issue a marriage license for a same-sex couple, should rot in jail. After all, as the critics said, she is just like ISIS.[27] Yes, a conservative Christian in a rural part of America that overwhelmingly rejected the concept of same-sex "marriage" is similar to a cold-blooded terrorist who literally chops off people's heads and burns others alive. Away with her!

That's why it was no surprise that the outspoken political commentator Keith Olbermann said this on October 8, 2020:

> The task is twofold. The terrorist Trump must be defeated, must be destroyed, must be devoured at the ballot box, and then he, and his enablers, and his supporters, and his collaborators, and the Mike Lees and the William Barrs and the Sean Hannitys, and the Mike Pences, and the Rudy Giulianis, and the Kyle Rittenhouses and the Amy Coney Barretts must be prosecuted and convicted and removed from our society while we try to rebuild it and to rebuild the world that Trump has nearly destroyed by turning it over to a virus. Remember it.[28]

Putting aside his hatred toward Trump (and your own views of Trump, whatever they may be), note carefully what Olbermann said: Christian conservatives like Attorney General William Barr, Vice President Mike Pence, and now Supreme Court justice Amy Coney Barrett "must be prosecuted and convicted and removed from our society." Away with them!

Back in 2013, Craig James was hired as a sports commentator by a regional Fox outlet. James had been a college football standout and an NFL star, a man praised by Fox Sports Southwest Executive Producer Mike Anastassiou as a "talented broadcaster who I've admired throughout his career....His knowledge of college football and the experience he brings as an analyst will be a tremendous asset to our coverage."[29]

But immediately after being hired by this regional Fox outlet, he was fired because of comments he made during his political campaign the previous year. Yes, Tony Perkins tells us, "after one day on the job—Fox gave James the boot for his conservative views on marriage. And here's the kicker: He made the comments not at the sports desk but during last year's Senate campaign!"[30]

What exactly did he say? In answer to a question during the campaign, he stated his opposition to same-sex "marriage." He explained that he didn't believe anyone was born gay (and therefore living a gay lifestyle was a choice), and he stated, "They are going to have to answer to the Lord for their actions."[31]

As reported by *Sports Illustrated*, "Fox Sports executives were not happy with the hire by the regional network, according to sources, and the hire had not been fully vetted at the highest levels of Fox Sports management."[32] As explained by a Fox spokesman, "We just asked ourselves how

Craig's statements would play in our human resources department. He couldn't say those things here."[33]

Yet around this very same time, Keith Olbermann went on a nine-minute rant against Russia's "antigay" laws, likening Putin's pro-family stance to Adolf Hitler's maniacal desire for world domination—and Olbermann did this on ESPN as part of his national sports broadcast. As I wrote, "Within a 10-day period, sportscaster Craig James was fired by Fox Sports for comments he had made against homosexuality during a political campaign last year while Keith Olbermann was lauded for his 9-minute anti-Russia, pro-homosexuality rant on ESPN. The double standards are as glaring as they are shocking."[34]

And Olbermann, of course, was praised by major gay websites such as *Advocate*, which noted, "Olbermann's nine-minute tirade brilliantly pointed out the ridiculousness of recent comments by President Vladimir Putin—who has tried to claim Russia's so-called gay propaganda law is not homophobic." And Olbermann "also highlighted the frightening similarities of the political climate surrounding the upcoming Winter Games regarding LGBT people and attitudes against other groups of people during the 1936 Olympics held in Berlin," pointing to America's pulling Jewish athlete Marty Glickman from the team. What was the result? According to Olbermann, "within three years Hitler was invading Czechoslovakia while America had an official policy of neutrality and within five years Hitler was in mid genocide."[35]

And remember: this took place back in 2013. Yet even then, two years before the Supreme Court overstepped its bounds and redefined marriage, Tony Perkins could write this:

> Is the grip of religious hostility so tight that Americans can't even have an open debate for fear it'll cost them their jobs?
>
> Dr. Angela McCaskill, Jerry Buell, Julea Ward, Damian Goddard, Senior Master Sgt. Phillip Monk, Crystal Dixon and Air National Guardsman Layne Wilson certainly think so. To a person, they were all suspended, fired or sued by their employers for their views on marriage—whether or not they expressed them at work. Like them, James' ousting had nothing to do with his job performance and everything to do with this new climate of Christian persecution.[36]

We've come a long way since then, haven't we? And things are getting worse by the day.

It Is Not Just Donald Trump Who Is Hated

Donald Trump was one of the most hated men in America during his presidency, as well as one of the most loved men in America. And this was largely his doing, since he was the type of person who left little room for neutrality. Those who loved him saw him as a fearless leader who fought for their cause and told it like it was, refusing to back down to anyone. Those who hated him saw him as a dangerous, mean-spirited, and reckless buffoon who was destroying the nation. And, to repeat, in many ways, Trump was directly responsible for these polar responses, giving one side a reason to love him and the other side a reason to hate him.

But the hatred toward Trump was not only directed against him (although, to be sure, he was the most direct recipient of it, for obvious reasons). It was also directed against those who voted for him and supported him, even if they differed with his methods and were often grieved by his words and tweets. Now, with Trump out of the While House, that hostility is coming their way—which, for many of us, means our way.

Writing on October 26, 2020, for the *Federalist* (and so, just one week before the elections), Stella Morabito listed "7 Open Leftist Threats That Political Terror Is Coming to America Whether Trump Wins or Not." She noted first how on Twitter, "agitator Nils Gilman called for the execution of journalist and former Trump adviser Michael Anton." Next, "former Twitter CEO Dick Costolo...accused Coinbase's CEO Brian Armstrong of being among the 'me-first capitalists' who would be the first lined up and 'shot in the revolution.'"[37] (Armstrong's crime was that he decided not to force social justice agendas like critical race theory on his employees. For this, he should be shot.)

The third example she gave was from an August 1, 2020, article in *Salon* calling for criminal charges against Trump and his key followers—likening the situation to the Nuremberg trials for Nazi war criminals, resulting in the death of thirty-seven Nazi leaders—along with what sounds like reeducation camps for those who voted for Trump.

Fourth, she cited the words of Keith Olbermann, which we discussed above. Fifth, she noted that "on Aug. 4, 2019, a supposed religious scholar and CNN contributor Reza Aslan announced on Twitter—a tweet still up as of Oct. 22—that all Trump supporters 'must be eradicated from society' along with Trump, and that there is 'no longer any room for nuance.' Aslan has nearly 300,000 followers." Sixth, Morabito pointed to the literal, physical attack on Senator Rand Paul and his wife outside the Republican

National Convention, one that Senator Paul and his wife felt could have been deadly were they not protected.[38]

She also wrote: "This represents a ramping up of the Antifa and Black Lives Matter attempt to normalize extreme violence against any perceived political opponent. Agitators even set up a mock guillotine on the spot with an effigy of Trump in it."[39] The guillotine? Again?

Finally, in her last example, Morabito detailed how the Left was encouraging the "doxing" of Trump supporters, meaning, revealing their personal information by posting their home addresses on social media or releasing their cell phone numbers to the general public.[40]

So, the anger is not simply directed toward Donald Trump, who gave it as well as he got it, lashing out with insults, attacking those he differed with, and using his massive Twitter account as a powerful, verbal weapon. The anger is also directed at Senator Rand Paul and his wife, although Senator Paul has never conducted himself as Trump did, nor, of course, has Paul's wife. As Republicans and Trump supporters, they were targeted for violence too—not just verbal but physical.

In that same spirit, comedian David Cross rejected President-Elect Joe Biden's tweet on December 26, 2020, which called for healing, answering with a categorical "No!" Biden had tweeted, "After a year of pain and loss, it's time to unite, heal, and rebuild."[41] Cross replied, "[Expletive] that. I want blood."[42] Cross had previously joked that he fantasized about beating Donald Trump "to a bloody pulp and then urinating and defecating on him."[43] Others, like Hollywood star Debra Messing, hoped that Trump would be arrested and imprisoned, expressing her desire that he would live a long life there while being raped by the male inmates. As she explained, "Rape is an act of violence. Trump has perpetrated violence on hundreds of millions of people. My hope is (and this is the first time in my life) that the tables are turned and he is the victim of perpetrators."[44]

Again, this ugly hatred is being directed against Trump himself. But as you quickly learn on social media (and in other social settings), if you dare to identify as a Trump voter or Trump supporter, or if you dare to say anything positive about the man, that hatred will soon be directed toward you as well. And what happens to those who simply stand for biblically based, socially conservative values? As I said at the outset of this book, there is a target on your back.

★ ★ ★

On January 12, 2021, Breitbart News posted a video showing Antifa demonstrators forcing the temporary closure of a prominent Portland bookstore. As the accompanying story explained, "Antifa wants the establishment to not sell a forthcoming book by a local conservative journalist that details 'Antifa's radical plans to destroy democracy.'

"Antifa protesters assembled outside Powell's Books on Monday and demanded the store not sell a book by independent journalist Andy Ngo—*Unmasked: Inside Antifa's Radical Plan to Destroy Democracy*, Reason.com reported. The demonstration forcing the store's closure continued on Tuesday."[45]

So, Antifa protestors strong-armed a respected local bookstore because it had the audacity to sell a book documenting Antifa's strong-arm tactics. This reminds me of a political cartoon I once saw featuring Muslim extremists yelling, "How dare you call us terrorists. We'll kill you!" Today, it might be radical leftists saying, "How dare you call us murderous people. Off with your heads!" (Note that on April 24, 2021, it was reported that a church in Seattle had to cancel a speaking engagement by Christian conservative Charlie Kirk after Antifa activists threatened to burn their building.)[46]

How, then, should we respond to hatred and intimidation like this? That's the subject of the rest of the book. Are you ready to be encouraged, challenged, and equipped?

PART II

THIS IS HOW WE OVERCOME

Chapter 8

"STOP BEING CHICKENS"

ONE OF THE most powerful tools of today's cancel culture is fear. Dare to speak up, and you will be shut down. Dare to cross the latest PC line, and you will be deplatformed. Dare to cause a ripple, and you will be banned. You had best comply, then, and save yourself a lot of trouble. After all, you've got a family (or a career or a dream or a future). Why hurt yourself and make things difficult for your loved ones just because you have a strong opinion? Better to censor yourself privately, fear tells you, than have the culture silence you publicly.

But this fear tactic is nothing new. Jesus warned His disciples about it frequently, telling them:

> The student is not above the teacher, nor a servant above his master. It is enough for students to be like their teachers, and servants like their masters. If the head of the house has been called Beelzebul, how much more the members of his household!
>
> So do not be afraid of them, for there is nothing concealed that will not be disclosed, or hidden that will not be made known. What I tell you in the dark, speak in the daylight; what is whispered in your ear, proclaim from the roofs. Do not be afraid of those who kill the body but cannot kill the soul. Rather, be afraid of the One who can destroy both soul and body in hell. Are not two sparrows sold for a penny? Yet not one of them will fall to the ground outside your Father's care. And even the very hairs of your head are all numbered. So don't be afraid; you are worth more than many sparrows.
>
> Whoever acknowledges me before others, I will also acknowledge before my Father in heaven. But whoever disowns me before others, I will disown before my Father in heaven.
>
> —MATTHEW 10:24–33

What sobering words! If the world treated Jesus as if He were the devil himself, how should we expect to be treated? And if people can kill only our bodies but God can destroy both our souls and bodies in hell, who is the one we should fear? Yet that same God has our lives in His hands and is intimately concerned with our well-being. In the end, the only opinion that really matters is God's opinion, and the only favor we need is His.

That's why Jesus also said this, repeatedly, in the Gospels: "Whoever finds his life will lose it, and whoever loses his life for my sake will find it" (Matt. 10:39, ESV).[1] Do you grasp the significance of these words? The Lord is saying that if we avoid following Him in order to save our lives—meaning, save our reputations; save our prestige; save our income; save our relationships; even save our own skin—we lose our lives. We become slaves to the will of others, slaves to human opinion, slaves to fear itself. In fact, something inside us dies as we surrender our integrity and deny our core convictions in order to save ourselves. In reality, we have lost what matters most: who we are on the inside. We have lost our very lives.

But if we lose our lives for Him—meaning, we die to the power of this world, die to popularity and praise, die to self, die to fear, die to threats—then we find ourselves. Now we really live. Now we really thrive. Now we are really free. How liberating it is to die to self and to the power of this age in order to live fully for God!

Wise Words From Dr. Martin Luther King

During the height of the civil rights movement, some of the leaders became concerned about the ongoing violent attacks on nonviolent protesters. They were beaten. Police dogs were unleashed against them. They were sprayed with fire hoses. In some cases, they were victims of bomb blasts. Perhaps it was wisest to step back for a time and be less confrontational?

Speaking at a church gathering in Selma, Alabama, on March 8, 1965, Dr. King addressed those very real concerns with these unforgettable words:

> Deep down in our non-violent creed is the conviction there are some things so dear, some things so precious, some things so eternally true, that they're worth dying for. And if a man happens to be 36-years-old, as I happen to be, some great truth stands before the door of his life—some great opportunity to stand up for that which is right.
>
> A man might be afraid his home will get bombed, or he's afraid that he will lose his job, or he's afraid that he will get shot, or beat

> down by state troopers, and he may go on and live until he's 80. He's just as dead at 36 as he would be at 80. The cessation of breathing in his life is merely the belated announcement of an earlier death of the spirit. He died...
>
> A man dies when he refuses to stand up for that which is right. A man dies when he refuses to stand up for justice. A man dies when he refuses to take a stand for that which is true.
>
> So we're going to stand up amid horses. We're going to stand up right here in Alabama, amid the billy-clubs. We're going to stand up right here in Alabama amid police dogs, if they have them. We're going to stand up amid tear gas!
>
> We're going to stand up amid anything they can muster up, letting the world know that we are determined to be free![2]

What an exposition of the words of Jesus. This is what Jesus meant when He said, "For whoever would save his life will lose it, but whoever loses his life for my sake and the gospel's will save it" (Mark 8:35, ESV). This is the path to freedom and liberation.

So, if God is calling you, or if your conscience is convicting you, then go ahead and cross that line. Take that stand. Hold to your conviction. If you have already died to this world, this world can take nothing from you. You are oblivious to human threats. They can no longer hurt you.

Of course, it may not *feel* like you are oblivious. You might still struggle with fear. In that case, say to the Lord, "You know I am weak on the inside. You know I am a compromiser by nature. You know I don't like confrontation. But You also know that I want to please You more than anything. So, I'm asking You for the courage to do what is right. And if it helps for You to make me miserable if I choose the way of carnal compromise, then make me so miserable in my heart that I will come running back to You, ready to take a stand. Father, demonstrate Your strength in my weakness!" That is a prayer the Lord will gladly answer.

Dr. Ben Carson Makes It Plain

Shortly after Senator Rand Paul questioned President Biden's nominee for assistant secretary for Health and Human Services—a biological male who identifies as a woman named "Rachel" Levine—pressing Levine about the dangers of hormone blockers and sex-change surgery for minors, radio host Alex Marlow asked Dr. Ben Carson for his opinion on the subject.

Dr. Carson agreed with Sen. Paul, explaining that transgender activists "have completely neglected biology," which teaches us that there are males and females and indicates that the human brain is "not fully developed until your mid- to late-twenties." In his view, these dangerous medical interventions are actually a form of "child abuse."[3]

And what did Carson make of "left-wing political censorship related to the left's rejection of human biology"? After all, Marlow noted, these days, if you simply state that a biological male will always be a male, you can be banned from social media and have your books canceled. Carson pointed to our national anthem, which celebrates America as "the land of the free and the home of the brave." In Carson's view, the only way that we can be the land of the free is by also being the home of the brave. He said, "You've got to be willing to stand up."[4]

Shades of the words of Jesus! And shades of the words of Dr. King. You can't be free if you're not willing to take a stand. Without bravery, there can be no liberty.

And what about the consequences for speaking truth to power? To that Carson answered with "so what?" reminding us that had our Founding Fathers not been willing to stand up to the homeland, we would be under the rule of the British to this very day. "So stop being chickens," he said, "and get out there and fight for what we believe in." Otherwise they'll be the only ones with a public platform, and without our resistance, they win automatically.[5]

Exactly. We lose only if we surrender. We can be silenced only if we capitulate. And in Dr. Carson's view, if we capitulate, all of America loses, which means the world loses too.

You may feel like a chicken. You may even act like a chicken. But if you are a born-again follower of Jesus, you are *not* a chicken. That's because Jesus Himself lives inside you. That's because the Holy Spirit has been given to you. That's because the Word of God—the sword of the Spirit—is available to you.

So, let's stop thinking of ourselves as scared chickens. Let's stop acting as if this world really has any power over us. And let us refuse to be canceled or silenced. In the end, the only ones who can silence God's people are God's people themselves. What will it be?

This doesn't mean that we respond with anger or hatred or that we try to provoke a conflict or act recklessly. And this doesn't mean we simply speak up whenever there is a disagreement. Instead it means that we really press into the Lord to deepen our relationship with Him, that we give ourselves to Him afresh every day, saying, "Lord, here I am. Send me; use me." And it means that when it is time to do the right thing, by His power and with wisdom and grace we stand and we speak and we act.

The chicken spirit is not in us. We are God's holy people, clothed with His Spirit, called and appointed for such a time as this. And so, in Jesus' name, we will not be silenced. Cancel culture will not cancel us. And we will certainly not self-censor and thereby cancel our very selves.

Dr. Richard Menger, a neurosurgeon like Dr. Ben Carson, said:

> The indifference of the silent majority on cancel-based culture has pushed everyone out of the room. Fear drives action. People are afraid to speak up. They are labeled with stigmas and names that end careers. And when everyone who disagrees has been pushed out, ideological progressive groupthink takes over the workplace, committees, and boardrooms. This is where we are, and I'll invoke a phrase normally used by progressives: *it's not safe.*[6]

The fact is, this can happen only if the silent majority stays silent. By God's grace, we will not.

Chapter 9

THE WORD OF GOD CANNOT BE BOUND

FOR TWELVE LONG years, John Bunyan (1628–1688) sat in prison while his wife and four children barely survived outside the prison walls. He made shoelaces in an effort to support them, but this was not nearly enough, so he also had to rely on "the charity of good people" to keep his family alive.[1] Yet he was in prison by his own choice, refusing to submit to the king's order to stop preaching. (Bunyan was a Baptist, and under King Charles II, all ministry had to be done under the authority of the Church of England.) When the local magistrates told Bunyan he could be released if he stopped preaching, he replied that he would rather stay in prison "until moss grew on his eyelids" than disobey God.[2] Compromise for the sake of comfort and convenience was not in his vocabulary.

Bunyan had enjoyed religious freedom in the Commonwealth under Oliver Cromwell. But with the restoration of the monarchy under Charles II, things changed dramatically, with Parliament passing the Act of Uniformity in 1662. The full title of the bill was "An Act for the Uniformity of Public Prayers and Administration of Sacraments, and other Rites and Ceremonies, and for establishing the Form of making, ordaining and consecrating Bishops, Priests and Deacons in the Church of England."[3] All ministers had to conform to these rules if they wanted to continue their work, but when the bill was passed, roughly two thousand ministers left the Anglican Church rather than conform, earning the name Nonconformists. There was even a bill passed in 1665 titled "The Five Mile Act," forbidding clergy from living within five miles of the parish from which they had been expelled.[4] The crackdown was very real, and it was quite severe.

That's why John Bunyan was in jail. He would not conform, he would not capitulate, and he would not be silenced. History also tells us that he would not be canceled. You see, it was during his time in prison[5] that he wrote *The Pilgrim's Progress*, one of the best-selling books ever published, continually in print from the year of publication (1678) until today. In fact, "for more than two centuries after its publication, *The Pilgrim's Progress* ranked just behind the King James Bible as the most common and important book in evangelical Protestant households. It has been translated into more than two hundred languages, including eighty in Africa alone."[6] There is a lesson here for us!

Bunyan had been raised in a dirt-poor family, destined to be one of the countless millions of nameless, faceless people who fill the corridors of history, leaving virtually no trace behind. As noted by *Christianity History* magazine:

> Successful English writers were, in John Bunyan's day, nearly synonymous with wealth. Men like Richard Baxter and John Milton could afford to write because they didn't need to earn a living. But Bunyan, a traveling tinker like his father, was nearly penniless before becoming England's most famous author. His wife was also destitute, bringing only two Puritan books as a dowry.[7]

We don't even know his first wife's name (she died in 1658; Bunyan married again in 1659), and their first child, a daughter, was born blind. Yet God used the two Christian books this poor, nameless woman owned to open Bunyan's heart and mind, and after years of deep spiritual struggle, he had a powerful and lasting conversion experience, subsequently obeying God's call to preach (yet doing so without a license). And that is how he wound up in prison.[8]

But God's Word and God's truth cannot be imprisoned, and it was from Bunyan's prison cell that one of the most important books ever written in the English language was produced. The authorities could imprison him, but they couldn't silence him. In fact it was their oppressive actions that completely backfired, since they put him in prison to shut him up but he had more free time in prison to write than he would have if he had been involved in pastoral ministry.

As a result, instead of reaching thousands through his preaching, he ended up reaching tens of millions through his writings. As D. L. Jeffrey explained, "One of the evident ironies of Bunyan's life is that his enemies afforded him, in effect, a series of enforced sabbaticals; it is highly unlikely that his normal pastoral duties would have permitted him to accomplish nearly so much of his most enduring writing without these periods of incarceration."[9] People meant it for evil. God used it for good. To say it again: there is a lesson here for us.

Jeffrey noted that "Bunyan claimed, honestly no doubt, that his Bible and his concordance were his only library. He was not in the least ashamed that he knew no biblical languages; Pontius Pilate, he remarked wryly, could speak Hebrew, Greek and Latin."[10] Yet this same man was used by God to write enduring works while imprisoned in a miserable British jail. The Lord really does turn bad things around for good. As Joseph said to his brothers, the very men who sold him into slavery in a foreign land, "You intended to harm me, but God intended it all for good. He brought me to this position so I could save the lives of many people" (Gen. 50:20, NLT).

This is similar to Paul's testimony. The Romans imprisoned him, but that just gave him a new opportunity for evangelism. As he wrote to the Philippians, who were obviously concerned that their spiritual father was suffering in chains with the real possibility he would be martyred:

> Now I want you to know, brothers and sisters, that what has happened to me has actually served to advance the gospel. As a result, it has become clear throughout the whole palace guard and to everyone else that I am in chains for Christ. And because of my chains, most of the brothers and sisters have become confident in the Lord and dare all the more to proclaim the gospel without fear.
>
> —PHILIPPIANS 1:12–14

The Roman attempts to muzzle Paul's message simply provided him with a new preaching platform. First, he got to reach the palace guards, people he never would have been able to reach before. They saw he was different from the other prisoners, who were in chains for their crimes. He was in chains for the gospel. And so, he got to share the good news with them, to the point that he has this wonderful little note at the end of his letter: "Give my greetings to each of God's holy people—all who belong to Christ Jesus. The brothers who are with me send you their greetings. And all the rest of God's people send you greetings, too, *especially those in Caesar's household*" (Phil. 4:21–22, NLT, emphasis mine). Paul was talking about the converts he had won to the Lord in prison—the palace guards, "those in Caesar's household." Paul could not be silenced!

Second, while in prison, Paul wrote some of the most amazing letters ever penned, read more widely than virtually any other letters in history (outside the other New Testament letters). I'm referring to the Letters to the Ephesians and Philippians and Colossians and Philemon, documents of extraordinary spiritual depth and incredible spiritual riches (with the tiny letter to Philemon actually playing a role in helping to free the slaves in England and America). Yet Paul wrote each of these while imprisoned for the gospel. That's why he could also write to Timothy, "Remember Jesus Christ, risen from the dead, the offspring of David, as preached in my gospel, for which I am suffering, bound with chains as a criminal. But the word of God is not bound!" (2 Tim. 2:8–9, ESV). Say it out loud with me: "The Word of God is not bound!"

Other translations speak of Paul being imprisoned, yet the Word of God is not imprisoned (see NET), or they refer to Paul being in chains, but the Word is not chained (see NKJV). This is something to shout about. The Word cannot be bound, imprisoned, or chained. We might be, but the Word will never be. The Lord will get His message out, and what Satan or the society mean for evil, the Lord will turn for good if we give ourselves to Him and His cause without reservation.

Will you be a tool in God's hands? Will you say, "Lord, use me to get Your message out to the world" rather than praying, "Lord, bless me with a nice, comfortable life"? I can assure you that John Bunyan and Paul would tell you that the jail cell was worth it. The deprivation was worth it. The hardship was worth it. Their imprisonment provided them an opportunity to reach new people and to reach out in new ways. The Word of God cannot be muzzled.

Even martyrdom can be used to advance the gospel, as Pastor Josef Tson declared to the Romanian secret police during an interrogation in 1977. He had preached a message urging the churches in his country not to submit to the demands of the communist government that wanted to have control of their ministries.

Now, he was arrested, totally at their mercy, with no way to fight for himself. When one of them ordered him to renounce his sermon, he refused. This shocked the policeman, who said, "Aren't you aware that I can use force against you?" Tson replied:

> You should know your supreme weapon is killing. My supreme weapon is dying....You know that my sermons are on tape all over the country. When you shoot me or crush me, whichever way you choose, [you] only sprinkle my sermons with my blood. Everybody who has a tape of one of my sermons will pick it up and say, "I had better listen again. This man died for what he preached." Sir, my sermons will speak 10 times louder after you kill me and because you kill

> me. In fact, I will conquer this country for God because you killed me. Go on and do it.[11]

As a result, he was released, since his captors realized that his martyrdom would present far more problems than his sermon. Talk about the mentality of an overcomer! Talk about turning the tables! "Go ahead and kill me," he was saying to his captors. "That will simply result in more people listening to my message. And the harder you try to silence me, the more the gospel will go out to the nation." The Word of God cannot be bound.

Tson also understood that "tribulation is never an accident but is part of God's sovereign plan for building His church." As he told his interrogator, "Sir, don't you understand that when you kill me you send me to glory? You cannot threaten me with glory." In his view, "The more suffering, the more troubles, the greater the glory. So, why say, 'Stop this trouble'? Because the more [suffering], the greater the glory up there."[12]

Paul wrote that not only do we "rejoice in hope of the glory of God" but we also "rejoice in our sufferings, knowing that suffering produces endurance, and endurance produces character, and character produces hope, and hope does not put us to shame, because God's love has been poured into our hearts through the Holy Spirit who has been given to us" (Rom. 5:2–5, ESV).

By all means, we should stand up for our liberties while we have them. But should we lose them for a season, that could become an opportunity for us to become stronger and more fearless and disciplined. Maybe some of us will even end up writing world-changing books from a prison cell somewhere. The Word of God cannot be bound!

Chapter 10

TELL YOUR STORY!

David Pickup is a professional therapist who, himself, is ex-gay. And for years now he has been testifying against the attempt to ban professional therapy for those struggling with same-sex attraction or gender confusion. (For more on this, see chapter 5.) In an email exchange with some conservative colleagues on February 21, 2021, he wrote:

> After many years now of testifying in about 13 states against these therapy bans, and after seeing footage I have of one of the lawyers for this LGBT movement say their real mission is eventually to fight religion, everyone on this list needs to know that professional therapists are not really the LGBT activists' target. Their target is Christianity and any religion that says LGBT lifestyles are sinful or unhealthy.
>
> They are coming for the churches, and in my opinion, most denominations are essentially ignoring this fact by either doing very little assertive work, or attempting to lay low to see if our laws will uphold the truth instead. Faith is going to be tested in very open ways around the US and world, and already is. Religious rights and the truth are being taken away as we speak. And, it's going to get worse whether we speak more candidly about it or not. Sooner or later Christians will have to make a decision to speak out and sacrifice.[1]

That time has really come. Christians *must* speak up and speak out, especially those whose stories threaten the PC narrative. And if enough of us do this at the same time, our voices will be irresistible.

Speaking of the ban on "conversion therapy" in Victoria, Australia, Bill Muehlenberg wrote:

> Since Christians are often the ones at the forefront of offering genuine help and healing in this area, this is a direct assault on biblical Christianity. Indeed, the Bible is a book about transformation—about

> how God can set people free and make them into new persons with new desires.
>
> So clearly the Bible itself is seen as a book filled with "hate speech" according to these militant misotheists. Surely Bibles and Christian literature will be among the documents seized by the authorities as they bring their reign of terror upon all those who dare to stand against the sexual revolutionaries.
>
> There you have it: Christianity, Scripture and prayer are all now being criminalised in Victoria. This is not some bit of futuristic science fiction, or the stuff of some dystopian novel. This is reality right now, right here in Victoria. Every person who claims to be a true disciple of Jesus Christ should be utterly appalled at what is taking place here.
>
> We are very quickly heading to the same things that we find in atheistic hellholes like North Korea. Hardcore persecution is always preceded by softcore persecution, and it builds up incrementally. Sadly I fear that by the time most Christians finally wake up to what is actually happening, it will be too late.[2]

I say we wake up now. Do you agree? With reference to things happening in America, Muehlenberg wrote, "If they can ban Dr Seuss books today, there is nothing to stop them from banning the Bible tomorrow. If even non-persons like Mr Potato Head and the Muppets can be considered to be hateful and the subject of bans today, you can count on it that Christians will be treated in the very same way tomorrow."[3]

David Acevedo, a young man who writes articles for the National Association of Scholars, came to this same conclusion, recognizing the need to speak openly and boldly. But at first he wrote under the pseudonym John David. Why? He didn't want his career to be hurt. He didn't want to be marginalized. He didn't want to be rejected because of his conservative views. Then one day he appeared online under his real name, picture and all. Why? He explained:

> First, I'm simply tired of living in fear. For many people, writing under a pseudonym is not a choice made out of fear or cowardice. But for me it was, and I feel compelled to leave it aside for the sake of my principles and character. How can I, for example, encourage you all to stand up to the academic cancel culture while at the same time avoiding my real name for fear of being canceled? This is exactly how the culture wins—by scaring people into silence.[4]

Well done, David. We will not allow the culture to scare us into silence.

The Stories That Must Be Told Today

We saw in chapter 5 that one of the major PC narratives is that homosexuality is innate and immutable, meaning you are born that way and you cannot change. Therefore, sexual orientation is equivalent to race or ethnicity. This is who you are, and there is nothing you can do to change that. How, then, can society not have special categories for those who identity as gay or lesbian, not to mention transgender, which, we are also told, is innate and immutable?

Hitching "LGBT rights" to the civil rights movement has been a brilliant strategy, one that has even become enshrined in our local and federal laws. But it is simply not true, as a host of scientific studies indicate[5] and as a host of personal testimonies demonstrate.[6] People can be changed, especially through the gospel. That's why it is imperative that those who came out of homosexual practice or who used to identify as transgender tell their stories to the world.

Of course there are some people who are ashamed of their past and who, for many good reasons, prefer not to talk about it. That is understandable. But others are held back only by fear. To each of them—to you?—I say this: We are standing with you. You are not alone. God has your back too! So let your voice be heard. The nation needs to hear what you have to say.

The Voices of the Multitudes Cannot Be Ignored

Did you ever see the movie *Miracle on 34th Street*? It tells the story of a man who believed he was Santa Claus, and he had an amazing effect on the people of New York City with his charitable spirit. But when he was tried for falsely claiming to be Santa, his attorneys shocked the court by bringing in mountains of supporting testimony in the form of thousands of letters addressed to him as Santa. The evidence was overwhelming.

That, of course, was just a movie, and Santa Claus is just a myth. But ex-gay and ex-trans Christians are anything but a myth and their stories anything but a movie. When thousands share their stories across the nation (and the world)—powerful stories, poignant stories, moving stories, marvelous stories—those stories cannot be denied.

Take a moment and visit the Changed Movement website.[7] As the home page explains, "We are a community of friends who once identified as LGBTQ+. Today, we celebrate the love of Jesus and His freedom in our lives." Then click on the page where many of them share their stories,[8] or check out the beautiful book they have published, containing many other stories.[9]

On October 30, 2019, NBC News reported:

> A group of people from across the country who formerly identified as gay and transgender have descended upon Washington this week to share their stories and lobby against two proposed LGBTQ-rights bills.
>
> The group is made up of 15 members of Church United and Changed, two California-based organizations that seek to provide community for, and protect the rights of, "formers"—individuals who formerly identified as lesbian, gay, bisexual or transgender.[10]

This has now happened in other parts of the country as well, as ex-gays and ex-trans believers testify before congressional hearings and stand as one before the media. It's hard to argue with their personal stories and smiling faces. It's hard to argue with life and hope and joy. And it's hard to pass a law saying, "We forbid you from seeking after that life and hope and joy."

As former lesbian Elizabeth Woning said on a large Christian radio station in Los Angeles with reference to a dangerous bill that was being considered by the state, "AB 2943 would seek to block me inviting other people to go on that same journey that I went on....My faith journey involved questioning my sexuality as a lesbian, and so this bill would seek to block any kind of invitation, or any kind of encouragement from me, to another person to do the same."[11]

Quoting scientific statistics is one thing, and it does have its place. Listening to expert witnesses is effective, but it is often lost in the midst of a back-and-forth debate. Personal, individual stories, however, carry tremendous weight, especially in today's generation.

That's why it is so important that all of you who feel the liberty to share your testimonies do so, be it in your local church or before your local government. Your message is simple and clear: "The world says I don't exist, but here I am! The world says that change is impossible, but I'm here to tell you that Jesus can change anyone. I am living proof!"

That doesn't mean you're living a perfect life (who of us is perfect?), nor does it mean you are never tempted. But it does mean you are not who you used to be. That is the power of the gospel. As Paul wrote:

> Or do you not know that wrongdoers will not inherit the kingdom of God? Do not be deceived: Neither the sexually immoral nor idolaters nor adulterers nor men who have sex with men nor thieves nor the greedy nor drunkards nor slanderers nor swindlers will inherit the

> kingdom of God. *And that is what some of you were.* But you were washed, you were sanctified, you were justified in the name of the Lord Jesus Christ and by the Spirit of our God.
>
> —1 Corinthians 6:9–11, emphasis mine

If that is who you used to be, especially if you are grounded and solid and mature in the Lord, then let your voice be heard. Nothing is more powerful than your testimony.

Some will ask, "But what about those who used to be ex-gay, only to renounce it? What do you say to those who are now in same-sex relationships and feeling happy and accepted by God? And how do you answer them when they say that ex-gay counseling almost destroyed their lives?"

My answer is simple. First, no one is forcing anyone to hear the gospel or to get counseling or seek out change. That is a personal choice. If someone else had a bad experience with counseling, that does not give them the right to stop someone else from seeking counseling. Second, we base our doctrine on what the Word says, not on personal experience. Third, I believe that this is their own story, and they have a right to tell it. I only ask them to believe those whose stories are different, whose stories point to the life-changing power of the gospel.

All things truly are possible with Jesus. Let us proclaim Him as both Lord and Savior, both King and Deliverer. That is who He is!

Chapter 11

TIME FOR PROFESSORS TO PRACTICE "KAMIKAZE ACADEMICS"

IN CHAPTER 2 we focused on what is happening on our college campuses, and the truth be told, it can be maddening. Just consider this sampling of headlines from the Campus Reform website from February 28, 2021:

- "Harvard Business School Club of NY Cancels Speaker From...Cancel Culture Talk: Report"[1]
- "Math Education Prof: 2 + 2 = 4 'Trope' 'Reeks of White Supremacy Patriarchy'"[2]
- "Academics Called Breastfeeding 'Ethically Problematic' Because It Endorses 'Gender Roles.' Their View Is Gaining Traction."[3]
- "Cancel Culture Comes for Thomas Jefferson...and Fails Miserably"[4]
- "UW Profs Attempt to Explain Away Devastating Free Speech Survey Results"[5]

And remember this is just a sampling of headlines from one day on one website. Can you imagine what happens over the course of a year on tens of thousands of campuses across America? Cancel culture continues to rise, free speech is assaulted more and more, and the voices of students and faculty and administration are being silenced. What can be done in response?

We have been reflecting on the words of Jesus when He said, "Whoever would save his life will lose it, but whoever loses his life for my sake will find it" (Matt. 16:25, ESV). As expressed in another passage, "Truly, truly, I say to you, unless a grain of wheat falls into the earth and dies, it remains alone; but if it dies, it bears much fruit. Whoever loves his life loses it, and whoever hates his life in this world will keep it for eternal life" (John 12:24–25, ESV). This is a cardinal, revolutionary principle, and by understanding it and implementing it, we can overcome cancel culture.

But what exactly does this principle mean in our practical, day-to-day lives? An Australian professor, Dr. Peter Ridd, fired by his university for telling the politically incorrect truth, has coined a term that says it all. He calls it "Kamikaze Academics," which, as explained by James Delingpole, means professors like Ridd will be "willing to get themselves fired for expressing opinions which go against the standard leftist narrative," exposing "how little free speech and diversity of thought there now is in academe."[6]

This is the practical application of the teachings of Jesus, fleshed out here in the academic world. You speak the truth and live the truth, regardless of cost or consequences. In the process, you save your integrity even if you lose your job. As a result, you become free. (In the words of Jesus, "you find your life.")

In contrast, as we have seen, if you try to save your job and preserve your reputation, refusing to question false narratives and choosing to compromise your convictions for the sake of your career, you actually "lose your life." You become a slave to the system, a slave to peer pressure, a slave to the dollar, a slave to the approval of people, a slave to expediency rather than a person of principle. And little by little, as you compromise your convictions time and again, you lose your very soul even more.

Dr. Ridd himself suggested that "it's only older academics like me who can do this....We have a duty to do this so that younger academics can have a proper academic career where they can say tough things or even stupid things and still be forgiven. You need to be able to make mistakes."[7]

But the call must be much broader. Both older and younger academics must speak the truth. The oppressive system must be challenged. To be silent is to enable. More broadly still, beyond the world of academia, we must all determine to stand up and speak out and be witnesses to the truth, regardless of cost or consequence.

Other Professors Are Speaking Out

On December 13, 2020, law professor Daniel B. Ravicher posted an op-ed on the *Miami Herald* website titled "As a Conservative UM [University of Miami] Professor, I'm Fighting the Campus Cancel Culture." He wrote:

> I'm a rare breed, a law professor that is an unashamed conservative. Over my 15 years of teaching, countless students of all genders, races, and religions, have confided in me as one of—if not the—only faculty member...with whom they could speak freely about political and social issues.
>
> This is because too many professors are intolerant of conservative ideas and students are rightfully afraid of being punished.[8]

Prof. Ravicher decided that the best way for him to fight back was not by speaking out on campus. He said his faculty manual said "anything a faculty member says in their personal life shall have no impact on their employment," so he went to battle on Twitter, posting his personal, conservative views plainly.[9] As a result, the university told him he had to retract his tweets or be fired. So much for the faculty manual! Students called for his dismissal. Other faculty called for his ouster. How dare he be an out-and-proud conservative! But he would not back down, explaining, "I'm too stubborn to give in to cancel culture and decided to fight as hard as I could against it."[10]

He appeared on the Laura Ingraham show on Fox. He offered to debate his law school faculty colleagues on any of his tweets. (None took up his offer.) He held his ground. And the university relented, but not before questioning his academic integrity. As he wrote, "The chilling effect on conservative speech, including by students in particular, has been achieved. But fighting cancel culture must be done, because without free exchange of ideas, we are not going to produce the best citizens and the best policies."[11]

And despite the cost, Ravicher said he would not retract his statements, apologize, or resign. This is what it is going to take to overcome cancel culture, and if enough professors and administrators and students speak up, the power of cancel culture will be broken.

Columbia University professor John McWhorter noted that in July 2020, he tweeted that since May 2020, he and a colleague (who was also his ideological sparring partner) had been receiving messages almost daily "from professors living in constant fear for their career because their opinions are incompatible with the current woke playbook."[12] Those are very strong words.

In response to those who accused him of lying (how convenient!), Prof. McWhorter wrote:

> This year, the Heterodox Academy conducted an internal member survey of 445 academics. "Imagine expressing your views about a

> controversial issue while at work, at a time when faculty, staff, and/or other colleagues were present. To what extent would you worry about the following consequences?" To the hypothetical "My reputation would be tarnished," 32.68 percent answered "very concerned" and 27.27 percent answered "extremely concerned." To the hypothetical "My career would be hurt," 24.75 percent answered "very concerned" and 28.68 percent answered "extremely concerned." In other words, more than half the respondents consider expressing views beyond a certain consensus in an academic setting quite dangerous to their career trajectory.[13]

Accordingly, he observed, no one should act surprised or express disbelief at his report that so many academics are contacting him, expressing their fears and concerns. Indeed, he states, in just three weeks in the early summer of 2020, he received 150 such messages. He wrote, "And what they reveal is a very rational culture of fear among those who dissent, even slightly, with the tenets of the woke left."[14]

Indeed, he noted, "Overall I found it alarming how many of the letters sound as if they were written from Stalinist Russia or Maoist China."[15] Need I say more? This is why it is imperative that faculty members in particular refuse to be intimidated or threatened, starting with those who are tenured professors and whom it would be harder to fire. Then let others rise up and do what is right, even at the potential cost of their careers.

Let Wisdom and Courage Work Hand in Hand

But the call to be bold doesn't mean that we abandon practical wisdom. There is a time to speak and a time to refrain from speaking. And the call to boldness doesn't mean that we cultivate pride and arrogance, as if we couldn't care less about what others think. To the contrary, we are called to humility, called to be peacemakers rather than troublemakers. But we must have the mentality of spiritual revolutionaries, understanding that we are here for something greater than earthly pleasures, here for a purpose that transcends the goals of ordinary life.

We are here to be witnesses, to make an eternal difference, to bring about positive change, and to live lives that count, both in this age and the age to come. As a result, we are willing to sacrifice something temporal to gain something eternal. In the words of missionary martyr Jim Elliot, "He is no fool who gives what he cannot keep to gain that which he cannot lose."[16]

Strikingly, while in college, Elliot journaled this prayer: "Father, take my life, yea, my blood, if Thou wilt, and consume it with Thine enveloping fire. I would not save it, for it is not mine to save. Have it, Lord, have it all. Pour out my life as an oblation for the world. Blood is only of value as it flows before Thine altars."[17] And this: "God, I pray, light these idle sticks of my life and may I burn up for Thee. Consume my life, my God, for it is Thine. I seek not a long life but a full one like Yours, Lord Jesus."[18]

Elliot, martyred by the Auca Indians at the age of twenty-eight in 1956, saw his prayers answered dramatically. And while he did not live a long life, he certainly lived a full life, one that continues to speak and make an impact long after his passing, one like that of Jesus Himself.

Of course the vast majority of us will not face the test of literal martyrdom. But there are many "deaths" we will be called to die in our daily obedience to God. That's why I devoted an entire chapter to the theme "To Save Your Life Is to Lose Your Life" in my book *Revolution: An Urgent Call to a Holy Uprising*.[19] It is a fundamental, revolutionary principle set forth by Jesus, and it is something we must live out in the home, in the workplace, on the campus, and online. And yet, in contrast to the original practitioners of "kamikaze," the Japanese pilots who gave their lives to kill others,[20] we give our lives to liberate and help others. We are here to save people's lives, not destroy them.

The moment we take hold of this reality—that by losing our lives we find our lives—cancel culture, along with the larger culture of peer pressure, loses it power. The moment we take hold of this reality, we are truly free.

Dr. Ridd is living this out in the world of academics, where he is in a pitched court battle with the university that dismissed him. Let each of us live this out in our own worlds, putting conviction before convenience. By losing our lives, we will find them.

Chapter 12

PARENTS, TAKE A STAND!

DOES YOUR HOLY blood boil when you read these headlines, all posted within one week's time in January 2021?

- "Joe Biden Day 1: Order on Transgender Rights in Sports and Bathrooms"[1]
- "Virginia Plans for All Public Schools to Allow Boys in Girls' Bathrooms and Sleepovers"[2]
- "Virginia's New Transgender Rules for Public Schools: Use Preferred Pronouns, Don't Question Bathroom Choices"[3]

Or how about this headline from November 2020? "Boy Scouts Must Settle 95,000 Abuse Claims by Next Summer—or Risk Running Out of Cash."[4] Yes, you read that correctly. Ninety-five thousand claims. Who can imagine the damage done to so many impressionable, innocent children? And all this, allegedly, under the oversight of the Boy Scouts.

What about this headline from March 6, 2021? How does this make you feel? "NY Lawmaker Wants Sex Ed for Kindergartners."[5] Or how about this, from March 7, 2021: "New York Democrat Pushes for Sex Ed That Would School 11-Year-Olds in Pansexuality and Anal Sex"?[6] Or this, from March 6, 2021: "Three Dads, a Baby and the Legal Battle to Get Their Names Added to a Birth Certificate"? The story begins:

> Meet Ian Jenkins and his partners, Alan and Jeremy.
>
> They're a "throuple": a committed polyamorous relationship involving three people.
>
> And after a complicated and expensive court battle to all become legal parents, the trio are raising two toddlers in Southern California—and proving how families come in all forms.[7]

Yes, this is the "normal" environment in which these children will be raised. The assault on our kids is real. There's even a school in New York City that doesn't want the students to use the words *mom* or *dad* because those words make "assumptions" about their home lives.[8] This is just plain crazy, especially when you consider that this is an Episcopal school, and so, claiming to be Christian. (Ironically, at the time the school made this announcement, the Twitter bio described the head of the school, Robbie Pennoyer, as "teacher, priest, husband, dad.")[9]

And how do you feel about the contents of this book, designed for children aged four to eight and titled *The GayBCs*?

> A playdate extravaganza transforms into a celebration of friendship, love, and identity as four friends sashay out of all the closets, dress up in a wardrobe fit for kings and queens, and discover the wonder of imagination. From **A is for Ally** to **F is for Family** to **Q is for Queer**, debut author/illustrator M. L. Webb's bright illustrations and lively, inclusive poems delight in the beauty of embracing one's truest self. A glossary in the back offers opportunity for further discussion of terms and identities. *The GayBCs* is perfect for fans of *A Is for Activist* and *Feminist Baby*—showing kids and adults alike that every identity is worthy of being celebrated.[10]

I've seen a video of a child well under four going through the pages of this book, pages which he had clearly memorized, including lines like "B is for bi" (as in bisexual) and "C is for coming out" and "D is for drag" and "N is for non-binary" and "S is for sashay."[11] What kind of madness is this? And what little child on the planet can possibly understand the meaning of these terms? Yet one professional reviewer stated, "*The GayBCs* should be required reading for all children."[12] This is shameless—and dangerous—indoctrination.

In chapter 6 I painted a picture of the terrible assault our children are under today (for some of us, our grandchildren or even great-grandchildren), so what I've written here to open this chapter is just another jolt, a reminder of the environment surrounding our young people. The question is, What will you who are parents do about it?

Time to Take a Stand

I understand that life itself can be challenging and that just making ends meet on a daily basis can be exhausting. And I understand that parenting is hard work, even in the best of environments. Parenting requires commitment and dedication and patience and perseverance. Parenting is not for the lazy or faint of heart.

But now is not the time for you who are parents to be casual in your commitment. There is an all-out war on your kids, and you are their last and most important line of defense as well as the most important influencers in their lives. And while it is true that they will make choices for themselves and are ultimately responsible for their own destiny, the impact you have on their lives, for better or for worse, can be the difference between success and failure, happiness and sadness, heaven and hell. Parents, it is time to take a stand! This means being vigilant and this means being involved.

First, I encourage you to set the spiritual tone of your home, not by putting on a religious show (which your kids will quickly see through and learn to resent) but rather by living out your faith, being people of godly character, people of devotion to Jesus, people serious about God and His Word. Set a consistent example, and don't allow yourself to get lax just because you're in the privacy of your own home. Impressionable eyes are watching! And when you fall short, acknowledge your failing, apologize, and get on with the race. Model what you want your kids to become.

Second, get aggressive spiritually. Take hold of God in prayer on behalf of your kids. Rebuke the devil and the forces of darkness in the power of the Spirit and by the name of Jesus. Speak the Word of God over them. And as much as it lies within you, and with the help and grace of God, do not allow the evil one to steal your children. Push back! Do spiritual warfare! Tell the devil, "Hands off!"

Wrestle in prayer in the morning and in the evening. Pour out your tears as you change diapers or as you drive to work. Contend for the souls of your children as if your prayers alone were responsible for their future. And then pray for yourselves, that God would pour His love into you, that He would pour His wisdom into you, that He would pour His life into you, that He would pour His resolve into you, that He would pour Himself into you. And if you are married, realize that if the devil can destroy your marriage, he has a much better shot at destroying your kids. Guard that sacred commitment with everything within you. Do not play games or flirt with evil. The consequences could be disastrous.

Third, get deeply involved in the lives of your children. I don't mean harassing them or giving them no privacy. But I mean being responsible, especially when they are younger. What kind of music are they listening to? What kind of videos are they watching? What kind of games are they playing? What are they viewing online? Who are their friends on social media? Who are they spending their time with? What kind of text messages are they sending? If your kids are in your home, especially if they are minors, these are things you need to know, and again, especially the younger they are.

There are some really evil people out there waiting to prey on your vulnerable kids. There is a lot of darkness on the internet. There is a lot of danger out there. Satan really is prowling and roaming and planning and plotting.

Of course it's easy to get overly paranoid, which isn't helpful either. But by all means, don't get complacent. And the more you are involved with your kids in a positive way, the more they'll enjoy spending time with you and the family, and the more you can pull them away from that which is destructive and lead them into that which is wholesome and healthy.

This also means getting involved in your kids' education. If you do not feel called to homeschool your children, or if you are not able to, then be sure you know what they're learning in school, especially if they are in a secular school. (Unfortunately, all too often this also applies to Christian schools, some of which are Christian in name only.) I know it can be difficult with all the other burdens of life. I know it's much easier simply to send your child into his or her room to do homework. But as parents, given how much dangerous material is being taught in our schools, it is imperative that you be aware.

When the school semester starts, ask your children to see the lesson plans or textbooks for the semester. Chat with your kids about what they're learning in school. You may not do this every single day, but you certainly need to do this on a regular basis. Often they are being indoctrinated with destructive, anti-Christian information and they don't have the slightest clue.

Meet with the teachers if necessary. Stand up to ungodly curricula. Meet with administrators if need be. Go to the school board meetings if things are heading in the wrong direction. Perhaps some of you are even called to serve on the school boards or be administrators or be teachers—and I mean right within the secular school system. Why not?

Recently one of my younger colleagues, a former student and a powerful evangelist, texted me. He and his wife were terribly grieved over an assignment that was given to their seven-year-old daughter. They found out about it because their children were being taught online because of the COVID lockdown, so the parents had to help their daughter with the assignment.

She was given a video to watch and asked to describe how she felt watching different parts of the video. It was a music video with many tens of millions of views, and it started with a long and ridiculous skit which featured a man dressed as a woman (in very obvious and flagrant ways), along with some very gay men acting in a very caricatured way. And their seven-year-old was asked to watch this video and explain how she felt while watching. To repeat a question from earlier in this chapter, what kind of madness is this? And who appointed a schoolteacher to give a little child an assignment like this?

My colleague and his wife asked for my input, and I affirmed their plan to meet with the school principal along with the teacher who gave the assignment. They reached out in a gracious, nonintimidating way, and they were immediately given an appointment to meet together. They showed the principal and the teacher the video, and to the surprise of this mother and father, the teacher apologized immediately. She had not actually watched the full video, thinking it was simply the music video itself, which apparently was not offensive and would have elicited different reactions from the student. She apologized immediately, and the principal assured these parents this would not happen again.

But what if the parents did not get involved? What if their daughter simply clicked on the link and watched for herself (or, worse still, watched at school with her peers)? What if she thought that this must be good because her teacher told her to watch and her parents didn't object? And how many other students would have been negatively impacted?

Thankfully, in this situation, things ended well. At other times things have not ended well at all, resulting in lawsuits and even the arrest of a parent.[13] But what else is a parent to do? You have no more sacred entrustment than the children God gives you to raise.

I also feel an especially strong burden to remind you that it is imperative that you fight on behalf of your teenagers. (I did not say fight *with* your teenagers but *on behalf of* your teenagers.) The pressures on them can be immense. Their emotions can be all over the place. The influences around them can be so dark and demonic. The challenges they face are, in many ways, unique. And it is often during the teen years that relationships between parents and children break down.

I appeal to you by the burden of the Lord: Fight on behalf of your teens. Be there for them. Battle for them before the Lord behind the scenes. Pray silently over their bedroom doors when they are asleep. Cry out for them during the day while they are at school or working their jobs. And make yourselves available to them when you sense they have a need.

Let them ask you the hard questions. Create an environment where they feel safe to come to you with their doubts and their questions and their pains and their unbelief.[14] And do what you can to help them encounter God for themselves. A personal relationship with the living God, coupled with real intimacy with the Holy Spirit, will be a bulwark for them against all the forces of hell.

Be compassionate toward your teens even when they are frustrating and infuriating. Sometimes they don't even understand their own feelings. You be the rock. You be the strong one. You be the stable one. And while you must draw the lines and hold to those lines, setting righteous standards and bringing stability in the home, do so with love and perseverance.

All across America there are teens who have run away from home and who have now been sold into sex trafficking. As much as it lies within you, don't let that happen to one of yours. All across America there are kids dying of drug overdoses, kids suffering from severe depression, kids with sexually transmitted diseases, kids who are cutting themselves, kids who are killing themselves. As much as it lies within you, don't let that happen to one of yours.

And while you cannot stop your children from making wrong decisions, your influence in their lives and your prayers on their behalf may genuinely be the thing that keeps them from death and destruction. In all your imperfection—I recognize my many imperfections as a father myself—ask the Perfect One to take holy action.

Finally, in keeping with the larger theme of this book, help to instill a spirit of courage in your children by setting an example for them. Help them stand for what is right regardless of social pressure. Help them to value the favor of God more than the favor of people. And when they take a stand, be there for them. Take the heat with them. Let them know that you are proud of them and prepare them to be bold in an increasingly hostile world. With God's help, the devil will *not* have your children. They will not be stolen, and as they grow up and mature, they will not be silenced.

Chapter 13

CALLING ALL EVANGELISTS

THE MORE THE culture tries to silence us, the louder we must shout. And no one shouts better than an evangelist. He stands on a chair, gets the attention of the audience, and cries out, "Hear the Word of the Lord!"

Think about this for a moment, not from an earthly perspective but from a divine perspective. The greatest offensive weapon we have is the gospel, which is "the power of God that brings salvation to everyone who believes: first to the Jew, then to the Gentile" (Rom. 1:16). It can transform a terrorist and save a serial killer. It can liberate a drug abuser and deliver a porn addict. It can set prisoners free and fill the despondent with hope. It can lift up the suicidal and bring joy to the depressed. It can bring light out of darkness and life out of death.

That's because the true gospel message doesn't put band-aids on a patient with heart disease, spiritually speaking. Instead it gives sinners a brand-new heart. They are literally born again, born anew, born from above, transferred from the kingdom of Satan to the kingdom of God's own Son.

This is the message that can change individuals and families, communities and cities, states and countries. This is the message that wreaks havoc on the enemy's territory, as we invade his strongholds in Jesus' name and, quite literally, rescue the perishing. And no one is more called to bring this message and to equip others to do the same than the evangelist. How we need a massive army of evangelists to arise from coast to coast! This could really rock the nation and turn today's cancel culture on its head.

No one is bolder than an anointed evangelist. No one is more determined to reach the lost than an anointed evangelist. No one is more effective in reaching the masses than an anointed evangelist. That's why I'm issuing a trumpet call to evangelists everywhere in America (along with evangelists from other nations who are called to join us here). Now is the time to arise and shine! May an army of evangelists come forth!

Wesley and Booth Understood This Well

History teaches us that an army of dedicated and anointed evangelists can literally shake a nation. That's why John Wesley, who was literally used to impact an entire generation and beyond, listed this as Rule 11 in his twelve rules for "helpers":

> You have nothing to do but to save souls. Therefore spend and be spent in this work. And go always, not only to those that want you, but to those that want you most.
>
> Observe: It is not your business to preach so many times, and to take care of this or that society; but to save as many souls as you can; to bring as many sinners as you possibly can to repentance, and with all your power to build them up in that holiness without which they cannot see the Lord. And remember! A Methodist Preacher is to mind every point, great and small, in the Methodist discipline! Therefore you will need all the sense you have, and to have all your wits about you![1]

This was a call to be focused and intentional. This was a call to keep the main thing the main thing. This was a call to follow in the footsteps of the apostles who, first and foremost, were called to be "fishers of men" (Matt. 4:19, ESV; see also Luke 5:10). Even Timothy, whose main calling was that of a pastor and teacher, was instructed by Paul to "do the work of an evangelist" (2 Tim. 4:5). That applies to each of us! And so, while we're praying for that army of evangelists to arise, let each of us seek to be fishers of men and women. The Great Commission is our commission too.

The lost are still lost, which is why the searing words of William Booth still burn the conscience today:

> "Not called" did you say? "Not heard the call," I think you should say. Put your ear down to the Bible, and hear him bid you go and pull sinners out of the fire of sin. Put your ear down to the burdened, agonized heart of humanity, and listen to its pitiful wail for help. Go stand by the gates of hell, and hear the damned entreat you to go to their father's house and bid their brothers and sisters and servants and masters not to come there. Then look Christ in the face—whose mercy you have professed to obey—and tell him whether you will join heart and soul and body and circumstances in the march to publish his mercy to the world.[2]

Perhaps you are now hearing this call yourself. As Booth also said, "Go straight for souls, and go for the worst."[3]

Sadly, in so many of our churches today, months or even years can pass by without us seeing a single new convert. We are ingrown. We are overtaught. We are complacent. We are self-centered. That's where the evangelist comes into play, jarring us out of our slumber, reminding us of our sacred mission, and equipping us to win the lost. Then, as sinners come to faith, the ripple effect is felt throughout the church as believers come alive because of the stream of new converts flowing into the congregation. Without this—the salvation of the lost and the renewal of the saved—America cannot be changed.

Booth, who had a tremendous burden to help the downtrodden and the poor and who absolutely believed in taking practical social action, understood that the best of our social programs could only go so far. As he said, "To get a man soundly saved it is not enough to put on him a pair of new breeches, to give him regular work, or even to give him a university education. These things are all outside a man, and if the inside remains unchanged you have wasted your labor. You must in some way or other graft upon the man's nature a new nature, which has in it the element of the Divine."[4]

That is the real way to transform a society—by bringing individuals into a life-changing encounter with the living God with the end result being that they receive a new nature. Then, as new creations in Jesus, they go out and change the world around them. That is the power of the gospel. And that is how our faith has made a nation-changing impact in centuries past. It starts with the message we preach and proclaim, and it starts with us living out the gospel. When the saved live like the saved, the lost will be saved as well.

The Vision of an Army of Evangelists

A few years ago, as I was deeply burdened over the state of our nation and giving thought to the culture wars, I saw a clear vision in my mind's eye. It was an army of evangelists flooding the cities of America, some preaching in tents, some on street corners, others in church buildings. They were fearlessly preaching the cross, confronting sin, lifting up the name of Jesus. And they were driven and carried by love. The Holy Spirit was moving, and there seemed to be a swirl of people around these evangelists, with multitudes being born again. God was on the move!

In 2020 we began to witness more signs of this army as evangelistically gifted believers hit the streets in the midst of the protests and riots, sharing the good news. At the same time, my colleague Daniel Kolenda, leader of Christ for all Nations, the powerful evangelistic ministry founded by Reinhard Bonnke, launched his evangelism boot camps, releasing this growing army in Africa first, but with a view to impact America and other nations as well.[5] Not long after that, another colleague, Joe Oden, a national evangelistic leader focused on the US, released an equipping series to help launch evangelists in every local church.[6]

And for years now, some of my other evangelistic colleagues have been ministering in local churches, not just to preach to the lost but to mobilize and equip the saints to do outreach themselves. Some of these friends will not accept an invitation to preach in a church unless the pastor agrees to set one day aside for equipping and mobilization—normally a Saturday, when most people are free—and he will do it only if the pastor agrees to hit the streets with the evangelist and the congregants. Those congregations that continue to reach out after the evangelist leaves continue to see great fruit. It is certainly harvest time in America!

It is true, of course, that these have been very difficult times for many Americans. COVID has turned our world upside down and taken many loved ones from us. The political divide has almost torn us apart, while racial unrest remains an ever-present reality. People are angry and hurting, confused and lonely, disillusioned and distrusting. But that also means people are ripe for the gospel. It is during times of upheaval and change that the greatest gospel advance can take place. May God raise up thousands of evangelists to help all of us reap this precious harvest of souls!

Getting the Right People in the Right Place

While ministering in England in 1987, I stayed at the home of a local pastor for a few days and was given full access to his library, where I found a little book on prayer written by a man named Ole Hallesby. One story in that book caught my attention, and I have never forgotten it to this day. Hallesby wrote:

> In this connection permit me to mention what an ordinary country girl, Bolette Hinderli, was able to accomplish for the great preacher of God, Lars Olsen Skrefsrud.
>
> In a vision she saw a prisoner in a prison cell. She saw plainly his face and his whole form. And a voice said to her, "This man will share the same fate as other criminals if no one takes up the work of praying

> for him. Pray for him, and I will send him out to proclaim my praises among the heathen."
>
> She was obedient unto the heavenly vision; she suffered and prayed and fought for this prisoner, although she did not know him. She waited longingly, too, to hear of a convict who had become converted and called to missionary work.
>
> Finally, during a visit in Stavenger, Norway, she heard that an ex-convict who had been converted was to preach in the city that evening. When Skrefsrud stepped up to the speaker's stand, she recognized him immediately as the one she had seen in her vision.
>
> This woman had learned the meaning of Jesus' words about praying forth the gifts of grace.
>
> As far as I am able to understand the Word of God, and as far as I can learn from the history of the kingdom of God, no prayer-task is more important than this. If the right man gets into the right place, there is almost no end to what he can do. Think of men like Martin Luther, Hans Nielsen Hauge, Lars Olsen Skrefsrud, Hans Peter Borresen, William Carey, Hudson Taylor.[7]

What a remarkable account, and what a testimony to the power of prayer and to the faithfulness of this simple country girl. God used her prayers to change the destiny of a common criminal, thereby impacting the nation of Norway with the gospel. In the same way, several generations later, God used the prayers of His people to help save a lost sinner named Steve Hill, the man who became the evangelist of the Brownsville Revival, thereby literally touching multiplied millions of lives. He, too, was a common criminal before Jesus saved him—and God saved him in answer to the prayers of the saints. May God hear our prayers for the next wave of converts whom the Lord has destined for this sacred task!

But it's not just lost sinners I'm thinking about, not just those who don't know the Lord today but will come to know Him in the days ahead and become powerful evangelists themselves. I'm thinking of all the called, gifted evangelists we already have in the body. Let us make room for their ministries and help turn them loose. Let us recognize that there is more to ministry than pastors and teachers, more to the Spirit than amazing prophetic words, more to God than basking at His feet in worship, although everything I just listed is wonderful and necessary and amazing. There must also be a reaching *out*—out to the streets, out to the lost, out to the hurting—and that means out of our comfort zone. Gifted evangelists can help lead the way.

Pastors, when is the last time you asked an equipping evangelist to help mobilize your people to reach the lost? And when is the last time you hosted an evangelistic outreach in your city? Now is the perfect time! And the meetings will not be about politics. They will be about Jesus. May all be drawn to Him!

And to every evangelist reading this book, is the fire still burning bright in you, or have you become more professional than passionate, with your eye on salaries more than souls? Or perhaps you've become discouraged, seeing little fruit over the years or having little backing from the churches. Perhaps you've accepted the fact that your calling will never be received or needed in the body. I encourage you, my friend, to think again. I encourage you to make a fresh consecration of your life to the Lord, saying, once again, "Here I am! Send me; use me." I encourage you to use your gift wherever you can—in your neighborhood, in the workplace, with your home congregation, on a missions trip. The more you give out what you have, the more the Lord will pour in. It is time!

★★★

In February 2021, I was speaking to a leading Christian strategist, a man with decades of international ministry experience and with a wide-ranging understanding of what is happening in our culture. He painted a very dark picture of our current state of affairs, with a specific focus on the attack on our liberties coming from the Left. I asked him, "So, what is your strategy for turning the tide? What is God calling us to do?"

He responded, "Where are the evangelists? We need evangelists more than ever!" When I told him about the theme of this book and about this very chapter, he was amazed to hear my words.

Evangelists, it is time to arise and shine! Lead the way in winning the lost, and help light a fire in the hearts of God's people to go and do the same. It is harvest time!

Chapter 14

WE DO NOT FIGHT WITH THE WEAPONS OF THIS WORLD

IN 2 CORINTHIANS 10:3–5 Paul wrote, "For though we live in the world [or, the flesh], we do not wage war as the world [or, flesh] does. The weapons we fight with are not the weapons of the world [or, the flesh]. On the contrary, they have divine power to demolish strongholds. We demolish arguments and every pretension that sets itself up against the knowledge of God, and we take captive every thought to make it obedient to Christ."

We live in this world. We are only flesh and blood. Yet we do not fight the way the world fights, in the power of the flesh. Instead we have divine power to demolish strongholds. What an incredible word. We are human, but we do not fight as humans.

The world fights by intimidation, by anger, by violence, by fear, by suppression, by oppression. We also fight, but with totally different weapons. They are counterintuitive weapons, weapons that seem weak in the eyes of the world. But when rightly used, they are unstoppable. To repeat Paul again: these weapons have divine power to demolish strongholds. Or, as rendered in the NASB, these weapons are "divinely powerful for the destruction of fortresses" (v. 4).

And how, exactly, does this take place? Paul states that "we destroy arguments and every lofty opinion raised against the knowledge of God, and take every thought captive to obey Christ" (v. 5, ESV). The lies of Paul's opponents, the lies by which some of the Corinthian believers were being led astray, the false arguments that created strongholds of deception in their minds—these lies would be destroyed by the divine weapons of the Spirit.

But do we know what these weapons are today? Do we understand the intent and power of Paul's words? Are we using these weapons within the church, let alone in the world? The Greek scholar A. T. Robertson wrote,

"Paul aims to pull down the top-most perch of audacity in their reasonings against the knowledge of God. We need Paul's skill and courage today."[1] He is absolutely right (and note that he wrote this in the early 1930s). But how do we do it?

We must first remember that ultimately we are not fighting people. As Paul stated clearly in Ephesians 6:12, "For our struggle is not against flesh and blood, but against the rulers, against the authorities, against the powers of this dark world and against the spiritual forces of evil in the heavenly realms." That means while people may oppose us and hate us and seek to silence us, our greatest battle is with the demonic powers that enslave and motivate them. And that means our greatest weapon is always prayer and fasting, coupled with the Word of God, which is the sword of the Spirit (v. 17). And in all that we do, we rely on the Spirit's anointing and empowerment. (See 1 Corinthians 2:1–4.) This is how we overcome.

As one commentator explained:

> Thus by the proclamation of the gospel Paul can destroy arguments *and take every thought captive to obey Christ*. The imagery is of a stronghold breached and those sheltering behind its walls taken captive. So the apostle's purpose is not only to demolish false arguments but also to bring people's thoughts under the lordship of Christ. His calling as an apostle was "to bring about the obedience of faith… among all the nations" (Rom. 1:5).[2]

And since we know that our battle is ultimately spiritual and that our political or ideological or cultural enemies are themselves people for whom Jesus died, we do not demonize our opponents as if they were totally and completely evil. Nor do we glorify ourselves (or our political party or cultural affiliation) as if we were all perfect, flawless, super-saints. Instead we stand up courageously and without compromise against the evils of the day, but we remember that the battle is between the kingdom of light and the kingdom of darkness more than it is between Republicans and Democrats or conservatives and liberals.

To quote 2 Corinthians 10 once more, but as paraphrased in *The Message*:

> The world is unprincipled. It's dog-eat-dog out there! The world doesn't fight fair. But we don't live or fight our battles that way—never have and never will. The tools of our trade aren't for marketing or manipulation, but they are for demolishing that entire massively corrupt culture. We use our powerful God-tools for smashing warped philosophies, tearing

> down barriers erected against the truth of God, fitting every loose thought and emotion and impulse into the structure of life shaped by Christ. Our tools are ready at hand for clearing the ground of every obstruction and building lives of obedience into maturity.
>
> —2 CORINTHIANS 10:3–6, MSG

Paul Lived This Out Himself

Paul didn't simply preach this. He lived it out himself. Just look at this amazing description of how Paul and his apostolic colleagues lived:

> We put no stumbling block in anyone's path, so that our ministry will not be discredited. Rather, as servants of God we commend ourselves in every way: in great endurance; in troubles, hardships and distresses; in beatings, imprisonments and riots; in hard work, sleepless nights and hunger; in purity, understanding, patience and kindness; in the Holy Spirit and in sincere love; in truthful speech and in the power of God; with weapons of righteousness in the right hand and in the left; through glory and dishonor, bad report and good report; genuine, yet regarded as impostors; known, yet regarded as unknown; dying, and yet we live on; beaten, and yet not killed; sorrowful, yet always rejoicing; poor, yet making many rich; having nothing, and yet possessing everything.
>
> —2 CORINTHIANS 6:3–10

When we live like this, we cannot be silenced or canceled, and the more that people cut us down, the more that we will rise up. Read those words again and then ask yourself: Can we learn something from a man whose writings are still shaking the world after almost two thousand years? Perhaps his strategy is better than ours.

Paul also wrote this in an attempt to wake up the Corinthian believers who were mistaking the power of the flesh for the power of the Spirit: "To this very hour we go hungry and thirsty, we are in rags, we are brutally treated, we are homeless. We work hard with our own hands. When we are cursed, we bless; when we are persecuted, we endure it; when we are slandered, we answer kindly. We have become the scum of the earth, the garbage of the world—right up to this moment" (1 Cor. 4:11–13).

And yet, to repeat, Paul and his colleagues changed the world. They did not fight as the world fought, and if we are to see lasting victory and societal change, it will not be through force and intimidation. Instead it will be with the power of the gospel, with the presence of the Spirit, and with the character of Jesus.

Bless Those Who Curse You

This is an important aspect of our spiritual warfare, another way that we do not fight the way the world fights. Of course this doesn't mean that we are totally uninvolved in the system of the world. It doesn't mean that we don't vote or that we don't get involved in politics or that we don't sign a petition or join in a boycott. It just means that we do not rely on methods of the world, that we do not fight with fleshly weapons, that we renounce sinful efforts, and that our mentality and demeanor and posture are different from those of the world.

Isn't that the whole message of the cross? God saves the world through weakness, not dominance. The Lord of all dies for our sins rather than wipes out all sinners. The Creator of the universe lowers Himself to serve His creation. And He calls us to follow His lead. Are we too big and proud to do so?

This does not mean that Christians cannot defend themselves against home intruders. It does not mean that believers cannot fight in the army to thwart an enemy invasion. It does not mean that a follower of Jesus cannot be a policeman or fire a gun. Those are not the issues here, nor is that the point of this book. We're talking here about overcoming cancel culture, about pushing back against the silencing of the lambs, about refusing to capitulate to the world's intimidation. This will not be accomplished by brandishing knives or flooding the streets with angry mobs. That is not how we, the followers of Jesus, fight.

Instead, as Paul wrote to the Romans, we are to follow these supernatural, countercultural guidelines:

> Do not repay anyone evil for evil. Be careful to do what is right in the eyes of everyone. If it is possible, as far as it depends on you, live at peace with everyone. Do not take revenge, my dear friends, but leave room for God's wrath, for it is written: "It is mine to avenge; I will repay," says the Lord. On the contrary: "If your enemy is hungry, feed him; if he is thirsty, give him something to drink. In doing this, you will heap burning coals on his head."
>
> Do not be overcome by evil, but overcome evil with good.
>
> —ROMANS 12:17–21

Or, in the words of Jesus:

> You have heard that it was said, "Love your neighbor and hate your enemy." But I tell you, love your enemies and pray for those who persecute you, that you may be children of your Father in heaven. He causes his sun to rise on the evil and the good, and sends rain on the righteous and the unrighteous. If you love those who love you, what reward will you get? Are not even the tax collectors doing that? And if you greet only your own people, what are you doing more than others? Do not even pagans do that? Be perfect, therefore, as your heavenly Father is perfect.
>
> —Matthew 5:43–48

The Lord also said this:

> But love your enemies, do good to them, and lend to them without expecting to get anything back. Then your reward will be great, and you will be children of the Most High, because he is kind to the ungrateful and wicked. Be merciful, just as your Father is merciful.
>
> Do not judge, and you will not be judged. Do not condemn, and you will not be condemned. Forgive, and you will be forgiven.
>
> —Luke 6:35–37

Did Jesus Really Mean It?

Was Jesus being serious when He said this? Did He really intend that we live this out? Are we really supposed to *love* our *enemies*—people who want to hurt us, bad people who are full of hate themselves? Dr. Martin Luther King addressed these very questions in a 1957 sermon, "Loving Your Enemies." He said:

> Certainly these are great words, words lifted to cosmic proportions. And over the centuries, many persons have argued that this is an extremely difficult command. Many would go so far as to say that it just isn't possible to move out into the actual practice of this glorious command. They would go on to say that this is just additional proof that Jesus was an impractical idealist who never quite came down to earth. So the arguments abound. But far from being an impractical idealist, Jesus has become the practical realist. The words of this text glitter in our eyes with a new urgency. Far from being the pious injunction of a utopian dreamer, this command is an absolute necessity for

> the survival of our civilization. Yes, it is love that will save our world and our civilization, love even for enemies.[3]

But how do we live this out? Dr. King said that we must first examine ourselves to recognize our own shortcomings and deficiencies and sins. Maybe people hate us because of something wrong in us. Next he said that we must discover some good within our enemies, "and every time you begin to hate that person and think of hating that person, realize that there is some good there and look at those good points which will over-balance the bad points."[4] How often do we think along these lines? This is a challenge indeed.

And we must not make our battles personal, as if our goal was to defeat or hurt a person. Instead, King said, we demonstrate genuine love in our interpersonal relationships—yes, even with our enemies. As a result, "when you rise to the level of love, of its great beauty and power, you seek only to defeat evil systems. Individuals who happen to be caught up in that system, you love, but you seek to defeat the system."[5] It is the system that we are battling more than people.

As to why we must respond with love when we are hated, Dr. King explained "that hate for hate only intensifies the existence of hate and evil in the universe. If I hit you and you hit me and I hit you back and you hit me back and go on, you see, that goes on ad infinitum. It just never ends. Somewhere somebody must have a little sense, and that's the strong person. The strong person is the person who can cut off the chain of hate, the chain of evil."[6]

Yes, "Somewhere somebody must have some sense. Men must see that force begets force, hate begets hate, toughness begets toughness. And it is all a descending spiral, ultimately ending in destruction for all and everybody. Somebody must have sense enough and morality enough to cut off the chain of hate and the chain of evil in the universe. And you do that by love."[7]

Not only so, but hate distorts the person who hates.

> For the person who hates, you can stand up and see a person and that person can be beautiful, and you will call them ugly. For the person who hates, the beautiful becomes ugly and the ugly becomes beautiful. For the person who hates, the good becomes bad and the bad becomes good. For the person who hates, the true becomes false and the false becomes true. That's what hate does. You can't see right. The symbol of objectivity is lost. Hate destroys the very structure of the personality of the hater.[8]

Finally, King stated, that

> love has within it a redemptive power. And there is a power there that eventually transforms individuals. That's why Jesus says, "Love your enemies." Because if you hate your enemies, you have no way to redeem and to transform your enemies. But if you love your enemies, you will discover that at the very root of love is the power of redemption. You just keep loving people and keep loving them, even though they're mistreating you.

Unfortunately, he said, most people "believe in hitting for hitting; they believe in an eye for an eye and a tooth for a tooth; they believe in hating for hating; but Jesus comes to us and says, 'This isn't the way.'"[9]

Jesus is saying the same thing to us today. There is a better way! In short, as expressed in one of King's most famous quotes, "Darkness cannot drive out darkness; only light can do that. Hate cannot drive out hate; only love can do that."[10]

This is one of the most powerful ways we overcome cancel culture: by refusing to become like it. To quote Dr. King once more: "Here then is the Christian weapon against social evil. We are to go out with the spirit of forgiveness, heal the hurts, right the wrongs and change society with forgiveness."[11]

Chapter 15

WE MUST BE BETTER THAN THE CANCELING CULTURE

IT HAPPENED IN a moment of time, and the fall was swift and severe. One day, Morgan Wallen was a famous country music star. The next day, he was largely deplatformed. What exactly caused his sudden fall? After a night out partying with his friends, Wallen was videotaped outside his own house using profanities, including the n-word. He had crossed the forbidden line. He was now an untouchable.

According to the *Daily Wire*, Cumulus Media was the first to pull Wallen's music, directing its more than four hundred stations to stop playing his songs, "effective immediately." Other media giants, including iHeartRadio, SiriusXM, and Pandora (among others), pulled his songs as well, while his music was dropped by some of the biggest online platforms, including Spotify and Apple Music (all this according to *Variety* magazine). Even the "Nashville-based label Big Loud has suspended their contract with Wallen 'indefinitely.' Additionally, as reported by the *New York Post*, Wallen 'has been disqualified from performing at or receiving any recognition during the upcoming Academy of Country Music Awards.'"[1]

Talk about swift justice. Talk about decisive action. One wrong word, one single time, and Wallen was suddenly out, despite the fact that he quickly apologized, writing, "I'm embarrassed and sorry. I used an unacceptable and inappropriate racial slur that I wish I could take back.... There are no excuses to use this type of language, ever. I want to sincerely apologize for using the word. I promise to do better."[2]

Unfortunately, as others have emphasized, in today's cancel culture climate there is no redemption, no forgiveness, no room for repentance and contrition and restitution.[3] One strike and you're out—or, at the least, tarnished for life. And as wrong as his actions were (obviously), he was drunk and apparently meant his comment in jest. Shouldn't his sober apology carry weight?

This did not sit well with Wallen's sister Ashlyn, who wrote:

> "There are only 3 things you should ever do about a mistake: admit it, learn from it, and don't repeat it." Cancel culture is the worst thing that has come out of our digital world. It leaves no room for forgiveness and growth, in turn, leaving no opportunity for individuals who have made mistakes to learn from them. If you make a mistake or do something stupid then apologize, correct your mistake, and learn through personal growth.

She added:

> The world we live in thrives off drama and bringing others down. I refuse to be part of that. If my family or my friends make a mistake and apologize, I'm going to listen, accept it, and expect them to learn from their mistake.
>
> Someone who is truly sorry should be forgiven—not continuously bashed. Your past mistakes do not define you; it is how you choose to move forward that does.[4]

Isn't that something all of us have learned in the course of life? Haven't we all made regrettable mistakes, learned from them, asked forgiveness from those we offended, and sought to make things right? Haven't many of us become better people as a result—more sensitive, more caring, more humble, more genuine? And couldn't the same thing happen with Morgan Wallen? (For the record, I know nothing of him beyond what I have written here, and I have not followed his musical career.)

For those of us who claim to be followers of Jesus, we are called to a higher standard, a standard of redemption and mercy and forgiveness and second and third chances (and more). And for all of us who want to be decent human beings, we must not emulate the culture that cancels and shames and silences. Instead, we must be better than it. And that means being people who welcome repentance, who are quick to forgive (from the heart), and who show the same mercy to others that we wish to receive ourselves.

We take our lead from Jesus, who said as He was being crucified, "Father, forgive them, for they know not what they do" (Luke 23:34, ESV).[5] Yes, He prayed that His Father would forgive those who were nailing Him to the cross. Talk about the polar opposite of cancel culture! He also taught His disciples to forgive those who sinned against them if they wanted to receive God's forgiveness. (See Mark 11:25 and Matthew 6:14–15.)

Teaching like this sounded quite challenging, and so Peter, in a different context, asked the Lord, "Lord, how often will my brother sin against me, and I forgive him? As many as seven times?" (Matt. 18:21, ESV). In other words, Peter was saying to Jesus, "I understand the principle well enough. If my brother sins against me, then I confront him, and if he repents, asking for my forgiveness, I am to forgive him. But how many times do I this? Do I do it over and over again, as many as seven times?"

Jesus replied, "I do not say to you seven times, but seventy-seven times" (Matt. 18:22, ESV). What a staggering reply. That is what you call mercy and grace.

But isn't this how God treats us? How many times does He forgive us, sometimes in the same day? How patient was He when we were in rebellion, living for ourselves? And how patient has He been with us once we professed faith in Him? That's how we should be toward others.

And the Lord doesn't want us to forgive in a superficial way. Rather, He commands us to forgive from the heart—just as He forgave us. (See Matthew 18:23–35; this parable of Jesus is very strong.) As expressed by Paul, "Put on then, as God's chosen ones, holy and beloved, compassionate hearts, kindness, humility, meekness, and patience, bearing with one another and, if one has a complaint against another, forgiving each other; as the Lord has forgiven you, so you also must forgive. And above all these put on love, which binds everything together in perfect harmony" (Col. 3:12–14, ESV).

Certainly there are crimes we can commit that will have lifelong consequences, putting us in jail for decades, even if others forgive us. And without question, justice and righteous judgment have their place in life as well. There are also times when a nation must declare war on its mortal enemies.

But in our interpersonal relationships, we must model grace and forgiveness and mercy and longsuffering, refusing to become like the cancel culture and to retaliate in kind. Instead let us demonstrate to the world that, by God's grace, we are different and we are better. And let our communities be known as places where the worst of sinners will receive a warm embrace when they humble themselves and ask for God's help. As those who have been forgiven much, let us offer much forgiveness to others.

Forgiving a Nazi Who Ordered the Extermination of Your Family?

Pastor Richard Wurmbrand told me this extraordinary story face to face in 1993.[6] When Germany occupied Romania in the 1940s, Pastor Wurmbrand would go into town to look for a lonely Nazi soldier with whom he could share the gospel. He would sit down in a bar where one of these men was having a drink, and speaking to him in fluent German, he would invite him over to his house, giving him a unique offer: "I will play the piano for you in my home if you let me share the gospel with you." And since these soldiers were away from their families in a foreign country, they would often take Wurmbrand up on his offer.

On this particular night, his wife, Sabina, was sick in bed, so when the Nazi soldier came home with Richard, she did not come out to greet him. But in keeping with his promise, Pastor Wurmbrand entertained the soldier with his fine piano playing, then began to speak with him. This proud Nazi then began to boast about his exploits, not knowing that Richard and Sabina were both Jewish believers.

So he spoke freely, mentioning specific Jewish villages where he had given the order for extermination, until he mentioned one particular village. At this point Pastor Wurmbrand said to him, "That was my wife's village, and that makes you the murderer of my wife's entire family."

Upon hearing this, the Nazi was undone, and Wurmbrand preached the gospel to him clearly until the man repented with tears, asking the Lord to forgive him. He recognized the depth of his guilt and put his trust in the blood of Jesus to wash him clean.

But that was just the beginning of this remarkable story. Pastor Wurmbrand then said to him, "We are now going to wake up my wife, who is sick in bed. I will tell her that you are the murderer of her entire family but that you have now received Jesus and are her brother in the Lord, and she will get out of bed and embrace you."

The Nazi was mortified. He would not do it. He could not do it. And there was no way she would forgive him. How could she?

Finally the man agreed to see her, and it happened just as Wurmbrand predicted. He woke Sabina up, told her what this man had done but that he was now her brother in Jesus, and she got out of bed and hugged him as they wept together. (I weep as I write these words.)

Sabina was there that day in 1993 when Pastor Wurmbrand shared this account with me, and I can honestly tell you that I never met two human beings like Richard and Sabina Wurmbrand. It was as if they came from another world, glowing with the love of Jesus—and this was despite (or because of?) years of unspeakable torture and deprivation in horrific prisons (for Richard) and slave labor camps (for Sabina).[7]

In a 1989 interview on Canadian Christian TV, the interviewer asked Pastor Wurmbrand, "Did you feel anger, bitterness about your situation?" After explaining that although he was imprisoned for fourteen years, it was a very short time compared to other Christian prisoners, he said, "I don't remember ever to have had desire of revenge or hatred. I pitied the Communists. I loved them. And I did the little which I could to try to bring the Communists and even torturers to Christ. And I believe that all Christians have these feelings."[8] Oh that all Christians *would* have such feelings.

Corrie ten Boom, immortalized in *The Hiding Place* book and movie, also forgave one of the Nazi prison guards where Corrie and her sister were imprisoned and mistreated. (Her sister died there.) After she preached a message on God's forgiveness in Germany in 1947, the man approached her, asking for her forgiveness. He had become a Christian after the war and received God's forgiveness. What about hers?

Although in the natural she found it all but impossible, she obeyed the Lord and reached out her hand to shake his. "And so," she explains, "woodenly, mechanically, I thrust my hand into the one stretched out to me. And as I did, an incredible thing took place. The current started in my shoulder, raced down my arm, sprang into our joined hands. And then this healing warmth seemed to flood my whole being, bringing tears to my eyes."[9]

The miracle had taken place. Her heart was changed. "I forgive you, brother!" she cried. "With all my heart!" Yes, she wrote, "For a long moment we grasped each other's hands, the former guard and the former prisoner. I had never known God's love so intensely as I did then."[10]

As for others who were abused by the Nazis, Corrie said, "Those who were able to forgive their former enemies were able also to return to the outside world and rebuild their lives, no matter what the physical scars. Those who nursed their bitterness remained invalids. It was as simple and as horrible as that."[11]

Let us be the opposite of today's cancel culture, a culture that is so unforgiving. Let us not become "invalids" ourselves—to use Corrie ten Boom's words—captives to bitterness and unforgiveness. Instead, as those who have been forgiven much, let us offer forgiveness to all who seek it, first from the Lord, then from us. And let us model this within our own communities of faith so that people are attracted to the life of Jesus within us and among us. That love is truly irresistible.

Chapter 16

THE CHURCH CANNOT BE CANCELED

TV HOST AND comedian Bill Maher is not just an irreligious man; he is a man often hostile to religion, to the point of making a 2008 documentary titled *Religulous*. Yet even Maher, as liberal and left-wing as he is, sounded the alarm against cancel culture. In his words, "cancel culture is real, it's insane, it's growing exponentially, coming to a neighborhood near you."[1] Indeed it is.

But Maher is not one to sit back and be silenced, nor does he recommend that others be intimidated. Instead, he said, "When the woke mob comes after you for some ridiculous offense...stand your ground, stop apologizing."[2] He also said, "This is called a purge. It's a mentality that belongs in Stalin's Russia. How bad does this atmosphere we are living in have to get before the people who say cancel culture is overblown admit that it is in fact an insanity that is swallowing up the world?"[3]

All the more does this apply to us, the people of God, especially when we're not talking about a ridiculous, minor offense, like using a politically charged word the wrong way twenty years ago. Instead we're talking about our sacred, Bible-based, life and death, core convictions. By all means we must stand our ground. By all means we must proclaim rather than apologize and stand tall rather than cower. Our beliefs—and our Lord—are worth defending to our very last breath.

And if Bill Maher could say this without belief in God and without recognizing Jesus as Savior or Lord, how much more can we say it when the Captain of our salvation has said that He will build His Messianic congregation (His church) and the gates of Hades will not prevail against it—or against us? (See Matthew 16:18.) We do not back down, and we do not apologize for our faith. How can we if God is for us? Who or what can possibly be against us?

Other unexpected voices have expressed similar sentiments, saying enough is enough with cancel culture, including Nicki Minaj, a woman *not* known for her conservative Christian views. Pushing back against those who condemned her for asking questions about the COVID-19 vaccines, she said, "I remember going to China, and they were telling us you cannot speak out against the people in power there, etc., and I remember all of us thinking, 'Oh, OK, we understand and we respect the laws here and that it's so different from where we live.'" But she added, "Don't y'all see that we are living now in that time, where people will turn their back on you for not agreeing? People will isolate you if you simply speak and ask a question."[4] People have had it with being stifled.

As noted by a conservative online commentator, "In essence, it is very possible that cancel culture will cancel itself. Of course, it is not easy to predict how long this rebellion will take to manifest, but judging by the hard left's doubling down on this odious political tactic, it could happen sooner than we think."[5]

How Much More?

Take one look at the pierced, tattooed face of rapper Tom MacDonald and it does not appear that, like Bill Maher and others, he is standing up to cancel culture from a biblically based perspective. Yet, as the *Daily Wire* reported:

> Rapper Tom MacDonald's father took his son aside after he released the first of many "controversial" songs.
>
> "You may be a rapper, but what you're doing right now is rock 'n' roll. It's more about the truth and less about the music," MacDonald recalls of his father's advice.
>
> Tracks like "Fake Woke," "Clown World" and "Cancelled" pack so much "truth" into their bombastic melodies they made MacDonald more than just a rapper on the rise.
>
> He's a musical revolutionary.
>
> Sound hyperbolic? What other musician, in rap or any other genre, stares down Cancel Culture with such precision?[6]

How ironic that, indirectly, the silence of many Americans Christians is being rebuked by a rapper like Tom MacDonald, who is not known as a man of deep Christian faith. How ironic that he is risking his career by calling out cancel culture while so many of us are reluctant to risk anything for our glorious, precious faith. May his boldness rebuke our cowardice, and may his openness rebuke our timidity. And may the light of eternity shine so brightly on us that we will see all opposition to the faith—even deadly opposition—from an entirely different perspective.

As Paul so powerfully wrote:

> Who shall separate us from the love of Christ? Shall trouble or hardship or persecution or famine or nakedness or danger or sword? As it is written: "For your sake we face death all day long; we are considered as sheep to be slaughtered."
>
> No, in all these things we are more than conquerors through him who loved us. For I am convinced that neither death nor life, neither angels nor demons, neither the present nor the future, nor any powers, neither height nor depth, nor anything else in all creation, will be able to separate us from the love of God that is in Christ Jesus our Lord.
>
> —Romans 8:35–39

Chew on those words one at a time, digesting their meaning and feeling their force. Then look at all the powers that oppose us here in America. Are they not like paper tigers? Are they not more like the Wizard of Oz, propped up with smoke and mirrors to look so intimidating but, in reality, small and weak themselves?

The truth is that there is only one force on earth that can silence the church—especially here in America—and that force is us. It is only we who can cancel ourselves, only we who can put ourselves in the closet, only we who can hide our light under a basket. We still have an incredible amount of freedom, and we still make up a significant portion of the population. If we speak and act and stand, we cannot be stopped.

Perhaps some of us will go to jail for our faith. Perhaps some will lose jobs or be kicked out of college. Perhaps some will be beaten violently or even killed. So be it, as long as it is for the gospel and not for our personal belligerence or fleshly aggression. But our pulpits will not be silenced. Our house meetings will not be stopped. Our books will not be removed from circulation. Our radio and TV stations will not be shut down—unless we capitulate more and more, yielding to cancel culture and censoring ourselves. If we stop shining the light, anything (bad) is possible. If we continue in obedience, anything (good) is possible.

Learning the Lessons From the Past

Think back to the first century. The Jewish followers of Jesus were a small sect within the larger Jewish community, and their leader, hailed as the Messiah, died a despicable, shameful, criminal's death. Surely their movement was doomed to fail. As for the growing Gentile church, it was completely overshadowed by the power of Rome, both politically and religiously. At best, these "Christians" were a curiosity, no more a threat to the Roman Empire than a small rowboat would be a threat to a battleship.

But Jesus said He would build this community of believers, and so, not even the forces of death itself—not persecution and imprisonment and martyrdom—could stop its growth and progress. That's why the Jesus movement continues to grow worldwide to this moment. In fact, as we can see from church growth around the globe, to the extent we hold fast to the Word, preach Jesus without fear, and allow the Spirit to move freely, the growth will be dramatic.[7]

As for persecution, it is nothing we look for or ask for, understanding the terrible suffering it brings. But if we live for God, on one level or another we will be persecuted. As Paul wrote, "everyone who wants to live a godly life in Christ Jesus will be persecuted" (2 Tim. 3:12). Or in the words of Jesus, "The student is not above the teacher, nor a servant above his master. It is enough for students to be like their teachers, and servants like their masters. If the head of the house has been called Beelzebul, how much more the members of his household!" (Matt. 10:24–25). And this: "If the world hates you, keep in mind that it hated me first. If you belonged to the world, it would love you as its own. As it is, you do not belong to the world, but I have chosen you out of the world. That is why the world hates you. Remember what I told you: 'A servant is not greater than his master.' If they persecuted me, they will persecute you also. If they obeyed my teaching, they will obey yours also" (John 15:18–20).

It was for good reason that Lactantius, an early Christian apologist (meaning defender of the faith) wrote about 1,800 years ago, "There is another cause why [God] permits persecutions to be carried on against us, that the people of God may be increased."[8] Today's attempts to cancel and silence the church are a divine opportunity for us to grow and increase, both spiritually and numerically. This is our time to shine.

The Price That Was Paid for the English Bibles You Own

Many of us own multiple copies of the Bible in English, plus we have access to an almost endless number of English translations on our Bible apps and software. But five hundred years ago, if you lived in England, you could not get a Bible in English. They simply did not exist. In fact, *Christian History Magazine* asked its readers if they knew that when William Tyndale (ca. 1494–1536) attempted to translate the Bible into English, "he did this in an era when the English Catholic church had in effect a law that made it a crime punishable by death to translate the Bible into English, and when on one day in 1519, the church authorities publicly burned a woman and six men for nothing more than teaching their children English versions of the Lord's Prayer, the Ten Commandments and the Apostles' Creed?!"[9]

And to think that we cringe and draw back when someone unfriends us on Facebook or insults us on Twitter. These simple, faithful Christian parents utterly put us to shame, while also encouraging us to stand and follow their example. We are called to do what is right because it is right, not because it is easy or convenient or beneficial to the flesh. No, we stand because it is right to stand, and we speak because it is right to speak. Are you with me?

Tyndale had to flee from England to continue his work, but he was ultimately captured and imprisoned, then locked in a miserable, rat-infested, cold, damp cell. From there he wrote a humble appeal to the authorities, asking if "the Procurer" would be kind enough to send from his goods "a warmer cap, for I suffer extremely from cold in the head, being afflicted with a perpetual catarrh [inflammation], which is considerably increased in the cell."

He continued:

> A warmer coat also, for that which I have is very thin; also a piece of cloth to patch my leggings: my overcoat has been worn out; my shirts are also worn out. He has a woolen shirt of mine, if he will be kind enough to send it. I have also with him leggings of thicker cloth for the putting on above; he also has warmer caps for wearing at night. I wish also his permission to have a candle in the evening, for it is wearisome to sit alone in the dark.
>
> But above all, I entreat and beseech your clemency to be urgent with the Procurer that he may kindly permit me to have my Hebrew Bible, Hebrew Grammar, and Hebrew Dictionary, that I may spend my time with that study. And in return, may you obtain your dearest wish, provided always it be consistent with the salvation of your soul.

> But if any other resolutions have been come to concerning me, before the conclusion of the winter, I shall be patient, abiding the will of God to the glory of the grace of my Lord Jesus Christ, whose spirit, I pray, may ever direct your heart. Amen.
>
> W. Tyndale[10]

Talk about devotion to a sacred calling and task. But in the natural it was all over for Tyndale and his work.

Not long after that, when he was about forty-two, Tyndale was "strangled and then burned at the stake for the heresies of translating the Bible into English and questioning the authority of the pope and the established church."[11] Yet his work lives on today, to the point that "more than 90 percent of his wordings appeared in the King James Version that was published nearly 100 years later, and more than 75 percent of his wordings appear in the Revised Standard Version of 1952."[12]

Tyndale could be hunted like a criminal, imprisoned, deprived, strangled, and burned, but his work could not be stopped. Jesus continues to build His church! (And note that there is often a *big* difference between the church Jesus is building and the church that people have built. In Tyndale's case, it was the corrupt, compromised church that put him to death—and, again, they did so because he made it his life's work to get the Bible into the hands of the people in their own language.)

About 150 years earlier, John Wycliffe, who died in 1384, produced the first English translation of the Bible, also challenging some of the prevailing teaching of the church. One of his most famous lines was this: "Trust wholly in Christ; rely altogether on his sufferings; beware of seeking to be justified in any other way than by his righteousness."[13] While this seems like basic gospel to us today, it was considered heresy by the church of his day. And so, centuries after his death (he died a natural death as a free man rather than a martyr's death), his work lived on, continuing to challenge the false traditions of men, which included their suppression of the Word of God in the language of the people.

Indeed,

> John Wycliffe left quite an impression on the church: 43 years after his death, officials dug up his body, burned his remains, and threw the ashes into the river Swift. Still, they couldn't get rid of him. Wycliffe's teachings, though suppressed, continued to spread. As a later chronicler observed, "Thus the brook hath conveyed his ashes into Avon; Avon into Severn; Severn into the narrow seas; and they into the main

> ocean. And thus the ashes of Wycliffe are the emblem of his doctrine which now is dispersed the world over."[14]

The more the corrupt church sought to suppress his views, the more they spread. Once again, there is a lesson here for us.

This also reminds me of the famous words of Tertullian, a second-century Christian apologist, who stated that the blood of the martyrs was the seed of the church.[15] In keeping with this, a historian speaking of the persecution of the English Puritans by church authorities stated, "As the blood of martyrs is the seed of the Church, so freedom is the sweet fruit of bitter persecution."[16] It was out of this persecution that America was born.

Also in keeping with this mentality, this same historian noted, "No great cause in church or state, in religion or science, has ever succeeded without sacrifice. Blood is the price of liberty. 'The blood of martyrs is the seed of Christianity.' Persecution develops the heroic qualities of human nature, and the passive virtues of patience and endurance under suffering."[17]

An Example From Our Day

As I said earlier, if we as believers simply hold our ground, stay true to our convictions, and proclaim the gospel publicly and openly, we cannot be silenced or canceled. And it is not simply because God is with us. It is also because America is not yet the same as ancient Rome or Communist China or Afghanistan or North Korea. We still have abundant freedoms, we still have large numbers, we still have significant societal influence, and we still have legal rights. It is only if we fail to use them that we could face really severe persecution.

That's why it is all the more urgent that we speak now while it is relatively easy to do so, rather than have to pay the kind of price that men like William Tyndale paid—or the woman and six men paid for teaching their children the Lord's Prayer in English. After all, I had complete liberty to write this book, my publisher had complete liberty to publish it, we had complete liberty to advertise it, I was able to speak about it freely on radio and TV and the internet, and it has not been banned or blacklisted (yet!) by Amazon. Let us not exaggerate our current situation.

Yet the dangers are real, as illustrated by the countless examples cited in this book, and these were chosen among a countless number of others that could not be cited, lest this book run to thousands of pages in length. And what of all the examples of cancel culture that could be cited since this book was published?

But to say it again, Jesus is building His Messianic community, and no force of men or demons can stop what He is doing. We must simply stand our ground.

Here's one last example from our day involving an 8-1 Supreme Court ruling that came down in March 2021 as I was writing some of these very pages.

While Chike Uzuegbunam was a student at Georgia Gwinnett College, he began to share the gospel on campus, passing out gospel pamphlets. (This began in 2016.) When students complained about his activities, which were perfectly legal, the school authorities clamped down. Uzuegbunam was told "that he was not allowed to distribute materials or talk to other students about his beliefs unless he had reserved a time in a campus 'speech zone.'"[18] But even this was highly misleading.

As related by the Alliance Defending Freedom (ADF), which argued his case before the Court:

> Georgia Gwinnett College had two speech zones—but don't be fooled into thinking the college broadly encouraged free expression. Combined, the two spaces made up about 0.0015% of campus. If the entire campus were the size of a football field, these "speech zones"—the only places students could exercise their First Amendment rights—would be the size of a piece of notebook paper. On top of that, they were only open for student use for 10% of the week—just 18 hours on weekdays and closed on the weekends.
>
> Despite having already been silenced once, Chike did what the officials asked, reserved a time, and even received approval from college officials for the literature he intended to distribute. But when he began sharing his faith in the speech zone during the time he had reserved, campus police approached him. The officers took his ID card and told him to stop speaking because someone had complained.[19]

Another student, Joseph Bradford, also ran into opposition on the campus, and so the ADF took the college to court, as a result of which "the college eventually abandoned this argument and amended its speech policies to allow for speech in any outdoor area of campus—consistent with the U.S. Constitution. Because of this and the fact that Chike graduated, two courts dismissed the case. But that doesn't change the fact that college officials violated Chike's right to free speech by silencing him twice and intimidated Joseph into silence."[20]

So, even though Uzuegbunam had graduated and the school had made changes, the ADF asked the Supreme Court to hear the case. They wanted a louder, clearer, national statement to be made. And the case was so open and shut that all the liberal justices joined in the 8-1 decision.[21]

As stated by Sarah Kramer for the ADF:

> Countless universities have adopted and enforced speech zones and speech codes like those that Georgia Gwinnett College enforced in this case. That is part of the reason that ADF has over 400 victories against public universities across the country. And far too often, once students try to hold university official[s] accountable, they do just what Georgia Gwinnett officials did here: change the policies and ignore how they mistreated students. Thankfully, the Supreme Court put a stop to this.
>
> Today's college students are tomorrow's voters, legislators, and judges. If they are being taught that the correct way to deal with speech you disagree with is to shut it down, they will carry that understanding with them once they leave campus. To preserve free speech for us all, we must protect free speech on college campuses so that students learn to respectfully interact with diverse viewpoints. And when our constitutional freedoms are violated, courts should say so, even when officials back down. Otherwise, very little stops them from doing so again.[22]

Free speech must be protected, and it is our sacred task, with God's help, to protect it for our generation and the next.[23] Will we rise to the occasion?

In the end, there remains only one way we can be silenced or canceled or banned: we must do it to ourselves. The world cannot—and will not—muzzle the people of God unless we muzzle ourselves. In Jesus' name, we will not!

Chapter 17

BOW THE KNEE ONLY TO JESUS

EARLIER IN THIS book I spoke about Richard and Sabina Wurmbrand, Jewish Christians from Romania who were imprisoned, mistreated, and (especially Richard) brutally tortured for their unwavering faith. They would not bow the knee to the spirit of the age. They would not submit to the godless Communist agenda (or any other godless agenda). They would bow the knee only to Jesus.

But they did not suffer hardship and imprisonment because of a one-time, cavalier act. They did not just wake up one day and say, "Let's do something radical for Jesus." Instead, year after year they determined to obey the Lord, regardless of cost or consequence. Then when the great crisis came, they were ready to obey once again.

When the Nazis occupied Romania, Richard risked his life preaching the gospel, being arrested and beaten for his unflinching faith. Then in 1944 the Nazis were displaced by the Russians, who began to establish their communist regime in Romania, with one million soldiers occupying the country. That's when the great test came.

Richard and Sabina were attending the government-sponsored Congress of Cults along with other national religious leaders, and the event was being broadcast on live, national radio. As one religious leader after another publicly praised communism—I'm talking about Christian leaders praising an atheistic regime, in the name of Christianity—the Wurmbrands became sickened in their spirits.

Sabina said to her husband, who by then was well known in Romania, "Richard, stand up and wash away this shame from the face of Christ! They are spitting in His face."

He replied, "If I do so, you lose your husband."

She answered, "I don't wish to have a coward as a husband."[1]

So he made his way forward to the podium and prepared to deliver his remarks (and I remind you: this was airing live on national radio). As reported by the Christian History Institute:

> When Wurmbrand stepped forward to speak at the congress, there was a hush as everyone anticipated his endorsement of the new government. Into the electrifying silence fell Wurmbrand's proclamation to 4,000 delegates that their duty as Christians was to glorify God and Christ alone. He was hustled from the podium and from that moment became a marked man. As he continued his ministry, the government watched him.[2]

Three years later:

> On the morning of February 29, 1948, as Wurmbrand walked to church to prepare for the morning service, a secret police van pulled up beside him. Two men pushed him into the van, which quickly drove away. Thrown into prison Wurmbrand ceased to exist as though he had disappeared from the face of the earth. His name was registered as Vasile Georgescu, and he was forbidden to pronounce his real name, even when speaking to the guards. When foreign ambassadors or family members inquired about him, "Wurmbrand" did not appear on any list.[3]

But that was not the end of the story. Hardly.

> Richard Wurmbrand endured two terms of prison totaling 14 years. Sabina continued their underground church work, but was also incarcerated for three years in Romania's terrible labor camps. Wurmbrand became so ill in prison that he was put into what was called the "dying room," where guards sent prisoners who were expected to live no longer than a few days. Wurmbrand survived for more than two years before being released from the dying room. During that time he ministered to many people before their deaths.
>
> Finally, in 1965, friends ransomed the now-freed Wurmbrand family from Romania.[4]

Multiplied millions of copies of Richard Wurmbrand's most famous book, *Tortured for Christ*, have been distributed worldwide, having been translated into scores of different languages. Wurmbrand also founded the Voice of the Martyrs, a ministry that for decades has brought awareness of the suffering church to believers across the globe. And what was meant to destroy the church only made it stronger. As Wurmbrand said, "Persecution has always produced a better Christian—a witnessing Christian, a soul-winning Christian. Communist persecution has backfired and produced serious, dedicated Christians such as are rarely seen in free lands. These people cannot understand how anyone can be a Christian and not want to win every soul they meet."[5]

For these persecuted believers, following Jesus was not a matter of convenience or comfort. It was not simply the choosing of a better, more prosperous life. Rather, as Wurmbrand said, "A man who visits a barber to be shaved, or who orders a suit from a tailor, is not a disciple, but a customer. So one who comes to the Savior only to be saved is the Savior's customer, not his disciple." A disciple is "one who says to Christ, 'How I long to do work like yours. To go from place to place taking away fear; bringing instead joy, truth, comfort and life eternal."[6]

We are called to be disciples, not customers, not consumers, not casual seekers of carnal convenience. Instead, with joy we deny ourselves and take up our cross daily. (See Luke 9:23.) And by God's grace, we walk worthy of our Lord. That means we love Him more than father or mother, more than son or daughter, even more than our own lives. That's what disciples do. (See Matthew 10:37–39 and Luke 14:25–33.) We bow the knee only to Jesus!

Refusing to Bow the Knee to the Gods of This World

Sometimes the pressure to bow the knee is literal, not metaphorical. I'm talking about situations where someone is expected to bow the knee in public, just as the Jews in Babylonian exile were required to bow their knees to the statue of Nebuchadnezzar in Daniel 3. In our day, in America and the West, it's not a matter of bowing down to a physical statue. Instead it's a matter of bowing the knee to an ideology. Will we swim against the tide and go against the grain, or will we conform to the culture? Will we risk our reputations and careers by doing what is right, or will we bow to the pressure of public opinion?

These are questions that professional athletes have faced in recent years. When their colleagues are kneeling in support of the Black Lives Matter agenda, what do they do if they do not agree with that agenda, even though they support biblical justice and racial reconciliation? What if they simply differ with the BLM leadership and organization? If they do not kneel, they will be called bigots. If they do kneel, they will be cowards in

God's sight. What then will they do? Will they put their career first? Will they put earthly fame before obedience? Will they put convenience before conviction?

Some Christian athletes have sent a clear message. They will kneel only to the Lord Jesus. They will not support an agenda that they believe is driven by Marxist ideology. If they are mocked and scorned, so be it. If it hurts their careers, so be it. It is more important to honor God than to honor man.

Other athletes have taken similar stands, even though they did not do so based primarily on Christian conviction. For example, in January 2021, British soccer player Lyle Taylor explained why he was refusing to kneel with his teammates in honor of BLM. Said Taylor, himself a person of color:

> My support for what it is we are trying to achieve is absolute.
>
> But I do not support Black Lives Matter as an institution, as an organisation.
>
> I'd request anyone who blindly supports Black Lives Matter to have a look to what that organisation does and what it stands for—because it's scandalous the fact that the whole world and the whole world's media got behind Black Lives Matter.
>
> Standing behind Black Lives Matter, all the big institutions, all of them sitting there saying Black Lives Matter, not a good idea.
>
> I've done my fair amount of research into it. The message is 100 per cent important, don't get me wrong on that.
>
> Black lives do matter but you will never hear me saying Black Lives Matter again in reference to that organisation.[7]

One month later, on live radio, Taylor reiterated his stand:

> I said before that I agree with the message that black lives do matter and something needs to be done about that to actually teach the message that the racial inequality and the societal injustice needs to stop.
>
> But by the same token we are hanging our hat on a Marxist group who are...looking to defund the police, they're looking to use societal unrest and racial unrest to push their own political agenda and that's not what black people are, we're not a token gesture or a thing to hang your movement on just because it's what's powerful and it's what's going on at the moment.[8]

At about that same time, *an entire British soccer team* announced their decision not to kneel:

> As a group of players, we have decided we will no longer take a knee before the start of matches. This will begin when we face Barnsley tomorrow, Sunday 14 February.
>
> This decision has come after lengthy discussions as a group. We have been taking a knee before games since June but, like many of our fellow players at other clubs, no longer believe that this is having an impact. We believe we can use our time and energies to promote racial equality in other ways.[9]

But what can you do if you are white, and your failure to kneel will be perceived as bigotry? (Taylor was sensitive to this issue, recognizing how hard it would be for a white player not to bow down to BLM.)[10] This was a question faced by Sam Coonrod, a pitcher for the San Francisco Giants baseball team. The date was July 23, 2020, the much-anticipated opening day of the baseball season after long delays because of COVID. As every single player on both baseball teams took a knee during a moment of silence before the national anthem, Coonrod stood erect. Can you imagine doing this in front of all your teammates and colleagues? Can you imagine doing this live on national television?

But for Coonrod, the decision was simple. "I'm a Christian," he said. "So I just believe that I can't kneel before anything besides God."[11] (I do recognize that other Christian athletes felt it was right to take a knee in the name of racial justice. For Coonrod, however, that would have been compromise.)

Sadly, others in our society have caved, including the nation's largest evangelical adoption organization, throwing out their historic, Bible-based policy in favor of placing orphaned children in same-sex households.[12] Why face lawsuits and constant pressure? Capitulating to the culture was much easier.

Others, like Christian universities we mentioned in a previous chapter, have discarded their scriptural standards to appease LGBTQ activism. Still others have bowed the knee in more subtle, private ways, choosing silence over confrontation and capitulation over conviction. In effect, they have canceled themselves.

In this regard, Dr. Albert Mohler said in March 2021:

> The moral revolutionaries are now demanding that every single individual in this society, every single institution, every single school, every single religious denomination, every single adoption and foster

> care agency must pivot. And the pivot, in this case [speaking of the Christian adoption agency] means capitulation.
>
> It means absolute surrender to the demands of the LGBTQ community, and now we're just talking about, generalized, the political left in the United States.[13]

Our answer must be simple and clear: having surrendered our lives to Jesus, we will surrender to no one else and to nothing else, whether by life or by death. That is the attitude of a disciple. That must be our attitude too. (See Philippians 1:20–21.)

One day, willingly or unwillingly, every knee will bow to Jesus and every tongue will confess Him as Lord, to the glory of God the Father. (See Philippians 2:5–11.) Until then the daily question for each of us is simple: To whom will we bow the knee? To the praise of man? To the spirit of the age? To self-preservation? To the temptations of the flesh? To cancel culture and political correctness? Or will we bow the knee only to Jesus? If we bow to Him, then we cannot bow—indeed, we will not bow—to any other gods.

Let us declare in our daily lives and conduct, with love and with grace and with wisdom and with truth, "We will bow the knee only to Jesus, to the glory of God the Father!"

Chapter 18

TURNING PITFALLS INTO PLATFORMS

BEFORE 2016, JORDAN Peterson was a respected but little-known psychology professor at the University of Toronto, and his first book, *Maps of Meaning: The Architecture of Belief*, which took him thirteen years to write and was published in 1999, was a light-selling 564-page academic tome.[1] Then, quite suddenly and unexpectedly, Peterson became an international best-selling author and a man hailed by some as "the most influential public intellectual in the Western world right now."[2] What launched him into worldwide fame?

Wikipedia paints an accurate picture of what happened:

> In 2016, Peterson released a series of YouTube videos criticizing the Act to amend the Canadian Human Rights Act and the Criminal Code (Bill C-16), passed by the Parliament of Canada to introduce "gender identity and expression" as a prohibited grounds of discrimination. He argued that the bill would make the use of certain gender pronouns into compelled speech, and related this argument to a general critique of political correctness and identity politics. He subsequently received significant media coverage, attracting both support and criticism.
>
> Afterwards, Peterson's lectures and conversations—propagated especially through podcasts and YouTube—gradually gathered millions of views. He put his clinical practice and teaching duties on hold by 2018, when he published his second book, *12 Rules for Life: An Antidote to Chaos*. Promoted with a world tour, it became a bestseller in several countries.[3]

Society wanted to shame him and silence him, and his own university refused to support him, but he refused to back down. In fact if there is one quote that launched him into the public eye, it was this one, from October 2016, when he was asked what would happen if the government required him to comply with its new speech rules. He answered, "If they fine me, I won't pay it. If they put me in jail, I'll go on a hunger strike. I'm not doing this. And that's that. I'm not using the words that other people require me to use, especially if they're made up by radical left-wing ideologues."[4]

But in Peterson's case, instead of going to jail or being taken to court or being disciplined by his university, Peterson became an overnight sensation. According to his publisher, his second book, "*12 Rules for Life*, has sold over five million copies worldwide and his global book tour has reached more than 250,000 people in 100 different cities."[5] His Twitter account now has 2 million followers,[6] and his YouTube channel has 4.2 million subscribers.[7]

Instead of his voice being silenced, Dr. Peterson's voice has now been amplified to reach multiplied millions around the globe. This is an amazing example of what can happen when you make a principled decision not to cave in.

How the Attack on Our Video Backfired

In May 2018 my ministry released a six-minute video lecture titled "Can You Be Gay and Christian?"[8] The video was produced on the pattern of the famous Prager U videos—in other words it was a focused, highly professional video with animation—and as soon as it was released, we began to promote it on YouTube. Our advertising budget was only a few thousand dollars, so we carefully targeted our audience: namely, Christian conservatives and Bible believers who wanted to know what the Scriptures said about homosexuality. As a result, and working with an employee at Google Ads, my producer chose words like *Bible* and *Christian* and *homosexuality* and *gay* to draw viewers to our video.

What happened next was completely unexpected. As the video began to attract tens of thousands of viewers, along with a wide range of passionate comments, it also attracted the attention of major gay and transgender channels on YouTube. That's because our video began to play on those channels as paid advertising, meaning if you wanted to see how Charlie's sex-change transition was going, I would appear on the screen first, asking, "Can you be gay and Christian?"

It was not what we intended since, to be candid, I would not intentionally invade someone else's space like that. But that is what happened. And at the same time, an ad for the Alliance Defending Freedom calling for support for a florist who had declined to do the flower design for a same-sex "wedding" also appeared on some of these channels.

As you can imagine, this created an immediate internet firestorm as different YouTube presenters, some of them with millions of subscribers, began to show clips of our video with their commentary added to it. The story got so big that it was reported on major gay and transgender websites, almost all of which featured a picture of our video with a link to it.[9] Not only so, but the story was also covered by *Forbes* and *Business Insider*.[10] That's how much controversy the video stirred up.

Things finally got to the point where YouTube and Google published a formal apology, saying that some videos had inappropriately run as ads on a number of channels.[11] Needless to say, when you're talking about a company as massive as Google–YouTube, it takes a lot for them to issue a formal statement like this. But that's how big our video controversy became.

We even got information from a Google employee who told us what happened on the inside. When our video came out in May 2018, just before gay pride month (something that was not on our minds at all), many employees were highly offended, especially because we were allowed to pay for advertising on YouTube. They began to write emails of protest, which made their way to a Google vice president. He watched the video for himself and decided it was not suitable for advertising.[12]

Thankfully the video was not banned by YouTube, although it was demonetized, meaning that even if it is viewed 10 million times, our ministry does not receive a dime from it. But we are not in this for the money. We are in this to get a message out. And as of this writing, the video has been viewed more than 197,000 times on our YouTube channel alone, with over 4,400 comments and more than 7,100 thumbs up compared to 5,200 thumbs down.[13]

More significantly, clips of the video have been played *more than 35 million times* on various LGBT sites on YouTube as the hosts attacked and criticized the video.[14] But that means the message got out to people who needed to hear it, even if it was presented in the worst possible way. Still, truth was being proclaimed.

Honestly, even if we had ten times the advertising budget that we had, we could not have received this amount of exposure, especially in these kinds of circles. And so the video got to people we could not have reached otherwise, and it was largely because some critics were determined to silence us. You never know how God will turn things around!

One Shut Door Can Lead to a Bigger Open Door

In October 2020, Simon & Schuster, a giant in the publishing industry, announced it would be releasing Senator Josh Hawley's book titled *The Tyranny of Big Tech*. As reported by AP News, Hawley had frequently criticized the various social media giants "for everything from alleged anti-conservative bias to monopolistic control of the online market."[15] As Hawley explained, "At a time when these platforms are determining elections, banning inconvenient political views, lining politicians' pockets with hundreds of millions of dollars, and addicting our kids to screens, I want to draw attention to the robber barons of the modern era....This is the fight to recover America's populist democracy. That is why I am writing this book."[16] The book was targeted for a June 2021 release date.

But on January 7, 2021, one day after the storming of the Capitol, which was also one day after Sen. Hawley called for an investigation into claims of election fraud, Simon & Schuster released this statement:

> After witnessing the disturbing, deadly insurrection that took place on Wednesday in Washington, D.C., Simon & Schuster has decided to cancel publication of Senator Josh Hawley's forthcoming book, THE TYRANNY OF BIG TECH. We did not come to this decision lightly. As a publisher it will always be our mission to amplify a variety of voices and viewpoints: at the same time we take seriously our larger public responsibility as citizens, and cannot support Senator Hawley after his role in what became a dangerous threat to our democracy and freedom.[17]

So, a book exposing the tyranny of big tech gets canceled because of a knee-jerk reaction to Hawley's actions on January 6, actions that were neither dangerous nor unpatriotic. And this happened at the same time that President Trump's Twitter account was being shut down for life, along with many other conservative accounts being purged. Oh, the irony!

But the story doesn't end there. On January 18, 2021, Regnery Publishing, mentioned in chapter 1 as one of the conservative publishing giants, announced that their company would now be publishing the senator's book, with a release date of May 2021. As Mollie Hemingway reported on *The Federalist*, "Simon and Schuster canceled the book Jan. 7, quickly caving to a pressure campaign organized by leftist activists and making the Missouri Republican one of the highest-profile victims of cancel culture." Said Thomas Spence, the president of Regnery, "It's discouraging to see them cower before the 'woke mob,' as Senator Hawley correctly calls it. Regnery is proud to stand in the breach with him. And the warning in his book about censorship obviously couldn't be more urgent."[18]

Not surprisingly, interest in the book exploded after its cancellation and reinstatement, because of which the book's sales appear to be doing much, much better than they would have without all the adverse publicity. Simon & Schuster inadvertently made Hawley into a living martyr, spiking interest in his book rather than drawing attention away from it. (Would the book have opened as a national best seller, as it did in May 2021,[19] if Simon and Schuster had not canceled it?)

As for country singer Morgan Wallen, mentioned in chapter 15, several months after being dropped by his talent agency and largely deplatformed by his industry, he "won several major awards at the Billboard Music Awards ceremony Sunday despite being banned from the event and purged from multiple music platforms."[20] The voice of his fans, which kept his songs at the top of the charts, was louder than the voice of cancel culture.

And when a Canadian father was thrown in jail for defying a court order and speaking out about his teen daughter's transitioning to male, a Canadian member of parliament, Derek Sloan, wrote to him, saying, "Stay strong. The biggest changes come from government overreach like this....This is a tough time, but know that you are in the hearts and minds of many....This is a low-point, but it's things like this that will cause your plight to spread and the government to eventually break....You're in all of our prayers."[21]

Back on our university campuses, Chicago University Professor Dorian Abbot found himself in hot water when he publicly challenged how his school was using its diversity, equity, and inclusion (DEI) policies to stifle all dissenting viewpoints and influence all decision-making, "from admissions, to faculty hiring, to course content, to teaching methods." He had also observed for years "the increasing number of issues and viewpoints [that had] become impossible to discuss on campus," which also alarmed him.[22] But because he dared to criticize these policies openly, he became the subject of a Twitter attack campaign, as a result of which MIT canceled a prestigious lecture he was scheduled to deliver on extrasolar planets. The good news is that Princeton University stepped in, inviting him to deliver the same lecture on the same date on its campus. And because of MIT's capitulation to extremism, resulting in the cancellation of Abbot's lecture, the online audience grew exponentially, into the multiplied thousands, leading to this headline: "UPDATE: Professor Canceled by Woke Outrage Mob Has Last Laugh."[23]

Let us, then, envision every attempt to silence us as a potential platform from which we can speak, seeing obstacles as opportunities. The harder society works to suppress us, the higher God will lift us—as we humble ourselves in His sight, align our message and life with His Word, and then speak the truth in love without compromise or fear. On with it!

Chapter 19

ANNOUNCING A NEW GOSPEL HOLIDAY TO HELP OVERCOME THE SILENCING OF THE LAMBS

MARK THIS DATE on your calendar: April 14. Circle it and highlight it, not just this year but every year. I'll explain why in a moment, but let me say this first: Together we can make history. Together we can send a message. Together we can help turn the tide. Together we can overcome cancel culture and push back against the silencing of the lambs. Together we can—and will—be heard.

But what's so special about April 14? Right now there's nothing of particular significance about that day in America, other than the fact that it's one day before Tax Day. As for annual celebrations on that date, the ones listed on the Holidays and Observances website for April 14 are very little known (although I'm sure they're of importance to those who celebrate them):

- Air Force Reserve Birthday
- Children with Alopecia Day
- Dictionary Day
- Dreams of Reason Feast Day
- International Moment of Laughter Day
- Look up at the Sky Day
- National Bookmobile Day—April 14, 2021
- National Dolphin Day
- National Ex-Spouse Day

- National Gardening Day
- National Pecan Day
- National Perfume Day
- Pan American Day
- Pathologists Assistant Day
- Reach as High as You Can Day
- School Librarian Day—April 14, 2021
- Vaisakhi—April 14, 2021 (Sikh Holy Day in India)[1]

In 2021 we can also add the International Day of Pink—April 14, 2021 (since it is celebrated on the second Wednesday in April).[2] Who knew?

What, then, is so important about April 14? You could call this presumptuous, but I believe the Lord put it on my heart to proclaim every April 14 as the National Not Ashamed of Jesus Day. On that day every one of us will make a public statement of our faith in whatever way we can.

You can wear a gospel-themed T-shirt to school or bring a Bible to work and put it on your desk. You can share the good news with someone new or make a loud and clear proclamation of your faith on social media. Whatever is permitted and whatever is good and right, this will be the day to send a simple and clear message: we are followers of Jesus and we are not ashamed.

After all, if on April 14 there can be a National Bookmobile Day and a National Dolphin Day and a National Ex-Spouse Day and a National Gardening Day and a National Pecan Day and a National Perfume Day, why can't we have a National Not Ashamed of Jesus Day?

On that day every single one of us, in whatever way we can, will let the world know that we are not ashamed of Jesus. No way, no how! He is our Lord and our Master and our Savior and our Deliverer and our King, and we are not ashamed to be identified with Him. Let the whole world know that we are His!

You might say, "But shouldn't we do that every day? Shouldn't we look for opportunities to lift up the Lord every day of the week? Shouldn't we always be known as believers?"

Absolutely we should, as the Lord leads and as the doors are open. Being witnesses is our 24/7 calling 365 days a year.

But here's the thing. Many have us have floated under the radar for years. Our colleagues at work don't know we are believers. Our friends don't know about our faith—at least, the depth of our faith. Our neighbors are unaware that we are believers. We may be sincere, but we are stealth.

In some cases it's because we have been ashamed of our faith, not wanting to suffer rejection or mockery or reproach. In other cases it's because we haven't found the right setting to share our testimonies or we haven't been forced to stand for our convictions. And so, despite the large number of Jesus followers in America—we could be over ninety or one hundred million—it feels as if we are an insignificant minority. We almost feel sorry for ourselves.

The fact is that we are not some tiny, hidden people group forced to cower in the corner in fear for our lives. We are represented in every area of society, from the government to the courts and from the media to the schools. We give tens of billions of dollars every year to Christian and humanitarian causes, we broadcast around the clock on every conceivable media outlet, and our messages flood the internet. How wrong of us to have a "Woe is me" mentality. How wrong of us to throw a pity party. How wrong to feel that the odds are stacked against us.

The reality is that if God is for us, no one and nothing can be against us, and even if the world literally kills us, even death does not scare us. We overcome in Him!

Now is our time to arise and shine. Now is the time to come out of hiding. Now is the time to follow Jesus outside the camp, as Hebrews 13:12–13 states, bearing the reproach He bore. When we are rejected for Him, that is our honor. The world is treating us the same way it treated our Savior. We are privileged! As Paul wrote to the Philippians, "For it has been granted to you on behalf of Christ not only to believe in him, but also to suffer for him" (1:29). That's why after being flogged by the Sanhedrin, the apostles rejoiced that they were counted worthy of suffering on behalf of His name. (See Acts 5:41.)

And note this: although the Jewish leadership forbade them from preaching and teaching in Jesus' name, giving them a stern warning, along with whipping them, the apostles went out and did the exact opposite. As Acts records: "Day after day, in the temple courts and from house to house, they never stopped teaching and proclaiming the good news that Jesus is the Messiah" (v. 42). May we follow their lead!

This is why I'm proposing a National Not Ashamed of Jesus Day. It's about all of us, on one particular day, declaring to the world around us, "We are followers of Jesus, and we are not ashamed of the gospel." It's about all of us raising our voices together. It's about finding mutual strength. It's about us telling the world, "We are here, we love the Lord, and we are not going to be silenced or shamed." It is also our way of saying to the world, "As followers of Jesus, we are here for you. How can we be a blessing in your life?"

Once that is done, the cat is out of the bag. You will no longer float under the radar. You will be approached with questions. You will be watched. You might even be targeted. But to repeat, this is why we are here: to be witnesses, to testify, to share our faith, to point people to Jesus, to serve this lost generation, to stand for what is right.

And so on April 14 every year, God helping, we will raise a shout together. We will proclaim to the entire nation, "We will not be silenced!"

Why April 14?

What's the significance of this particular date? Why not another day of the year? The reason for this date is Esther 4:14 (thus, 4-14, as in April 14), which quotes the famous words of Mordecai to Queen Esther when their Jewish people were facing mass attack and even annihilation at the provocation of Haman. Mordecai said to her, "For if you remain silent at this time, relief and deliverance for the Jews will arise from another place, but you and your father's family will perish. And who knows but that you have come to your royal position for such a time as this?"

If we are alive today, we are alive by God's will, and that means He put us here in this generation at this very hour, for such a time as this. We are the lambs who will not remain silent, the believers who will not be canceled, the followers of Jesus who will not be muzzled.

We are not ashamed of our Lord. We are not ashamed of His Word. We are not ashamed of His ways. We are not ashamed of His standards. We are not ashamed to be identified with Him. To the contrary, Jesus is our pride and joy, our life. Without Him, we are nothing. With Him, we have everything. Why should we be ashamed of Him?

Really now, when you think about it, it's an odd thing to say, "For I am not ashamed of the gospel, because it is the power of God that brings salvation to everyone who believes: first to the Jew, then to the Gentile" (Rom. 1:16). Who would think of being ashamed of the most wonderful message in the world, a message of forgiveness and freedom, of liberation and love?

If you are a husband, would you introduce your wife whom you love and adore and say, "This is my wife, and I'm not ashamed of her"? Perish the thought. Grandparents, would you introduce your beloved, amazing grandchildren and say, "These are my grandkids, and I'm not ashamed of them"? Never!

Why, then, did Paul say he was not ashamed of the gospel? Why did Jesus say that if we were ashamed of Him, He would be ashamed of us? (See Mark 8:38 and Luke 9:26.) Why on earth would we be ashamed of Jesus?

Paul's words to Timothy, written from jail, give us some insight: "So do not be ashamed of the testimony about our Lord or of me his prisoner. Rather, join with me in suffering for the gospel, by the power of God" (2 Tim. 1:8). And then this: "May the Lord show mercy to the household of Onesiphorus, because he often refreshed me and was not ashamed of my chains" (v. 16).

Do you see it? In the first-century Roman world, Jesus was not viewed as a hero. Quite the contrary. The man died a shameful, criminal's death, the most barbaric death known to man, a death reserved for the lowest and worst of transgressors. To be associated with Jesus was to be associated with reproach. It would be equivalent to saying today, "So, you follow that guy on Death Row who was just electrocuted?" In fact it would be even worse.

As for Paul, he must have been a criminal too. After all, the man was considered a troublemaker. The man was in jail. The man was in chains. If you are one of Paul's supporters, then there must be something wrong with you too. And that's how it is in every age: there is reproach associated with Jesus.

But that is a reproach we wear boldly, a reproach we carry with honor, a reproach we are proud to endure. That's because we know who He really is. That's because we have encountered His beauty and glory and power. That's because we understand the depth of His love. And that's why we are not ashamed of Jesus.

Now Is the Time to Take a Stand

On December 20, 2020, feeling deeply gripped by the Spirit, I wrote this in my journal: "I believe God has given me a plan to combat the attempt to silence God's people. April 14, every year (in commemoration of Esther 4:14): National 'Not Ashamed of the Gospel' Day. I believe God has given me a plan!!"

Could it be so? Could this one small step help spark a Spirit-backed, love-empowered movement of holy boldness? Why not?

Now is the time for us to join together and stand and speak and act. In Jesus' name, we will not be silenced. Cancel culture will be overcome by the cross. Our Savior died, and we died with Him. But Jesus also rose from the dead, conquering sin and death. We rose with Him too, and now we live by Him.

For many years now we have watched LGBT activists overcome the stigma associated with identifying as gay or lesbian or bisexual or transgender or queer by being out and proud, also launching the Day of Silence in public schools and National Coming Out Day.[3] This in turn has emboldened countless thousands of others to come out of the closet, to overcome their sense of rejection, to face their pain, and to be out and proud themselves.

But that was only the beginning. Today things have shifted to the point that many of those who fought shame and stigma in the past are seeking to shame and stigmatize those who oppose their ideology. Those who came out of the closet want to put us in the closet. But as I've said before, we are not about to go into the closet. No way, no how. And there is no way under heaven that we will allow gays and lesbians and drag queens and trans activists to march proudly down our streets while we are too ashamed to be who we are. Not a chance!

And so, while we pray for those who identify as LGBTQ, while we reach out to those on the radical Left, while we bless those who curse us, we also stand up in the power of the Spirit and proclaim to the world WE ARE NOT ASHAMED OF THE GOSPEL. WE ARE NOT ASHAMED OF JESUS. WE ARE NOT ASHAMED OF GOD'S WORD. AND WE WILL NOT BE SILENCED.

Let's make a statement on April 14, and let's live by that statement every day of the year. And let's refuse to be silenced or canceled. As Dr. King famously said, "The time is always right to do what's right."[4]

And whatever we opposition we face, never forget this: the Lamb has gone before us!

> Then I saw in the right hand of him who sat on the throne a scroll with writing on both sides and sealed with seven seals. And I saw a mighty angel proclaiming in a loud voice, "Who is worthy to break the seals and open the scroll?" But no one in heaven or on earth or under the earth could open the scroll or even look inside it. I wept and wept because no one was found who was worthy to open the scroll or look inside. Then one of the elders said to me, "Do not weep! See, the Lion of the tribe of Judah, the Root of David, has triumphed. He is able to open the scroll and its seven seals."
>
> Then I saw a Lamb, looking as if it had been slain, standing at the

center of the throne, encircled by the four living creatures and the elders. The Lamb had seven horns and seven eyes, which are the seven spirits of God sent out into all the earth. He went and took the scroll from the right hand of him who sat on the throne. And when he had taken it, the four living creatures and the twenty-four elders fell down before the Lamb. Each one had a harp and they were holding golden bowls full of incense, which are the prayers of God's people. And they sang a new song, saying: "You are worthy to take the scroll and to open its seals, because you were slain, and with your blood you purchased for God persons from every tribe and language and people and nation. You have made them to be a kingdom and priests to serve our God, and they will reign on the earth."

Then I looked and heard the voice of many angels, numbering thousands upon thousands, and ten thousand times ten thousand. They encircled the throne and the living creatures and the elders. In a loud voice they were saying: "Worthy is the Lamb, who was slain, to receive power and wealth and wisdom and strength and honor and glory and praise!"

Then I heard every creature in heaven and on earth and under the earth and on the sea, and all that is in them, saying: "To him who sits on the throne and to the Lamb be praise and honor and glory and power, for ever and ever!"

The four living creatures said, "Amen," and the elders fell down and worshiped.

—REVELATION 5:1–14

Let all of God's people shout Amen! We will not be silenced.

NOTES

PREFACE

1. Michael Brown, "The Silencing of the Lambs," *The Stream*, March 18, 2019, https://stream.org/the-silencing-of-the-lambs/.
2. Wikipedia, s.v. "cancel culture," accessed October 29, 2021, https://en.wikipedia.org/wiki/Cancel_culture.
3. Brown, "The Silencing of the Lambs."

INTRODUCTION

1. Glenn Greenwald (@ggreenwald), "In the prevailing climate, the rational choice is to avoid social scorn and ostracization no matter how baseless the grievances one must appease. Unleash this monster," Twitter, January 22, 2021, 11:50 a.m., https://twitter.com/ggreenwald/status/1352659921175793664.
2. Glenn Greenwald, "The Moronic Firing of Will Wilkinson Illustrates Why Fear and Bad Faith Mob Demands Reign Supreme," Glenn Greenwald, January 22, 2021, https://greenwald.substack.com/p/the-moronic-firing-of-will-wilkinson.
3. Greenwald, "In the prevailing climate, the rational choice is to avoid social scorn and ostracization no matter how baseless the grievances one must appease."
4. Claude Thompson, "Social Media Chiefs Left Speechless When Asked if Mother Teresa Abortion Quotation Is Hate Speech," *Washington Examiner*, April 10, 2019, https://www.washingtonexaminer.com/news/social-media-chiefs-left-speechless-when-asked-if-mother-teresa-abortion-quotation-was-hate-speech.
5. Kristi Burton Brown, "Live Action: Twitter's Ban on Pro-Life Ads Is Discriminatory and Wrong," Live Action, September 26, 2017, https://www.liveaction.org/news/live-action-twitters-ban-pro-life-ads-discriminatory-wrong/.
6. Jennifer Roback Morse, "'Cancel Culture Has Us in the Crosshairs,' Ruth Institute Says," *The Stream*, February 25, 2021, https://stream.org/cancel-culture-has-us-in-the-crosshairs-ruth-institute-says/.
7. Erwin W. Lutzer, *We Will Not Be Silenced: Responding Courageously to Our Culture's Assault on Christianity* (Eugene, OR: Harvest House, 2020), 34–35.
8. Bill Muehlenberg, "Criminalising Christianity, Prayer, and the Bible," Culture Watch, March 1, 2021, https://billmuehlenberg.com/2021/03/01/criminalising-christianity-prayer-and-the-bible/.

9. "About: Frequently Asked Questions," Philadelphia Statement, accessed October 29, 2021, https://thephillystatement.org/about/.
10. "Read the Statement," Philadelphia Statement, accessed October 29, 2021, https://thephillystatement.org/read/.
11. Jake Jacobs, *Mobocracy: The Cultural and Political War to Destroy Our Republic Under God* (Abbotsford, WI: Life Sentence Publishing, 2012), 9.
12. David Acevedo, "Tracking Cancel Culture in Higher Education," National Association of Scholars, updated October 15, 2021, https://www.nas.org/blogs/article/tracking-cancel-culture-in-higher-education.
13. Acevedo, "Tracking Cancel Culture in Higher Education"; see further David Acevedo, "From John David to David Acevedo: Why I'm Leaving Behind My NAS Pseudonym for Good," National Association of Scholars, December 22, 2020, https://www.nas.org/blogs/article/from-john-david-to-david-acevedo-why-im-leaving-behind-my-nas-pseudonym-for-good.
14. Ryan T. Anderson (@RyanTAnd), "I hope you've already bought your copy, cause Amazon just removed my book 'When Harry Became Sally: Responding to the Transgender Moment' from their cyber shelves," Twitter, February 21, 2021, 3:34 p.m., https://twitter.com/RyanTAnd/status/1363587820565184521; see further Jeffrey A. Trachtenberg, "Amazon Won't Sell Books Framing LGBTQ+ Identities as Mental Illnesses," *Wall Street Journal*, March 11, 2021, https://www.wsj.com/articles/amazon-wont-sell-books-framing-lgbtq-identities-as-mental-illnesses-11615511380.
15. Brian Flood, "Amazon Pulls Justice Clarence Thomas Doc as Censorship of Conservative Content Continues," *New York Post*, March 4, 2021, https://nypost.com/2021/03/04/amazon-pulls-justice-clarence-thomas-doc-as-censorship-of-conservative-content-continues/.
16. Emily Wood, "Christians Respond After 6 Dr. Seuss Books Were 'Canceled' for 'Hurtful' Portrayal," *Christian Post*, March 4, 2021, https://www.christianpost.com/news/6-dr-seuss-books-canceled-how-should-christians-respond.html?uid=07ed4df3d9; see further Al Perrotta, "Dr. Seuss and the Woke Army's Nonsensical, Fanatical Thirst to Cancel American Treasures," *The Stream*, March 4, 2021, https://stream.org/dr-seuss-and-the-woke-armys-nonsensical-fanatical-thirst-to-cancel-american-treasures/.
17. See also Megan Basham, "Five Conservative Films Amazon and Jeff Bezos Have Censored," Daily Wire, June 3, 2021, https://www.dailywire.com/news/five-conservative-films-amazon-and-jeff-bezos-have-censored.

18. Tim Wildmon, "Amazon Prime Cancels AFA," American Family Association, accessed November 4, 2021, https://inform.afa.net/optiext/optiextension.dll?ID=F98F4e30InSwa3E7eNBbJOdok3C3fjDh16_x5sguX10K9Z4VxWVtYGUW_dvmXVD_oAysxg%2BjH4%2BL_1MLexe1u4bH%2BkpFc&fbclid=IwAR06aQFNcv4_xlV1qrowXMk4BN1NIIt1imtt16nVZve6TaQ2dpU5mypQT3Y.
19. Megan Basham, "American Booksellers Association Implements New 'Oversight' to Prevent Accidentally Promoting Authors Like Candace Owens," Daily Wire, August 11, 2021, https://www.dailywire.com/news/american-booksellers-association-implements-new-oversight-to-prevent-accidentally-promoting-authors-like-candace-owens; for the ABA and Abigail Shrier's important book, *Irreversible Damage*, mentioned in chapter 1 of this book, see Jim Thompson, "Code Red Comics: Book Burners Are Coming for Your Books," Red State, July 16, 2021, https://redstate.com/jimthompson/2021/07/16/code-red-comics-book-burners-are-coming-for-your-books-n411742.
20. Kristian Jenkins, "Introduction," in *Cancel Culture and the Left's Long March*, ed. Dr. Kevin Donnelly (Melbourne, Australia: Wilkinson Publishing, 2021), 10.
21. Jenkins, "Introduction," 10.
22. Susan Svrluga, "Berkeley Free-Speech Fight Flares Up Again Over Ben Shapiro," *Washington Post*, July 20, 2017, https://www.washingtonpost.com/news/grade-point/wp/2017/07/19/berkeley-free-speech-fight-flares-up-again-over-ben-shapiro/.
23. Rebecca Savransky, "Trump Threatens Funding Cut if UC Berkeley 'Does Not Allow Free Speech,'" The Hill, February 2, 2017, https://thehill.com/homenews/administration/317494-trump-threatens-no-federal-funds-if-uc-berkeley-does-not-allow-free.
24. Thomas Fuller, "Berkeley Cancels Ann Coulter Speech Over Safety Fears," *New York Times*, April 19, 2017, https://www.nytimes.com/2017/04/19/us/berkeley-ann-coulter-speech-canceled.html.
25. Lois Beckett, "Arrests Made After More Than a Thousand Protest Ann Coulter Speech," *The Guardian*, November 21, 2019, https://www.theguardian.com/us-news/2019/nov/21/ann-coulter-berkeley-protesters-arrests.
26. Ben Zeisloft, "5 Times Anti-Christian Sentiment Manifested on Campus in 2020," Campus Reform, January 1, 2021, https://www.campusreform.org/article?id=16526.
27. Christopher F. Rufo (@realchrisrufo), "SCOOP: A Cupertino elementary school forces third-graders to deconstruct their racial and sexual identities, then rank themselves according to their 'power and

privilege,'" Twitter, January 13, 2021, 4:47 p.m., https://twitter.com/realchrisrufo/status/1349473089331974144.

28. Tom Gilson, "Totalitarianism in America Is Nearer Than You Think," *The Stream*, January 4, 2021, https://stream.org/totalitarianism-america-nearer/.
29. Victor Davis Hanson, "Victor Davis Hanson: The Capitol Incursion Offered the Perfect Crisis the Left Needed to Cancel Conservatives," *Western Journal*, January 13, 2021, https://www.westernjournal.com/victor-davis-hanson-capitol-incursion-offered-perfect-crisis-left-needed-cancel-conservatives/. On May 5, 2021, it was reported that Facebook was upholding its ban on Trump. See Susan Milligan, "Facebook Upholds Ban on Trump," *US News & World Report*, May 5, 2021, https://www.usnews.com/news/national-news/articles/2021-05-05/facebook-upholds-ban-on-trump.
30. Hanson, "The Capitol Incursion Offered the Perfect Crisis the Left Needed to Cancel Conservatives."
31. Hanson, "The Capitol Incursion Offered the Perfect Crisis the Left Needed to Cancel Conservatives."
32. Hanson, "The Capitol Incursion Offered the Perfect Crisis the Left Needed to Cancel Conservatives."

CHAPTER 1

1. History.com Editors, "Stalin Banishes Trotsky," History.com, A&E Television Networks, updated January 14, 2021, https://www.history.com/this-day-in-history/stalin-banishes-trotsky.
2. Erin Blakemore, "How Photos Became a Weapon in Stalin's Great Purge," History.com, updated April 8, 2020, https://www.history.com/news/josef-stalin-great-purge-photo-retouching.
3. Glenn Kucha and Jennifer Llewellyn, "Dealing With Opposition," Alpha History, September 29, 2019, https://alphahistory.com/chineserevolution/dealing-with-opposition/#Mass_hearings_and_punishments.
4. Yanan Wang, "The People China 'Disappeared' in 2018," *The Diplomat*, December 31, 2018, https://thediplomat.com/2018/12/the-people-china-disappeared-in-2018/.
5. Wang, "The People China 'Disappeared' in 2018."
6. Joseph Wulfsohn, "Maher Panel Blasts 'Cancel Culture': It's a Form of 'Social Murder,'" Fox News, August 1, 2020, https://www.foxnews.com/entertainment/maher-panel-blasts-cancel-culture.

7. Bari Weiss, "Resignation Letter," Bari Weiss, accessed November 1, 2021, https://www.bariweiss.com/resignation-letter.
8. arthur ezepov, "Bari Weiss Calls Out Cancel Culture 1," YouTube, August 4, 2020, https://www.youtube.com/watch?v=Oq2ubRIP4Ig; Joe Concha, "Bari Weiss Rips Cancel Culture as 'Social Murder' on Bill Maher Show," The Hill, August 1, 2020, https://thehill.com/homenews/administration/510115-bari-weiss-rip-cancel-culture-as-social-murder-on-bill-maher-show.
9. Concha, "Bari Weiss Rips Cancel Culture as 'Social Murder' on Bill Maher Show."
10. Bindi Cole Chocka (@bindicolechocka), Twitter, accessed November 1, 2021, https://twitter.com/bindicolechocka.
11. Dana Kennedy, "Northwestern Professor Alec Klein: 'Unfounded #MeToo Accusations Destroyed My Life,'" *New York Post*, December 26, 2020, https://nypost.com/2020/12/26/alec-klein-unfounded-metoo-accusations-destroyed-my-life/. More fully, see Alec Klein, *Aftermath: When It Felt Like Life Was Over* (Alexandria, VA: Republic Book Publishers, 2020).
12. Elliot Ackerman et al., "A Letter on Justice and Open Debate," *Harper's Magazine*, July 7, 2020, https://harpers.org/a-letter-on-justice-and-open-debate/.
13. Nardine Saad, "How a 2005 Sarah Silverman Joke Sparked Death Wishes From Two Baptist Pastors," *Los Angeles Times*, August 9, 2019, https://www.latimes.com/entertainment-arts/tv/story/2019-08-09/sarah-silverman-baptist-pastor-death-clip.
14. Leah Simpson, "You Would Say That Wouldn't You! Sarah Silverman Says Progressives Should Allow Cancel-Culture Victims a 'Path to Redemption'—After She Was Fired From Film Role for Blackface," *Daily Mail*, October 26, 2020, https://www.dailymail.co.uk/news/article-8880547/Sarah-Silverman-slams-non-forgiving-cancel-culture-progressives-warns-digging-mistakes.html.
15. Simpson, "You Would Say That Wouldn't You!"
16. Nick Cave, "What Is Mercy for You?," The Red Hand Files #109, August 2020, https://www.theredhandfiles.com/what-is-mercy-for-you/.
17. Cave, "What Is Mercy for You?"
18. David Rutz, "SNL, Liberal Comedians 'Scared' to Criticize Joe Biden, Gov. Cuomo: Adam Carolla," Fox News, February 1, 2021, https://www.foxnews.com/media/snl-liberal-comedians-scared-criticize-biden-cuomo-carolla; see also the relevant comments by comedian and actor Chris Rock at Tyler McCarthy, "Chris Rock Speaks Out Against Cancel Culture, Says It Creates 'Unfunny' and 'Boring' Comedy Content," Fox

News, May 20, 2021, https://www.foxnews.com/entertainment/chris-rock-cancel-culture-create-unfunny-boring-content.

19. Alec Baldwin (@AlecBaldwin), "Cancel culture is like a forest fire in constant need of fuel," Twitter, May 14, 2021, 11:09 a.m. https://twitter.com/AlecBaldwln____/status/1393221991126036488.
20. Pop Crave (@PopCrave), ".@MileyCyrus offers to educate DaBaby after his homophobic remarks at Rolling Loud," Twitter, August 4, 2021, 5:24 p.m., https://twitter.com/popcrave/status/1423032239651233794?lang=en.
21. Julius Young, "Sharon Stone Tears Into Cancel Culture: 'The Stupidest Thing I Have Ever Seen Happen,'" Fox News, March 25, 2021, https://www.foxnews.com/entertainment/sharon-stone-cancel-culture.
22. "About Regnery Publishing," Regnery Publishing, accessed November 1, 2021, https://www.regnery.com/our-story/.
23. Brandon Showalter, "Amazon Bans Ads for Book on How Transgender Ideology Harms Girls, Young Women," *Christian Post*, June 22, 2020, https://www.christianpost.com/news/amazon-bans-ads-for-book-on-how-transgender-ideology-harms-girls-young-women.html.
24. Consider this heartbreaking story: J. D. Robertson, "Double Mastectomy at 15, Detrans 16-Year-Old Now Seeks Reversal," The Velvet Chronicle, July 10, 2020, https://thevelvetchronicle.com/double-mastectomy-at-15-detrans-16-year-old-now-seeks-reversal/. See also Rachel Cooke, Tavistock Trust Whistleblower David Bell: 'I Believed I Was Doing the Right Thing,'" *The Guardian*, May 2, 2021, https://www.theguardian.com/society/2021/may/02/tavistock-trust-whistleblower-david-bell-transgender-children-gids.
25. Regnery Publishing (@Regnery), "Our full statement," Twitter, June 21, 2020, https://twitter.com/Regnery/status/1274557435231866881.
26. "Curriculum Vitae," Joseph Nicolosi, PhD, accessed November 1, 2021, https://www.josephnicolosi.com/resume.
27. Jules Gomes, "Homofascists Force Amazon to Ban Catholic Clinician's Books on Reparative Therapy," Church Militant, July 8, 2019, https://www.churchmilitant.com/news/article/homofascists-force-aamazon-to-ban-catholic-clinicians-books-on-conversion-therapy.
28. Daniel Newhauser, "Exclusive: House Republicans Are Pressuring Amazon to Sell Books on Gay Conversion Therapy," Vice, July 19, 2019, https://www.vice.com/en/article/qv7yqq/amazon-gay-conversion-therapy.
29. "Cancel Culture: Our Renowned Health Book Suddenly Banned by Amazon—After 3 1/2 Years of Successful Sales," MassResistance,

August 22, 2020, https://www.massresistance.org/docs/gen4/20c/Amazon-bans-MR-Health-Book/index.html.

30. "Cancel Culture: Our Renowned Health Book Suddenly Banned by Amazon," MassResistance.
31. Newhauser, "Exclusive: House Republicans Are Pressuring Amazon to Sell Books on Gay Conversion Therapy"; Glenn T. Stanton, "Amazon Bans Books About Same-Sex Attraction, But Not Nazi Propaganda," *The Federalist*, July 15, 2019, https://thefederalist.com/2019/07/15/amazon-bans-books-sex-attraction-not-nazi-propaganda/.
32. Stanton, "Amazon Bans Books About Same-Sex Attraction, But Not Nazi Propaganda."
33. Jardine Malado, "Vimeo Removes Videos of Christian Ministry That Preaches Against Homosexuality," Christian Times, April 3, 2017, https://www.christiantimes.com/article/vimeo-removes-videos-of-christian-ministry-that-preaches-against-homosexuality/71919.htm.
34. Michael Brown, "Vimeo Allows Jihadists and Porn but Shuts Down Ex-Gay Christian Testimony," *Christian Post*, March 27, 2017, https://www.christianpost.com/news/vimeo-jihadists-porn-shuts-down-ex-gay-christian-testimony.html.
35. See Stoyan Zaimov, "Ex-Gay Christian Group Says It's 'Saving Lives,' Not 'Inciting Hatred,' as Branded by Vimeo Shutdown," *Christian Post*, March 31, 2017, https://www.christianpost.com/news/ex-gay-christian-group-saving-lives-not-inciting-hatred-vimeo-shutdown-179130/.
36. Brown, "Vimeo Allows Jihadists and Porn but Shuts Down Ex-Gay Christian Testimony."
37. James Troupis, quoted in Mike Huckabee, "Election Aftermath: Since When Are These Things Acceptable?," *The Stream*, December 21, 2020, https://stream.org/election-aftermath-since-when-are-these-things-acceptable/.
38. Harriet Sherwood, "US Preacher Franklin Graham Tries to Reverse UK Tour Cancellations," *The Guardian*, February 7, 2020, https://www.theguardian.com/world/2020/feb/07/us-preacher-franklin-graham-will-try-to-reverse-uk-tour-cancellations. For some positive pushback on another front related to Rev. Graham's meetings in the UK, see Michael Gryboski, "UK Council Apologizes for Censoring Franklin Graham Event Ads; Pays Over $150K in Damages," *Christian Post*, July 16, 2021, https://www.christianpost.com/news/uk-council-apologizes-to-bgea-franklin-graham-for-censoring-ads-pays-damages.html?uid=07ed4df3d9&utm_source=The+Christian+Post+List&utm_campaign=CP-Newsletter&utm_medium=email; Lynn Williams, "A Statement From the Leader of the Council," Blackpool Council, July 9,

2021, https://www.blackpool.gov.uk/News/2021/July/A-statement-from-the-Leader-of-the-Council.aspx.

39. Matthew Hyndman, "I Escaped LGBT Conversion Therapy, but Not Everyone Is So Lucky—Ban It Now to Stop More Damage to Lives," *Independent*, February 20, 2021, https://www.independent.co.uk/voices/lgbt-conversion-therapy-ban-mental-health-b1805080.html; Tyler O'Neil, "LGBT Activist Urges the Government to Fight 'The Pernicious Power of Prayer,'" PJ Media, April 24, 2021, https://pjmedia.com/news-and-politics/tyler-o-neil/2021/04/24/uk-australia-bans-on-conversion-therapy-may-criminalize-preaching-counseling-even-prayer-n1442414. For the position of Prime Minister Boris Johnson, see Boris Johnson, letter to Mr. Peter Lynas, March 27, 2021, https://www.eauk.org/assets/files/downloads/Boris-Johnson-letter-of-response.pdf.
40. Tyler McCarthy, "'The Walking Dead' Actor Ilan Srulovicz Talks Cancel Culture, Media Censorship: 'It Is Orwellian,'" Fox News, January 25, 2021, https://www.foxnews.com/entertainment/walking-dead-ilan-srulovicz-cancel-culture-media-censorship.
41. Phyllis Chesler, "How I Got Canceled," *The Spectator*, August 7, 2020, https://spectator.us/got-canceled-phyllis-chesler-israel-palestine.
42. Chesler, "How I Got Canceled."
43. Rachael Melhuish, "Cardiff University: Do Not Host Germaine Greer," Change.org, 2015, https://www.change.org/p/cardiff-university-do-not-host-germaine-greer.
44. Steven Morris, "Germaine Greer Gives University Lecture Despite Campaign to Silence Her," *The Guardian*, November 18, 2015, https://www.theguardian.com/books/2015/nov/18/transgender-activists-protest-germaine-greer-lecture-cardiff-university.
45. See Michael Brown, "J. K. Rowling vs. Harry Potter Stars and the Supreme Court," *The Stream*, June 16, 2020, https://stream.org/j-k-rowling-vs-harry-potter-stars-and-the-supreme-court/.
46. Ruth Barrett, ed., *Female Erasure: What You Need to Know About Gender Politics' War on Women, the Female Sex and Human Rights* (Pacific Palisades, CA: Tidal Time Publishing, 2016).
47. *The Telegraph* (@Telegraph), "Lesbian are facing 'extinction' because of the 'disproportionate' focus on transgenderism in schools, a controversial campaign group for gay rights has claimed," Twitter, December 26, 2020, 4:00 p.m., https://twitter.com/telegraph/status/1342938307362172930. For the story, see Camilla Tominey, "Lesbians Facing 'Extinction' as Transgenderism Becomes Pervasive, Campaigners Warn," *The Telegraph*, December 25, 2020, https://

www.telegraph.co.uk/news/2020/12/25/lesbians-facing-extinction-transgenderism-becomes-pervasive/.

48. J. D. Robertson, "Lesbian Playwright Canceled by Thought Police," The Velvet Chronicle, October 7, 2020, https://thevelvetchronicle.com/lesbian-playwright-canceled-by-thought-police/.
49. Cormac Watson and Mairead Maguire, "The Hist Will 'Not Be Moving Ahead' With Richard Dawkins Address," *University Times*, September 27, 2020, https://universitytimes.ie/2020/09/the-hist-will-not-be-moving-ahead-with-richard-dawkins-address/.
50. "Now They've No Platformed Richard Dawkins," Spiked, September 28, 2020, https://www.spiked-online.com/2020/09/28/now-theyve-no-platformed-richard-dawkins/; see also Brendan O'Neill, "Cancelling Richard Dawkins Is Absurd," Facebook, September 29, 2020, https://www.facebook.com/watch/?v=267053551085265.
51. The Free Speech Union (@SpeechUnion), "Richard Dawkins has been NO PLATFORMED," Twitter, September 28, 2020, 12:21 p.m., https://mobile.twitter.com/speechunion/status/1310615711543431169; see also "Now They've No Platformed Richard Dawkins."
52. Tyler O'Neil, "Atheist Group Excommunicates Richard Dawkins for Transgender Heresy," PJ Media, April 20, 2021, https://pjmedia.com/news-and-politics/tyler-o-neil/2021/04/20/atheist-group-excommunicates-richard-dawkins-for-transgender-heresy-n1441403.
53. Steven Pinker (@sapinker), "Letter to the @American Humanist Association from myself (AHA Humanist of the Year 2006) and Rebecca Goldstein (AHA Humanist of the Year 2011) protesting its withdrawal," Twitter, April 21, 2021, 7:23 p.m., https://twitter.com/sapinker/status/1385011253924478981?lang=en.
54. Dennis Prager, "Why the Left Has to Suppress Free Speech," Townhall, January 19, 2021, https://townhall.com/columnists/dennisprager/2021/01/19/why-the-left-has-to-suppress-free-speech-n2583317.
55. Prager, "Why the Left Has to Suppress Free Speech."
56. David Ng, "Bryan Cranston: Cancel Culture Has Made Us 'Harder and Less Understanding, Less Tolerant, Less Forgiving,'" Breitbart, January 12, 2021, https://www.breitbart.com/entertainment/2021/01/12/bryan-cranston-cancel-culture-has-made-us-harder-and-less-understanding-less-tolerant-less-forgiving/.
57. Lydia Moynihan, "Harvard Students Seek to Revoke Trump Graduates' Diplomas After Capitol Hill Violence," Fox Business, January 14, 2021, https://www.foxbusiness.com/politics/harvard-students-seek-to-revoke-diplomas-of-trump-supporting-graduates-following-capitol-hill-violence.

58. Adam Michael Molon, "I'm Sounding the Alarm: PRC-Style Censorship Has Arrived in the United States," *Epoch Times*, January 14, 2021, https://www.theepochtimes.com/im-sounding-the-alarm-prc-style-censorship-has-arrived-in-the-united-states_3655220.html. For other relevant op-ed pieces, see Michael Knowles, "The Bad Faith Debate Over 'Cancel Culture,'" *Daily Wire*, accessed November 2, 2021, https://www.dailywire.com/news/knowles-the-bad-faith-debate-over-cancel-culture; Matt Walsh, "Stop Apologizing to the Cancel Culture Mob," *Daily Wire*, accessed November 2, 2021, https://www.dailywire.com/news/walsh-stop-apologizing-to-the-cancel-culture-mob.
59. Stephen Green, "More Than 250 Authors, Agents Compare Trump to 'Son of Sam' Killer," PJ Media, January 18, 2021, https://pjmedia.com/vodkapundit/2021/01/18/more-than-250-authors-agents-compare-trump-to-son-of-sam-killer-n1394417.
60. Stacey Lennox, "Governor Ron DeSantis Vows to Put an End to the Censorship of Conservative Ideas," PJ Media, January 18, 2021, https://pjmedia.com/news-and-politics/stacey-lennox/2021/01/18/governor-ron-desantis-vows-to-put-and-end-to-the-censorship-of-conservative-ideas-n1394460.
61. Paul Bois, "Kristy Swanson Demands Her Removal From All John Hughes Movies If Trump Gets Erased From 'Home Alone 2,'" *Daily Wire*, January 18, 2021, https://www.dailywire.com/news/kristy-swanson-demands-her-removal-from-all-john-hughes-movies-if-trump-gets-erased-from-home-alone-2.
62. Zachary Stieber, "My Pillow CEO Says Bed Bath and Beyond, Kohl's to Stop Selling His Products," *Epoch Times*, January 19, 2021, https://www.theepochtimes.com/my-pillow-ceo-says-bed-bath-and-beyond-kohls-to-stop-selling-his-products_3662460.html.
63. Ben Zeisloft, "Five Universities Who Canceled Trump Officials and GOP Lawmakers," *Daily Wire*, January 21, 2021, https://www.dailywire.com/news/five-universities-who-canceled-trump-officials-and-gop-lawmakers.
64. Christopher Seitz, "Canceling Culture," First Things, January 21, 2021, https://www.firstthings.com/web-exclusives/2021/01/canceling-culture.
65. Lily Cooper, "I Read the Book Target Banned That's Critical of Transgenderism in Girls—It's Essential Reading for This Day and Age," *Western Journal*, January 24, 2021, https://www.westernjournal.com/i-read-the-book-target-banned-thats-critical-of-transgenderism-in-girls-its-essential-reading-for-this-day-and-age/.
66. McCarthy, "'The Walking Dead' Actor Ilan Srulovicz Talks Cancel Culture, Media Censorship."

67. Thomas Fuller, "It's Liberals vs. Liberals in San Francisco After Schools Erase Contested Names," *New York Times*, January 28, 2021, https://www.nytimes.com/2021/01/28/us/san-francisco-school-name-debate.html.
68. Michael Brown, "The Hypocritical Canceling of Gina Carano," *The Stream*, February 11, 2021, https://stream.org/the-hypocritical-canceling-of-gina-carano/.
69. Alexandra Steigrad, "Hasbro Scraps Gina Carano's 'Star Wars' Action Figures," *New York Post*, February 16, 2021, https://nypost.com/2021/02/16/hasbro-scraps-gina-caranos-star-wars-action-figures/.
70. Andreas Wiseman, "Gina Carano Hits Back, Announces New Movie Project With Ben Shapiro's Daily Wire: 'They Can't Cancel Us If We Don't Let Them,'" *Deadline*, February 12, 2021, https://deadline.com/2021/02/gina-carano-mandalorian-ben-shapiro-hits-back-cancel-culture-1234692971/.
71. Emily Ekins, "Poll: 62% of Americans Say They Have Political Views They're Afraid to Share," Cato Institute, July 22, 2020, https://www.cato.org/publications/survey-reports/poll-62-americans-say-they-have-political-views-theyre-afraid-share.
72. Quoted in Michael Brown (@DrMichaelLBrown), "From an email: 'Your resistance to the 'progressive' culture encourages me to do the same,'" Twitter, August 3, 2020, 5:56 p.m., https://twitter.com/DrMichaelLBrown/status/1290406099938680833.
73. Chesler, "How I Got Canceled."

CHAPTER 2

1. Jon A. Shields, "The Disappearing Conservative Professor," National Affairs, Fall 2018, https://www.nationalaffairs.com/publications/detail/the-disappearing-conservative-professor. See the complete data from the study here: Mitchell Langbert, "Homogenous: The Political Affiliations of Elite Liberal Arts College Faculty," *Academic Questions* 31 (2018): 192 (table 1), https://www.nas.org/academic-questions/31/2/homogenous_the_political_affiliations_of_elite_liberal_arts_college_faculty/pdf.
2. John Gage, "Harvard Newspaper Survey Finds 1% of Faculty Members Identify as Conservative," *Washington Examiner*, March 4, 2020, https://www.washingtonexaminer.com/news/harvard-newspaper-survey-finds-1-of-faculty-members-identify-as-conservative. For an individual professor's perspective, see Jerry Bergman, "Ratio of Liberal to Conservative Professors Has

Profoundly Changed," KPC News, October 10, 2019, https://www.kpcnews.com/opinions/article_72a36307-576f-517e-8a43-64eb7f024e27.html.

3. Paul McCants, "Campus Ministry Link: Connecting Youth to College Ministries," Campus Renewal, September 2016, https://www.campusrenewal.org/wp-content/uploads/2016/09/Campus-Renewal-Campus-Link-Grant-Proposal.pdf.
4. Shields, "The Disappearing Conservative Professor."
5. Shields, "The Disappearing Conservative Professor."
6. Christopher Ingraham, "The Dramatic Shift Among College Professors That's Hurting Students' Education," *Washington Post*, January 11, 2016, https://www.washingtonpost.com/news/wonk/wp/2016/01/11/the-dramatic-shift-among-college-professors-thats-hurting-students-education/.
7. Acevedo, "Tracking Cancel Culture in Higher Education."
8. Jessica Custodio, "Prof Threatens to Punish Students for Pro-life, Anti-BLM Views," Campus Reform, August 18, 2020, https://www.campusreform.org/?ID=15472. For the record, I had to look up *sorophobia* too. My spell checker didn't recognize it either. I learned that the word is actually *sororophobia*, and it "designates the complex and shifting relations between women's attempts to identify with other women and their often simultaneous desire to establish and retain difference." But of course. See "Description," Helena Michie, *Sororophobia: Differences Among Women in Literature and Culture* (New York: Oxford University Press, 1998), https://www.oxford.co.za/book/9780195073874-sorophobia-h#.X9_GT9hKiF4.
9. Michael L. Brown, *A Queer Thing Happened to America: And What a Long, Strange Trip It's Been* (Concord, NC: EqualTime Books, 2011), 495–546.
10. Peter Wood and Pete Peterson, "Thought Control and Cancel Culture Overtakes Colleges and Universities," *Washington Times*, August 10, 2020, https://www.washingtontimes.com/news/2020/aug/10/thought-control-and-cancel-culture-overtakes-colle/.
11. Anna Fazackerley, "Sacked or Silenced: Academics Say They Are Blocked From Exploring Trans Issues," *The Guardian*, January 14, 2020, https://www.theguardian.com/education/2020/jan/14/sacked-silenced-academics-say-they-are-blocked-from-exploring-trans-issues.
12. "List of Pronouns!," Ask a Non-Binary, January 25, 2014, https://askanonbinary.tumblr.com/post/74544202338/list-of-pronouns (emphasis in the original); see also Michael Brown, "Fee, Fi, Fo, Fum: I Smell the Marks of Trans-Activism," Townhall, August 9, 2016, https://

townhall.com/columnists/michaelbrown/2016/08/09/fee-fi-fo-fum-i-smell-the-marks-of-transactivism-n2202989.

13. Associated Press, "Teacher Fired for Refusing to Use Transgender Student's Pronouns," NBC News, December 10, 2018, https://www.nbcnews.com/feature/nbc-out/teacher-fired-refusing-use-transgender-student-s-pronouns-n946006.
14. Owen Stevens (@owen_stevens_), Instagram video, November 22, 2020, https://www.instagram.com/tv/CH6R687JKWm/?igshid=xgfihz4oa2aq.
15. Alex Parker, "'A Man Is a Man and a Woman Is a Woman': Student Suspended for Violating Students' Dignity 'Til He Completes a 'Remediation Plan,'" RedState, February 25, 2021, https://redstate.com/alexparker/2021/02/25/a-man-is-a-man-and-a-woman-is-a-woman-student-suspended-for-violating-students-dignity-til-he-completes-a-remediation-plan-n333184. According to the *Daily Wire*, "Other videos on Steven's Instagram page include him explaining how Columbus Day isn't about celebrating every facet of Christopher Columbus' life and how race-based clubs can be toxic to racial progress." Chrissy Clark, "Student Suspended From Education Program for Saying, 'A Man Is a Man, a Woman Is a Woman,'" *Daily Wire*, February 25, 2021, https://www.dailywire.com/news/student-suspended-from-education-program-for-saying-a-man-is-a-man.
16. The Foundation for Individual Rights in Education is unrelated to FIRE School of Ministry, which I helped found; our acronym stands for Fellowship for International Revival and Evangelism.
17. "10 Worst Colleges for Free Speech: 2021," FIRE, February 17, 2021, https://www.thefire.org/10-worst-colleges-for-free-speech-2021/.
18. "10 Worst Colleges for Free Speech," FIRE.
19. Jonathan Sacks, *Morality: Restoring the Common Good in Divided Times* (New York: Basic Books, 2020), 180, https://www.amazon.com/dp/1541675312.
20. Michael Brown, "Are Our Universities Producing Spoiled Brats?," *The Stream*, April 23, 2017, https://stream.org/universities-producing-spoiled-brats/.
21. Aaron Couch, Tatiana Siegel, and Borys Kit, "Behind Disney's Firing of 'Mandalorian' Star Gina Carano," *Hollywood Reporter*, February 16, 2021, https://www.hollywoodreporter.com/news/general-news/behind-disneys-firing-of-mandalorian-star-gina-carano-4133813/.
22. Michael Brown, "Tampons in the Men's Room and Other Campus Insanity," *The Stream*, September 9, 2016, https://stream.org/tampons-mens-room-and-other-campus-insanity/.

23. Sarah Dean, "College Students Are Told They Can't Say 'You Guys' Because It Might Be Sexist and They Can't Ask Asian Strangers for Help With Math," *Daily Mail*, September 8, 2016, https://www.dailymail.co.uk/news/article-3779932/College-students-told-t-say-guys-sexist-t-ask-Asian-strangers-help-math.html.
24. Tom Ciccotta, "Princeton Wants Students to Stop Using the Word 'Man,'" Breitbart, August 18, 2016, http://www.breitbart.com/tech/2016/08/18/princeton-wants-students-stop-using-word-man/.
25. Ciccotta, "Princeton Wants Students to Stop Using the Word 'Man.'"
26. Jeremy Beaman, "Princeton HR Department: Don't Use Word 'Man,'" The College Fix, August 18, 2016, https://www.thecollegefix.com/princeton-hr-department-dont-use-word-man/.
27. Beaman, "Princeton HR Department."
28. Beaman, "Princeton HR Department."
29. Lela Gallery, "College Warns Students Against 'Fatphobic' Phrases Like 'You Have Such a Pretty Face,'" Campus Reform, August 17, 2020, https://www.campusreform.org/?ID=15457.
30. Peter Schmidt, "Supreme Court Decision on Law School's Anti-Bias Policy May Have Limited Impact," *Chronicle of Higher Education*, June 28, 2010, http:/chronicle.com/article/Supreme-Court-Decision-on-Law/66077/.
31. "Christian Club Sues UC Hastings Over Membership Policy," Alliance Defending Freedom, October 18, 2017, https://adflegal.org/press-release/christian-club-sues-uc-hastings-over-membership-policy.
32. Christian Legal Society Chapter v. Martinez, 561 U.S. 661 (2010), https://casetext.com/case/christian-legal-soc-chapter-v-martinez.
33. Christian Legal Society v. Martinez.
34. Bob Smietana, "Catholic Group Leaves Vanderbilt Over Membership Rules," *Washington Post*, April 5, 2012, http://www.washingtonpost.com/national/on-faith/catholic-group-leaves-vanderbilt-over-membership-rules/2012/04/05/gIQA1DWcxS_story.html.
35. See Adelle M. Banks, "Supreme Court Decision on Religion Upends Campus Religious Groups," *Christianity Today*, May 10, 2012, https://www.christianitytoday.com/ct/2012/mayweb-only/supreme-court-decision-upends-religious-groups.html.
36. Todd Starnes, "Harvard Punishes Christian Student Club," Todd Starnes, February 26, 2018, https://www.toddstarnes.com/faith/harvard-punishes-christian-student-club/.
37. Nicole Russell, "Universities Keep Kicking Christian Groups off Campus in Violation of Their Rights," *The Federalist*, March 9, 2018,

https://thefederalist.com/2018/03/09/universities-keep-kicking-christian-groups-off-their-campuses/.

38. Quinn Gawronski, "Duke Student Government Rejects Christian Group Over LGBTQ Policy," NBC News, September 19, 2019, https://www.nbcnews.com/feature/nbc-out/duke-student-government-rejects-christian-group-over-lgbtq-policy-n1056586.
39. Kaitlyn Choi, "DSG Rejects Christian Organization Young Life as Chartered Student Group," *The Chronicle*, September 12, 2019, https://www.dukechronicle.com/article/2019/09/duke-university-student-government-rejects-young-life-christian.
40. Kathleen Harris, "Trinity Western Loses Fight for Christian Law School as Court Rules Limits on Religious Freedom 'Reasonable,'" CBC News, June 15, 2018, http://www.cbc.ca/news/politics/trinity-western-supreme-court-decision-1.4707240. See also "Community Covenant Agreement," Trinity Western University, accessed November 2, 2021, https://www.twu.ca/sites/default/files/twu_community_covenant.pdf.
41. Harris, "Trinity Western Loses Fight for Christian Law School as Court Rules Limits on Religious Freedom 'Reasonable.'" See also Kate Shellnutt, "Canada's Supreme Court Rejects Country's Only Christian Law School," *Christianity Today*, June 15, 2018, https://www.christianitytoday.com/news/2018/june/canada-supreme-court-rejects-trinity-western-law-school.html.
42. Michael Brown, "Canada's Supreme Court Rules Against the Bible," *Christian Post*, June 19, 2018, https://www.christianpost.com/voices/canadas-supreme-court-rules-against-the-bible.html.
43. Robert G. Kuhn, "TWU Reviews Community Covenant," Trinity Western University, August 14, 2018, https://www.twu.ca/twu-reviews-community-covenant.
44. Note that here in the US, the American Bar Association leans strongly to the left. This could lead to potential problems with Christian law schools here as well. See Carrie Campbell Severino, "Yes, the ABA Is Still a Left-Wing Advocacy Group," *National Review*, September 27, 2019, https://www.nationalreview.com/bench-memos/yes-the-aba-is-still-a-left-wing-advocacy-group/; Adam Bonica et al., "The Legal Academy's Ideological Uniformity," *Journal of Legal Studies* 47 (January 2018), https://scholar.harvard.edu/files/msen/files/law-prof-ideology.pdf.
45. Azusa Pacific University, home page, accessed November 2, 2021, https://www.apu.edu/.
46. Azusa Pacific University, "Our Motto," accessed November 2, 2021, https://www.apu.edu/about/motto/. See further Joshua Arnold, "Fallout Continues From Azusa Pacific Sexuality Compromise,"

Juicy Ecumenism, December 19, 2018, https://juicyecumenism.com/2018/12/19/fallout-continues-azusa-pacific-sexuality-compromise/.

47. For Raleigh Washington's position, see Dean R. Broyles, "Azusa Pacific University Trustees Struggle With Cultural Sexual Pressures," Christian News Journal, March 26, 2019, https://christiannewsjournal.com/azusa-pacific-university-trustees-struggle-with-cultural-sexual-pressures/; Sophia Lee, "Mission Drift at Azusa Pacific?," World News Group, December 14, 2018, https://world.wng.org/2018/12/mission_drift_at_azusa_pacific.
48. Stephanie Martin, "Azusa Pacific University Lifts Ban on LGBT Relationships," September 24, 2018, https://churchleaders.com/news/334107-azusa-pacific-university-lifts-ban-lgbt-relationships.html.
49. Christopher Kane, "Evangelical University Reinstates Ban on Gay Relationships," *Los Angeles Blade*, October 3, 2018, https://www.losangelesblade.com/2018/10/03/evangelical-university-reinstates-ban-on-gay-relationships/.
50. Jeremy Bauer-Wolf, "Christian U Flip-Flops on Gay Relationships," Inside Higher Ed, March 19, 2019, https://www.insidehighered.com/quicktakes/2019/03/19/christian-u-flip-flops-gay-relationships.
51. Sex Change Regret (website), accessed November 2, 2021, https://sexchangeregret.com/.
52. Sarah Pulliam Bailey, "Transgender Theology Professor Asked to Leave California Christian College After Coming Out," Religion News Service, September 20, 2013, https://religionnews.com/2013/09/20/transgender-theology-professor-asked-leave-california-christian-college-coming/.
53. Dwight D. Eisenhower, "Personal To Robert J. Biggs," Document No. 1051, February 10, 1959, 2, in *The Presidential Papers of Dwight David Eisenhower*, ed. Louis Galambos (Baltimore: The Johns Hopkins University Press, 1996), http://www.agriculturedefensecoalition.org/sites/default/files/file/constitution_1/1B_1959_President_Dwight_D._Eisenhower_February_10_1959_Letter_on_Government.pdf.
54. Nicole Russell, "After Getting Kicked off Campus, This Christian Group Got Justice," *Daily Signal*, October 15, 2019, https://www.dailysignal.com/2019/10/15/after-getting-kicked-off-campus-this-christian-group-got-justice/.
55. Margery A. Beck, "Court Upholds Ruling in Favor of InterVarsity at U of Iowa," *Christianity Today*, July 19, 2021, https://www.christianitytoday.com/news/2021/july/court-iowa-intervarsity-ruling-discrimination.html; "Court Rules Against University That Targeted Christian Group, Saying They Were 'Hard-Pressed' to Find a More

Blatant Example of 'Discrimination,'" Duty to America News, accessed November 2, 2021, https://dutytoamericanews.com/2021/07/16/court-rules-against-university-that-targeted-christian-group-saying-they-were-hard-pressed-to-find-a-more-blatant-example-of-discrimination/.

CHAPTER 3

1. This is a summary of what many different headlines were saying.
2. Michelle Obama (@MichelleObama), "Like all of you, I've been feeling so many emotions since yesterday. I tried to put my thoughts down here," Twitter, January 7, 2021, 3:49 p.m., https://twitter.com/MichelleObama/status/1347284244763127810.
3. Austin Williams, "Trump Tweets Video Message Condemning Violent Mob of His Supporters Day After They Stormed US Capitol," Fox 10 Phoenix, January 7, 2021, https://www.fox10phoenix.com/news/trump-tweets-video-message-condemning-violent-mob-of-his-supporters-day-after-they-stormed-us-capitol.
4. Victor Davis Hanson, "Assault on the Capitol Has Let Loose the Electronic Octopus," *National Review*, January 14, 2021, https://www.nationalreview.com/2021/01/assault-on-the-capitol-has-let-loose-the-electronic-octopus/.
5. Nikki Haley (@NikkiHaley), "Silencing people, not to mention the President of the US, is what happens in China not our country," Twitter, January 8, 2021, 6:56 p.m., https://twitter.com/nikkihaley/status/1347693768825180160?lang=en.
6. Allum Bokhari, "Apple to Parler: Crack Down on Free Speech or Face Ban," Breitbart, January 8, 2021, https://www.breitbart.com/tech/2021/01/08/apple-to-parler-crack-down-on-free-speech-or-face-ban/; see also Alana Mastrangelo, "Google Blacklists Parler App From Play Store," Breitbart, January 8, 2021, https://www.breitbart.com/tech/2021/01/08/google-blacklists-parler-app-from-play-store/.
7. Glenn Greenwald, "How Silicon Valley, in a Show of Monopolistic Force, Destroyed Parler," Glenn Greenwald, January 12, 2021, https://greenwald.substack.com/p/how-silicon-valley-in-a-show-of-monopolistic.
8. Thanks to a great deal of resourcefulness, Parler was able to reconstruct its database and relaunch on new servers in February 2021.
9. Jesse O'Neill, "Steve Bannon's Podcast Shuttered by YouTube Over False 2020 Election Claims," *New York Post*, January 8, 2021, https://nypost.com/2021/01/08/

youtube-axes-steve-bannons-podcast-over-false-2020-election-claims/; Salvador Rodriguez, "Twitter Bans Michael Flynn, Sidney Powell, and Other QAnon Accounts," CNBC, January 8, 2021, https://www.cnbc.com/2021/01/08/twitter-bans-michael-flynn-sidney-powell-and-other-qanon-accounts.html.

10. Greg Gutfeld (@greggutfeld), "okay, this IS my last tweet," Twitter, January 9, 2021, 4:02 p.m., https://twitter.com/greggutfeld/status/1348012372653469709.
11. Zachary Stieber, "Facebook's Trump Ban an Example of Uneven Standards, Republicans Tell Oversight Board," *Epoch Times*, February 13, 2021, https://www.theepochtimes.com/republicans-tell-oversight-board-facebooks-trump-ban-example-of-uneven-standards_3695410.html.
12. Wolfgang Saxon, "The New York Post Has a Long History," *New York Times*, November 20, 1976, https://www.nytimes.com/1976/11/20/archives/the-new-york-post-has-a-long-history-from-alexander-hamilton.html.
13. Douglas A. McIntyre, "New York Post Stands Out as Newspaper Carnage Grows," 24/7 Wall St., September 1, 2020, https://247wallst.com/media/2020/09/01/new-york-post-stands-out-as-newspaper-carnage-grows/.
14. Todd Spangler, "Twitter Unblocks Account of New York Post, Which Claims Victory in Standoff Over Biden Stories," *Variety*, October 31, 2020, https://variety.com/2020/digital/news/twitter-unblocks-new-york-post-hunter-biden-hacked-materials-1234820449/.
15. Evan Perez and Pamela Brown, "Federal Criminal Investigation Into Hunter Biden Focuses on His Business Dealings in China," CNN, December 10, 2020, cnn.com/2020/12/09/politics/hunter-biden-tax-investigtation/index.html.
16. Jack Dorsey (@jack), "Our communication around our actions on the @nypost article was not great," Twitter, October 14, 2020, 7:55 p.m., https://twitter.com/jack/status/1316528193621327876.
17. Mollie Hemingway (@MZHemingway), "YOU SHOULD NOT BE INTERFERING IN ELECTIONS ON BEHALF OF YOUR PREFERRED CANDIDATE PERIOD," Twitter, October 14, 2020, 8:11 p.m., https://twitter.com/MZHemingway/status/1316532064754323461 (all caps in the original).
18. Rebecca Klar, "Cruz in Heated Exchange With Twitter's Dorsey: 'Who the Hell Elected You?,'" The Hill, October 28, 2020, https://thehill.com/policy/technology/523169-cruz-in-heated-exchange-with-twitters-dorsey-who-the-hell-elected-you. For Piers Morgan's similar

challenge to Google, see Piers Morgan, "Free Speech Is Dying and Woke Google Is Helping to Dig Its Grave: Piers Morgan Reveals How the Unaccountable Search Giant Ruled That His Criticism of Simone Biles Was Socially Unacceptable," *Daily Mail*, updated August 3, 2021, https://www.dailymail.co.uk/news/article-9856467/PIERS-MORGAN-Free-speech-dying-woke-Google-helping-dig-grave.html.

19. Newt Gingrich, "Why I Will Not Give Up," Gingrich 360, December 18, 2020, https://www.gingrich360.com/2020/12/why-i-will-not-give-up/.
20. Ryan Lovelace, "Joseph R. Biden Voters Experience Regret After New Revelations, Poll Finds," *Washington Times*, November 24, 2020, https://www.washingtontimes.com/news/2020/nov/24/joseph-r-biden-voters-experience-regret-after-new-/.
21. Sam Levin, "Is Facebook a Publisher? In Public It Says No, but in Court It Says Yes," *The Guardian*, July 3, 2018, https://www.theguardian.com/technology/2018/jul/02/facebook-mark-zuckerberg-platform-publisher-lawsuit.
22. Levin, "Is Facebook a Publisher?"
23. Statista Research Department, "Facebook: Number of Monthly Active Users Worldwide 2008–2021," Statista, November 1, 2021, https://www.statista.com/statistics/264810/number-of-monthly-active-facebook-users-worldwide/.
24. M. Szmigiera, "World Population by Age and Region 2020," Statista, March 30, 2021, https://www.statista.com/statistics/265759/world-population-by-age-and-region/.
25. Glenn Greenwald, "Facebook and Twitter Cross a Line Far More Dangerous Than What They Censor," *The Intercept*, October 15, 2020, https://theintercept.com/2020/10/15/facebook-and-twitter-cross-a-line-far-more-dangerous-than-what-they-censor/.
26. Kirsten Grind et al., "How Google Interferes With Its Search Algorithms and Changes Your Results," *Wall Street Journal*, November 15, 2019, https://www.wsj.com/articles/how-google-interferes-with-its-search-algorithms-and-changes-your-results-11573823753.
27. Ashley Oliver, "Exclusive—Watch: Sen. Ted Cruz Labels Google the 'Most Dangerous Company on the Face of the Planet,'" Breitbart, January 3, 2021, https://www.breitbart.com/2020-election/2021/01/03/exclusive-watch-ted-cruz-labels-google-most-dangerous-company-face-planet/.
28. Tucker Carlson, "Forget Trump Phone Call, Here's What Really Matters About Georgia Senate Runoffs," Fox News, January 4, 2021, https://www.foxnews.com/opinion/georgia-senate-runoffs-tucker-carlson-trump-phone-call. According to Bari Weiss (referenced in chapter 1),

"Twitter is not on the masthead of The New York Times. But Twitter has become its ultimate editor" (Weiss, "Resignation Letter"). For an attempt to get Carlson removed from Fox, see Jocelyn Grzeszczak, "Petition to Remove Tucker Carlson From Fox News Surpasses 100,000 Signatures," *Newsweek*, September 3, 2020, https://www.newsweek.com/petition-remove-tucker-carlson-fox-news-surpasses-100000-signatures-1529439. See also Brad Bird, "On the Efforts to Silence Tucker Carlson and Sean Hannity," *Epoch Times*, updated January 24, 2021, https://www.theepochtimes.com/on-the-efforts-to-silence-tucker-carlson-and-sean-hannity_3667979.html.

29. Alex Parker, "The Brilliant Rowan Atkinson Cans Cancel Culture: It's a 'Medieval Mob,'" RedState, January 5, 2021, https://redstate.com/alexparker/2021/01/05/rowan-atkinson-cancel-culture-mr-bean-johnny-english-comedy-woke-n305164.
30. Mark Judge, "'It's Terrifying.' The Who's Roger Daltrey Blasts Woke Anti-Culture," *The Stream*, May 7, 2021, https://stream.org/its-terrifying-the-whos-roger-daltrey-blasts-woke-anti-culture/.
31. Michael Brown, "The Facebook Censor Strikes," Townhall, June 13, 2012, https://townhall.com/columnists/michaelbrown/2012/06/13/the-facebook-censor-strikes-n1314358.
32. Michael Brown, "It Turns Out We Weren't Crazy After All," *Christian Post*, May 10, 2019, http://cdn.christianpost.com/voice/it-turns-out-we-werent-crazy-after-all.html.
33. Michael Brown, "Can You Be Gay and Christian?," AskDrBrown, video, May 2, 2018, 6:37, https://www.youtube.com/watch?v=5l_GY6mXgQg&lc=z22buvgaslvbwbfrt04t1aokgzoadpcpulcgwvyh3tyqrk0h00410.
34. Michael Brown, "How LGBT Activism Works, Illustrated in Front of Our Eyes," *The Stream*, June 7, 2018, https://stream.org/lgbt-activism-works-illustrated-front-eyes/.
35. See, for example, the legal battles of Steven Crowder (Julia Alexander, "YouTube Will Let Steven Crowder Run Ads After Year-Long Suspension for Harassment," The Verge, August 12, 2020, https://www.theverge.com/2020/8/12/21365601/youtube-steven-crowder-monetization-reinstated-harassment-carlos-maza) and Prager U (Isobel Asher Hamilton, "YouTube Isn't Bound by the First Amendment and Is Free to Censor PragerU Videos, a Court Ruled," *Business Insider*, February 27, 2020, https://www.businessinsider.com/youtube-google-censor-court-prageru-first-amendment-2020-2). See further Tyler O'Neil, "Breaking: James O'Keefe to Sue Twitter Over Suspension Following CNN Sting Videos," PJ Media, April 15, 2021, https://pjmedia.com/news-and-politics/tyler-o-neil/2021/04/15/

breaking-james-okeefe-to-sue-twitter-over-suspension-following-cnn-sting-videos-n1440360.

36. Tyler O'Neil, "Whistleblower: Google HR Slammed Christian YouTube Ads as 'Homophobic,'" PJ Media, March 13, 2019, https://pjmedia.com/faith/tyler-o-neil/2019/03/13/whistleblower-google-hr-slammed-christian-youtube-ads-as-homophobic-n102710.
37. Peter Hasson, "Exclusive: Google VP Stepped In After Employees Offended by Christian Video on Marriage," *Daily Caller*, March 18, 2019, https://dailycaller.com/2019/03/18/google-banned-christian-marriage-video-advertisements/.
38. Hasson, "Exclusive: Google VP Stepped In After Employees Offended by Christian Video on Marriage."
39. Culture Watch, website, accessed November 2, 2021, https://billmuehlenberg.com/.
40. Bill Muehlenberg, "Facebook Prisoner #9473782," Culture Watch, April 18, 2019, https://billmuehlenberg.com/2019/04/18/facebook-prisoner-9473782/.
41. Bill Muehlenberg, "Erased!," Culture Watch, May 27, 2021, https://billmuehlenberg.com/2021/05/27/erased/.
42. For a wide-ranging critique, see Tyler O'Neil, *Making Hate Pay: The Corruption of the Southern Poverty Law Center* (New York: Bombardier Books, 2020); for a list of my relevant articles and broadcasts, see "SPLC: Search Results," AskDrBrown, accessed November 2, 2021, https://askdrbrown.org/library/search/site/splc.
43. Kay C. James, "Amazon Doubles Down on Excluding Some Conservative Nonprofits From Customer Donations," Heritage Foundation, June 17, 2020, https://www.heritage.org/progressivism/commentary/amazon-doubles-down-excluding-some-conservative-nonprofits-customer.
44. Wikipedia, s.v. "List of Court Cases Involving Alliance Defending Freedom," last modified September 17, 2021, 6:20, https://en.wikipedia.org/wiki/List_of_court_cases_involving_Alliance_Defending_Freedom.
45. In February 2021, Amazon removed Ryan T. Anderson's important book *When Harry Became Sally*, along with a documentary on Justice Clarence Thomas in early March. For Abigail Shrier's tweet in response, see Abigail Shrier (@AbigailShrier), "Just one book, just two films... How many ideas and accounts and viewpoints will Amazon have erased before we recognize the problem?," Twitter, March 2, 2021, 9:03 p.m., https://twitter.com/AbigailShrier/status/1366932202584383488; see also Jason L. Riley, "Why Did Amazon Cancel Justice Thomas?," *Wall*

Street Journal, March 2, 2021, https://www.wsj.com/articles/why-did-amazon-cancel-justice-thomas-11614727562.

46. "Facebook and Google Comply with Sharia Law," MILO, video, February 25, 2018, https://www.youtube.com/watch?v=PriBWYvKA1A&feature=em-subs_digest&utm_source=dlvr.it&utm_medium=facebook; see also Michael Brown, "The Left Really Is Trying to Silence Us," Townhall, March 2, 2018, https://townhall.com/columnists/michaelbrown/2018/03/02/the-left-really-is-trying-to-silence-us-n2456652/print.
47. "Facebook and Google Comply with Sharia Law," MILO; Brown, "The Left Really Is Trying to Silence Us."
48. "#1538—Douglas Murray," *The Joe Rogan Experience*, transcript, September 17, 2020, https://www.happyscribe.com/public/the-joe-rogan-experience/1538-douglas-murray.
49. Robert Kraychik, "Dave Rubin on Big Tech Censorship: '2021 Will Be the Year of the Bannings,'" Breitbart, December 22, 2020, https://www.breitbart.com/tech/2020/12/22/dave-rubin-on-big-tech-censorship-2021-will-be-the-year-of-the-bannings/.
50. Charlie Spiering, "Exclusive—Mike Pence on Big Tech Censorship: 'We Got to Call Them Out,'" Breitbart, July 20, 2020, breitbart.com/tech/2020/07/20/mike-pence-big-tech-censorship-got-call-them-out/.
51. Brian Monteith, "Cancel Culture Will Deny Us the Ability to Tell Lies From Truth," *The Scotsman*, February 15, 2021, https://www.scotsman.com/news/opinion/columnists/cancel-culture-will-deny-us-ability-tell-lies-truth-brian-monteith-3134575.
52. Monteith, "Cancel Culture Will Deny Us the Ability to Tell Lies From Truth."
53. See further "NRB Project for Digital Free Speech," National Religious Broadcasters, accessed November 2, 2021, https://nrb.org/digitalfreespeech/; Ron Paul, "The 'War on Terror' Comes Home," Ron Paul Institute, January 11, 2021, http://ronpaulinstitute.org/archives/featured-articles/2021/january/11/the-war-on-terror-comes-home/; Jan Jekielek, "Video: Heather Higgins: How to Counter Runaway Narratives and Big Tech Censorship," American Thought Leaders, January 21, 2021, https://www.theepochtimes.com/video-heather-higgins-how-to-counter-runaway-narratives-and-big-tech-censorship_3666678.html.
54. "Governor Ron DeSantis Signs Bill to Stop the Censorship of Floridians by Big Tech," Governor Ron DeSantis, May 24, 2021, https://www.flgov.com/2021/05/24/governor-ron-desantis-signs-bill-to-stop-the-censorship-of-floridians-by-big-tech/.

55. "Governor Ron DeSantis Signs Bill to Stop the Censorship of Floridians by Big Tech," Governor Ron DeSantis.
56. "Governor Ron DeSantis Signs Bill to Stop the Censorship of Floridians by Big Tech," Governor Ron DeSantis.

CHAPTER 4

1. Michael L. Brown, *Jezebel's War With America: The Plot to Destroy Our Country and What We Can Do to Turn the Tide* (Lake Mary, FL: FrontLine, 2019).
2. Michael Brown, "This Is Why the Official BLM Statement Is So Disturbing," *The Stream*, July 8, 2020, https://stream.org/this-is-why-the-official-blm-statement-is-so-disturbing/.
3. Scott Walter, "The Founders of Black Lives Matter," First Things, March 29, 2021, https://www.firstthings.com/web-exclusives/2021/03/the-founders-of-black-lives-matter.
4. "'We Are Trained Marxists'—Patrisse Cullors, Co-Founder, #BlackLivesMatter," Martyn Iles, June 19, 2020, video, 1:13, https://www.youtube.com/watch?v=HgEUbSzOTZ8. For a more recent statement by Cullors, who in no way denies her Marxist heritage, see Patrisse Cullors, "Am I A Marxist?," December 14, 2020, video, https://www.youtube.com/watch?v=rEp1kxg58kE&feature=emb_logo.
5. Anthony B. Bradley, "The Marxist Roots of Black Liberation Theology," Acton Institute, April 2, 2008, https://www.acton.org/pub/commentary/2008/04/02/marxist-roots-black-liberation-theology.
6. "Meet the Lesbians Who Tech and Allies Speakers: Patrisse Cullors," Lesbians Who Tech, accessed November 2, 2021, https://lesbianswhotech.org/speakers/patrisse-cullors/.
7. Will Whitmire, "HRC Celebrates the Contributions of Black LGBTQ Leaders and Activists During Pride Month," Human Rights Campaign, June 30, 2020, https://www.hrc.org/news/hrc-celebrates-the-contributions-of-black-lgbtq-leaders-and-activists.
8. Sony Salzman, "From the Start, Black Lives Matter Has Been About LGBTQ Lives," ABC News, June 21, 2020, https://abcnews.go.com/US/start-black-lives-matter-lgbtq-lives/story?id=71320450.
9. "What We Believe," Black Lives Matter, accessed November 2, 2021, https://web.archive.org/web/20200716003500/https://blacklivesmatter.com/what-we-believe/ (emphasis mine).
10. "What We Believe," Black Lives Matter (emphasis mine).

11. “What We Believe,” Black Lives Matter.
12. “What We Believe,” Black Lives Matter (emphasis mine).
13. “What We Believe,” Black Lives Matter.
14. Michael Brown, “Are BLM Leaders Calling on the Spirits of the Dead?,” *The Stream*, September 1, 2020, https://stream.org/are-blm-leaders-calling-on-the-spirits-of-the-dead/.
15. Fowler Museum at UCLA, “Patrisse Cullors @osopepatrisse with Melina Abdullah @docmellymel. June 13, 2020. #blacklivesmatter,” Facebook, June 13, 2020, https://www.facebook.com/FowlerMuseum/videos/291479432259187.
16. This obviously refers to eighteen-year-old Michael Brown, who was shot and killed by police in Ferguson, Missouri, in 2014.
17. Hebah Farrag, “The Fight for Black Lives Is a Spiritual Movement,” Berkley Center for Religion, Peace and World Affairs, Georgetown University, June 9, 2020, https://berkleycenter.georgetown.edu/responses/the-fight-for-black-lives-is-a-spiritual-movement.
18. Abraham Hamilton III, “The BLM Connection to Witchcraft,” Hamilton Corner, August 19, 2020, video, https://www.youtube.com/watch?v=xGJSEoirF90.
19. Farrag, “The Fight for Black Lives Is a Spiritual Movement”; Brown, “Are BLM Leaders Calling on the Spirits of the Dead?”
20. “Rob McCoy and Dr. Michael Brown—FSC 159,” Godspeak Calvary Chapel, September 6, 2020, video, https://www.youtube.com/watch?v=JppPAsXek2I.
21. Peter Montgomery, “Michael Brown Says BLM Calling Out Names of the Dead Is ‘Witchcraft,’” Right Wing Watch, September 9, 2020, https://www.rightwingwatch.org/post/michael-brown-says-blm-calling-out-names-of-the-dead-is-witchcraft/.
22. “Vote YES on the Black Lives Matter at Schools Resolution at the UFT Delegates Assembly,” More Caucus, November 16, 2020, https://web.archive.org/web/20201116120422/https://morecaucusnyc.org/2020/11/16/wed-11-18-vote-yes-on-the-black-lives-matter-at-schools-resolution-at-the-uft-delegates-assembly/.
23. “Vote YES on the Black Lives Matter at Schools Resolution at the UFT Delegates Assembly,” More Caucus.
24. Laleña Garcia, “Talking to Young Children About the Guiding Principles of the Movement for Black Lives,” Black Lives Matter at NYC Schools, accessed November 2, 2021, https://blmedu.wordpress.com/guiding-principles/.
25. Garcia, “Talking to Young Children About the Guiding Principles of the Movement for Black Lives.”

26. Wesley Yang (@wesyang), "NYC teachers union passes 'Black Lives Matter at School' resolution calling for, among many other things, 'disrupting the Western-prescribed nuclear family," Twitter, November 19, 2020, 6:15 p.m., https://twitter.com/wesyang/status/1329564019942973441.
27. MORE-UFT (@MOREcaucusUFT), "And here's the language for the Black Lives Matter At Schools @UFT resolution that passed the Delegate Assembly by 90% today!," Twitter, November 18, 2020, 9:41 p.m., https://twitter.com/MOREcaucusUFT/status/1329253369135984640. For further reflections, see Brett T., "Teachers Union Adopts 'Black Lives Matter at School' Resolution Calling for 'Disrupting the...Nuclear Family,'" Twitchy, December 15, 2020, https://twitchy.com/brettt-3136/2020/12/15/teachers-union-adopts-black-lives-matter-at-school-resolution-calling-for-disrupting-the-nuclear-family/.
28. Lia Eustachewich, "Megyn Kelly Pulls Sons From 'Woke' UWS School Over Anti-white Letter," *New York Post*, November 18, 2020, https://nypost.com/2020/11/18/megyn-kelly-pulls-sons-from-woke-uws-school-over-anti-white-letter/.
29. "Remarks by President Trump at South Dakota's 2020 Mount Rushmore Fireworks Celebration," White House, July 4, 2020, https://web.archive.org/web/20200704134513/https://www.whitehouse.gov/briefings-statements/remarks-president-trump-south-dakotas-2020-mount-rushmore-fireworks-celebration-keystone-south-dakota/.
30. Judd Legum (@JuddLegum), "'Cancel culture' is something that does not exist but is a very popular concept among people who do terrible things and don't like being held accountable," Twitter, July 4, 2020, 11:39 a.m., https://twitter.com/JuddLegum/status/1279439762806517761.
31. William A. Jacobson, "Cancel Culture Is Real," Real Clear Politics, July 15, 2020, https://www.realclearpolitics.com/articles/2020/07/15/cancel_culture_is_real.html.
32. Jacobson, "Cancel Culture Is Real."
33. See Michael Brown, "If 'Hands Up, Don't Shoot' Is a Myth, Why Do So Many Black Americans Believe It?," *The Stream*, September 26, 2017, https://stream.org/hands-dont-shoot-myth-many-black-americans-believe/ and Michael Brown, "The Ferguson Lie That Will Not Die," *The Stream*, July 31, 2020, https://stream.org/the-ferguson-lie-that-will-not-die/.
34. Jacobson, "Cancel Culture Is Real."
35. The Free Speech Union (@SpeechUnion), "1/An alarming number of people are losing their jobs at the moment—or being suspended from

them, pending investigations—because they've criticized some aspect," Twitter, June 6, 2020, 1:03 p.m., https://twitter.com/SpeechUnion/status/1269314030663012352.

36. The Free Speech Union (@SpeechUnion), "13/ The editor-in-chief of Bon Appetit, Adam Rapoport, has stood down after a piece he wrote genuflecting to BLM was judged to be insufficiently pious by his staff (and he wore an inappropriate Halloween costume 13 years ago)," Twitter, June 9, 2020, 5:46 a.m., https://twitter.com/SpeechUnion/status/1270291244552466432.
37. The Free Speech Union (@SpeechUnion), "18/ LA Galaxy player Aleksandar Katai has been 'released' by the club following critical posts made by his wife Tea Katai about BLM protestors on Instagram," Twitter, June 10, 2020, 10:34 a.m., https://twitter.com/SpeechUnion/status/1270726121039056896.
38. The Free Speech Union (@SpeechUnion), "19/ Leading economists, including Paul Krugman, are calling for Harald Uhlig, a professor of economics at the University of Chicago, to be fired as editor of the Journal of Political Economy because he criticised the BLM movement," Twitter, June 10, 2020, 10:34 a.m., https://twitter.com/SpeechUnion/status/1270726122934874113.
39. The Free Speech Union (@SpeechUnion), "21/ BLM activists are demanding that Paw Patrol, the popular children's cartoon on the Nick Jr. channel, should be cancelled because it shows a positive view of police," Twitter, June 10, 2020, 7:51 p.m., https://twitter.com/SpeechUnion/status/1270866170258866183.
40. The Free Speech Union (@SpeechUnion), "23/ David Shore, a 28-year-old data scientist, has been fired for tweeting an article by a biracial Princeton African-American studies scholar suggesting that rioting is politically counterproductive," Twitter, June 11, 2020, 10:57 a.m., https://twitter.com/SpeechUnion/status/1271094177389072385.
41. The Free Speech Union (@SpeechUnion), "25/ Disney, T-Mobile, Papa John's, SmileDirectClub and Vari have pulled their ads from Tucker Carlson Tonight because of the Fox host's criticisms of the Black Lives Matter movement," Twitter, June 11, 2020, 5:23 p.m., https://twitter.com/SpeechUnion/status/1271191266571714568.
42. The Free Speech Union (@SpeechUnion), "28/ Jessica Mulroney, has been fired from Canadian reality show I Do, Redo and Meghan Markle's best friend, after getting into an argument about BLM with a black influencer on Instagram," Twitter, June 12, 2020, 5:27 a.m., https://twitter.com/SpeechUnion/status/1271373468941066240.

43. The Free Speech Union (@SpeechUnion), "30/ Lego has suspended advertising building sets and products including police stations, city police vests and the White House in solidarity with the BLM movement," Twitter, June 14, 2020, 6:15 a.m., https://twitter.com/SpeechUnion/status/1272110311630389248.
44. The Free Speech Union (@SpeechUnion), "32/ Tiffany Riley, the headmistress of a high school in Windsor, Vermont, has been forced to take 'administrative leave' after writing a Facebook post in which she said, 'Just because I don't walk around with a BLM sign should not mean I am a racist,'" Twitter, June 17, 2020, 8:27 p.m., https://twitter.com/SpeechUnion/status/1273411899783290880.
45. The Free Speech Union, (@SpeechUnion), "41/ The Chair of the Board of Governors at British Columbia University, Michael Korenberg, has resigned after liking tweets criticising Antifa and Black Lives Matter protestors," Twitter, June 26, 2020, 4:33 a.m., https://twitter.com/SpeechUnion/status/1276433498761572353.
46. For the story of a high school football coach who was fired for questioning BLM curricula that was being taught in one of his children's world history classes, see Chrissy Clark, "High School Football Coach Fired for Privately Questioning Black Lives Matter Curricula," *Daily Wire*, February 18, 2021, https://www.dailywire.com/news/high-school-football-coach-fired-for-privately-questioning-black-lives-matter-curricula.
47. Michael Brown, "There Is No Mercy and No Redemption in Today's Cancel Culture," *The Stream*, December 29, 2020, https://stream.org/there-is-no-mercy-and-no-redemption-in-todays-cancel-culture/. See also Luke Kenton, "'I Taught Her a Lesson': Black High School Student Insists He Doesn't Regret Getting White Classmate, 18, Kicked Out of Her Dream College by Sharing Video of Her Using a Racist Slur When She Was 15," *Daily Mail* (UK), December 27, 2020, https://www.dailymail.co.uk/news/article-9090959/Student-says-no-regrets-sharing-video-white-high-school-classmate-using-racial-slur.html.
48. Brown, "There Is No Mercy and No Redemption in Today's Cancel Culture"; Kenton, "'I Taught Her a Lesson.'"
49. "In a statement given to Fox News, Groves said: 'I'm not perfect. What I said several years ago as an [adolescent], in a short 3 second clip was wrong, irresponsible, degrading and I take full responsibility for my actions—and will continue to learn and understand the history and true meaning of that word. I hope others learn from [my] mistake and understand that words can hurt deeply, and it's never OK to say a racial slur to anyone'" (Olivia Burke, "'She Lost Her Dreams': College

Accused of 'Caving In to Hysteria' by Kicking Out Mimi Groves for Using N-word When She Was 15," *The Sun*, December 29, 2020, https://www.thesun.co.uk/news/us-news/13600019/college-accused-caving-in-to-hysteria-kicking-out-mimi/).

50. Martin Luther King Jr., *A Gift of Love: Sermons From* Strength to Love *and Other Preachings* (Boston: Beacon Press, 1963/2012), 46–47, https://www.amazon.com/Gift-Love-Sermons-Strength-Preachings/dp/0807000639/.
51. Jessica Napoli, "'Bachelor' Host Chris Harrison Apologizes for 'Speaking in a Manner That Perpetuates Racism,'" Fox News, February 11, 2021, https://www.foxnews.com/entertainment/bachelor-chris-harrison-apologizes-racism-defending-contestant.
52. Melissa Roberto, "Chris Harrison's Removal From 'Bachelor' Is 'Unconscionable' Example of Cancel Culture, Critics Say," Fox News, February 18 2021, https://www.foxnews.com/entertainment/chris-harrisons-bachelor-removal-unconscionable-example-cancel-culture-critics.
53. Roberto, "Chris Harrison's Removal From 'Bachelor' Is 'Unconscionable' Example of Cancel Culture, Critics Say."

CHAPTER 5

1. Susan Miller, "'Society Is Changing': A Record 5.6% of US Adults Identify as LGBTQ, Poll Shows. And Young People Are Driving the Numbers," *USA Today*, February 24, 2021, https://www.usatoday.com/story/news/nation/2021/02/24/lgbtq-gallup-poll-more-us-adults-identify-lgbtq/4532664001/.
2. Joe Biden (@JoeBiden), "Let's be clear: Transgender equality is the civil rights issue of our time," Twitter, January 25, 2020, 1:20 p.m., https://twitter.com/JoeBiden/status/1221135646107955200.
3. "Clinton to United Nations: 'Gay Rights Are Human Rights,'" Amnesty International, December 8, 2011, https://www.amnestyusa.org/clinton-to-united-nations-gay-rights-are-human-rights/.
4. Michael Brown, "Exposing the Hypocrisy of GLAAD," Townhall, March 19, 2012, https://townhall.com/columnists/michaelbrown/2012/03/19/exposing-the-hypocrisy-of-gladd-n1087600.
5. For other names on the original list, see Brown, "Exposing the Hypocrisy of GLAAD." The current list has expanded considerably; see "GLAAD Accountability Project," GLAAD, accessed November 2, 2021, https://www.glaad.org/gap.

6. "GLAAD's Commentator Accountability Project," GLAAD, accessed November 2, 2021, https://web.archive.org/web/20210204140859/https://www.glaad.org/cap.
7. See chapter 3.
8. See again Tyler O'Neil, *Making Hate Pay: The Corruption of the Southern Poverty Law Center.*
9. Southern Poverty Law Center, "30 New Activists Heading Up the Radical Right," *Intelligence Report* (May 26, 2012), https://www.splcenter.org/fighting-hate/intelligence-report/2012/30-new-activists-heading-radical-right.
10. Michael Brown, "Malik Zulu Shabbaz, David Duke, and Me," Townhall, May 25, 2012, http://townhall.com/columnists/michaelbrown/2012/05/25/malik_zulu_shabbaz_david_duke_and_me/page/full.
11. Aidan Moyer, "Students to Protest Speaker Michael Brown," *The Appalachian*, February 12, 2018, https://theappalachianonline.com/students-protest-speaker-michael-brown/.
12. Ben Kamisar, "Conservative Groups Cry Foul Over Controversial Group's Role in YouTube Moderation," The Hill, March 8, 2018, https://thehill.com/homenews/campaign/377310-conservatives-cry-foul-over-controversial-groups-role-in-youtube-moderation.
13. Dennis Prager, "Tell Big Tech to Stop Relying on the SPLC," Facebook Watch, April 11, 2019, video, https://www.facebook.com/watch/?v=340694433471373; Jolie O'Dell, "Facebook Working With GLAAD to Stop Anti-gay Bullying," CNN, October 14, 2010, http://www.cnn.com/2010/TECH/social.media/10/14/facebook.glaad.bullying/index.html.
14. Michael Brown, "Locked Out by Twitter for Telling the Truth," *The Stream*, January 25, 2021, https://stream.org/locked-out-by-twitter-for-telling-the-truth/.
15. "The Twitter Rules," Twitter Help Center, accessed November 2, 2021, https://help.twitter.com/en/rules-and-policies/twitter-rules.
16. John Zmirak, "Farewell Twitter, Goodbye YouTube," *The Stream*, December 15, 2020, https://stream.org/farewell-twitter-goodbye-youtube/.
17. Michael Brown, "This Is Child Abuse, This Is Madness, This Must Stop," *The Stream*, March 19, 2021, https://stream.org/this-is-child-abuse-this-is-madness-this-must-stop/.
18. "Hostile Judge Rejects Rob Hoogland's Plea Agreement With BC Attorney General in 'Criminal Contempt' Case for Breaking Gag Order. Sentences Rob to Six Months in Prison and $30,000 fine!,"

MassResistance, April 16, 2021, https://www.massresistance.org/docs/gen4/21b/Rob-Hoogland-given-prison-sentence-fined/index.html.

19. Jeremiah Keenan, "Canadian Father Jailed for Talking About Court-Ordered Transgendering of His Teenage Daughter," *The Federalist*, March 26, 2021, https://thefederalist.com/2021/03/26/canadian-father-jailed-for-talking-about-court-ordered-transgendering-of-his-teenage-daughter/.
20. Michael Brown, "Being Found Guilty of 'Transphobia' Could Cost You $250,000," *Christian Post*, January 8, 2016, https://www.christianpost.com/news/transgender-transphobia-gender-identity-fine-250000-dollars-new-york-city-washington-state.html.
21. Michael Brown, "If You Think We're Exaggerating, Just Look to Norway," *The Stream*, December 2, 2020, https://stream.org/if-you-think-were-exaggerating-just-look-to-norway/.
22. Anugrah Kumar, "Christian MP Faces 6 Years in Prison for Tweeting Bible Verses on Marriage, Sexuality," *Christian Post*, May 1, 2021, https://www.christianpost.com/news/christian-mp-faces-prison-for-tweeting-bible-verses-on-marriage.html.
23. Kumar, "Christian MP Faces 6 Years in Prison for Tweeting Bible Verses on Marriage, Sexuality."
24. "When a Tweet Can Land You in Jail: Criminal Charges Brought Against Finnish MP," ADF International, accessed November 2, 2021, https://adfinternational.org/news/when-a-tweet-can-land-you-in-jail-criminal-charges-brought-against-finnish-mp/.
25. See Joy Pullmann, "In Case With Global Implications, Finland Puts Christians on Trial for Their Faith," *The Federalist*, November 23, 2021, https://thefederalist.com/2021/11/23/in-case-with-global-implications-finland-puts-christians-on-trial-for-their-faith/.
26. For a recent example, see Katie Feehan and Rory Tingle, "Christian Pastor Arrested for Making 'Homophobic Statements' After Preaching From the Bible Says He Was Treated 'Shamefully'—and Was 'Doing What My Job Description Says,'" *Daily Mail* (UK), April 28, 2021, https://www.dailymail.co.uk/news/article-9521123/Moment-police-arrest-elderly-preacher-71-street-quoting-homophobic-statements-Bible.html; for some previous examples, see "Preacher Locked Up for Hate Crime After Quoting Bible to Gay Teenager," *The Telegraph*, February 5, 2017, https://www.telegraph.co.uk/news/2017/02/05/preacher-locked-hate-crime-quoting-bible-gay-teenager/; Laura Churchill, "Christian Street Preachers Who Read From Bible Found Guilty of Abusing Bristol Shoppers and Causing Angry Scenes," *Bristol Post*, updated June 29, 2017, https://www.bristolpost.co.uk/news/bristol-news/

christian-street-preachers-who-read-4603; Michael Gryboski, "British Police Pay $3,000 to Street Preacher for Wrong Arrest, Taking Away Bible," *Christian Post*, July 29, 2019, https://www.christianpost.com/news/british-police-pay-3000-to-street-preacher-for-wrong-arrest-taking-away-bible.html.

27. Christian Concern, "School Chaplain Reported to Terrorist Watchdog and Forced Out of Job for Sermon on Identity Politics," news release, May 9, 2021, https://christianconcern.com/ccpressreleases/school-chaplain-reported-to-terrorist-watchdog-and-forced-out-of-job-for-sermon-on-identity-politics/.
28. Educate & Celebrate, website, accessed November 2, 2021, https://www.educateandcelebrate.org/.
29. Christian Concern, "School Chaplain Reported to Terrorist Watchdog and Forced Out of Job for Sermon on Identity Politics."
30. Tom Gordon, "Feminist Campaigner Charged With 'Hate Crime,'" *The Herald* (Scotland), June 3, 2021, https://www.heraldscotland.com/news/19349054.feminist-campaigner-charged-hate-crime/.
31. "Corporate Equality Index Archive," Human Rights Campaign, accessed November 2, 2021, https://www.thehrcfoundation.org/professional-resources/corporate-equality-index-archive.
32. "Dr. Brown Puts the Human Rights Campaign on Notice," AskDrBrown, September 30, 2014, video, https://youtu.be/CaBSJKOPIsc.
33. R. Albert Mohler Jr., "A Direct Threat to Christian Education—The Human Rights Campaign Demands That the Biden Administration Deny Accreditation to Christian Colleges and Schools," Albert Mohler, November 18, 2020, https://albertmohler.com/2020/11/18/a-direct-threat-to-christian-education-the-human-rights-campaign-demands-that-the-biden-administration-deny-accreditation-to-christian-colleges-and-schools.
34. Mohler Jr., "A Direct Threat to Christian Education."
35. Mohler Jr., "A Direct Threat to Christian Education." For specific language and details, going well beyond the Department of Education, see HRC staff, "The HRC Blueprint for LGBTQ Equality Under Biden," Human Rights Campaign, press release, November 11, 2020, https://www.hrc.org/press-releases/human-rights-campaign-charts-bold-path-for-equality-under-biden-administration; Human Rights Campaign, *Blueprint for Positive Change 2020* (Washington, DC: Human Rights Campaign, 2020), https://hrc-prod-requests.s3-us-west-2.amazonaws.com/Blueprint-2020.pdf.

36. Stephanie Condon, "Pastor Drops Out of Inauguration Over Anti-gay Sermon," CBS News, January 10, 2013, https://www.cbsnews.com/news/pastor-drops-out-of-inauguration-over-anti-gay-sermon/.
37. R. Albert Mohler Jr., "The Giglio Imbroglio—The Public Inauguration of a New Moral McCarthyism," Albert Mohler, January 10, 2013, https://albertmohler.com/2013/01/10/the-giglio-imbroglio-the-public-inauguration-of-a-new-moral-mccarthyism.
38. Mohler Jr., "The Giglio Imbroglio."
39. Some, like Professor Robert Oscar Lopez, were forced to take stands and speak out. Thankfully he and others have refused to be silenced. See, for example, Robert Oscar Lopez and Brittany Klein, eds., *Jephthah's Children: The Innocent Casualties of Same-Sex Parenting* (London: Wilberforce Publications, 2016).
40. For a major statement filled with grace, see "Statement on Biblical Sexuality," Changed Movement, accessed November 2, 2021, https://changedmovement.com/statement-of-belief.
41. Wikipedia, s.v. "List of U.S. Jurisdictions Banning Conversion Therapy," last edited October 21, 2021, 03:40, https://en.wikipedia.org/wiki/List_of_U.S._jurisdictions_banning_conversion_therapy. (This article reflects the prevailing hostile attitude toward "conversion therapy.")
42. Tim Fitzsimons, "Germany Is 5th Country to Ban Conversion Therapy for Minors," NBC News, May 8, 2020, https://www.nbcnews.com/feature/nbc-out/germany-5th-country-ban-conversion-therapy-minors-n1203166 (again, stated in hostile terms); "Israel: 'Gay Conversion' Therapy Ban Bill Passed by MPs," BBC, July 23, 2020, https://www.bbc.com/news/world-middle-east-53511329.
43. Tim Fitzsimons, "UN Calls for Global End to Conversion Therapy, Says It 'May Amount to Torture,'" NBC News, June 13, 2020, https://www.nbcnews.com/feature/nbc-out/u-n-calls-global-end-conversion-therapy-says-it-may-n1230851.
44. Michael Brown, "California's Shocking 'You Must Stay Gay' Bill," *The Stream*, April 5, 2018, https://stream.org/californias-shocking-must-stay-gay-bill/.
45. Matilda Marozzi, "Here Is What We Know About Victoria's Gay Conversion Bill," ABC News, February 3, 2021, https://www.abc.net.au/news/2021-02-04/victorian-gay-conversion-bill-what-is-it/13116998.
46. "Victorian Bill Banning Gay Conversion Therapy Passes Upper House as Amendments Fail," ABC News, February 4, 2021, abc.net.au/news/2021-02-05/victorias-gay-conversion-bill-passes-upper-house/13122058. It subsequently passed both houses and is currently going into effect. See Department of Justice and Community

Safety, "Change or Suppression Practices—Legislative Ban," Engage Victoria, accessed November 2, 2021, https://engage.vic.gov.au/changeorsuppression.

47. Brandon Showalter, "Amazon Pulls Books by Authors Who Once Identified as Gay, Lesbian," *Christian Post*, July 9, 2019, https://www.christianpost.com/news/amazon-pulls-books-by-authors-who-once-identified-as-gay-lesbian.html.
48. Beth Schwartzapfel, "Born This Way?," American Prospect, March 14, 2013, https://prospect.org/power/born-way/; Abigail Shrier, *Irreversible Damage: The Transgender Craze Seducing Our Daughters* (Washington, DC: Regnery, 2020), 123–126. Dr. Paul McHugh is also viewed as an enemy of the trans community; see Andrea James, "Paul McHugh vs. Transgender People," Transgender Map, accessed November 2, 2021, https://www.transgendermap.com/politics/psychiatry/paul-mchugh/.
49. Brown, "California's Shocking 'You Must Stay Gay' Bill."
50. Muehlenberg, "Criminalising Christianity, Prayer, and the Bible."
51. See David H. Pickup, "New Jersey Governor Christie Makes Himself Complicit in the Effects of Sexual Abuse Onto Children," Voice of the Voiceless, accessed November 2, 2021, https://www.voiceofthevoiceless.info/tag/brielle-goldani; Michael Brown, "Did a Gay Activist Lie to the New Jersey Senate?," Townhall, March 25, 2013, https://townhall.com/columnists/michaelbrown/2013/03/25/did-a-gay-activist-lie-to-the-new-jersey-senate-n1548304.
52. Michael Brown, "The Truth About So-Called 'Conversion Therapy,'" *Christian Post*, July 10, 2019, https://www.christianpost.com/voices/the-truth-about-so-called-conversion-therapy.html.
53. Otto v. City of Boca Raton, 981 F.3d 854, Casetext, November 20, 2020, https://casetext.com/case/otto-v-city-of-boca-raton-1. For an important, groundbreaking study pointing to the positive effects of counseling therapy, see https://www.reintegrativetherapy.com/news-release-2.
54. See "Stories," Changed Movement, accessed November 2, 2021, https://changedmovement.com/stories/.

CHAPTER 6

1. One of my ministry school graduates working in the Philippines told me how it felt to hold in his arms a three-year-old child who had been rescued from sex slavery. Who can imagine such evil?
2. Right to Life of Michigan, "National Statistics," *Black Abortions by the Numbers*, updated June 14, 2021, https://rtl.org/wp-content/uploads/2018/12/HopeForTomorrow_brochure.pdf.

3. Jason L. Riley, "Let's Talk About the Black Abortion Rate," *Wall Street Journal*, July 10, 2018, https://www.wsj.com/articles/lets-talk-about-the-black-abortion-rate-1531263697.
4. "Genocide: Black Abortions in America," Grand Rapids Right to Life, accessed November 2, 2021, https://www.grrtl.org/genocide.
5. Michael Brown, "The Soon-to-Be No. 1 Song Underscores Why We Need a Moral and Cultural Revolution," *The Stream*, August 13, 2020, https://stream.org/the-soon-to-be-no-1-song-underscores-why-we-need-a-moral-and-cultural-revolution/.
6. Several months after writing these words, I saw that Pastor John MacArthur had given a similar, much shorter summary during an interview with Laura Ingraham. He said, "America's in a moral free fall. You murder the babies in the womb. If they survive the womb, you try to seduce them into transgender sexual deviation when they're young. If they survive that, you corrupt them with a godless education....If they survive that, you have divorce in the family and if they grow to be adults, you drown them in a sea of pornography.... This is a nation so far down in the sewer of immorality and wickedness that nothing surprises me." Quoted in Ryan Foley, "'America Is in a Moral Free Fall,' John MacArthur Warns," *Christian Post*, November 20, 2020, https://www.christianpost.com/news/america-is-in-a-moral-free-fall-john-macarthur-says.html.
7. "Youth Suicide Statistics," The Jason Foundation: The Parent Resource Program, accessed November 2, 2021, http://prp.jasonfoundation.com/facts/youth-suicide-statistics/ (emphasis in the original). The number one cause of death for this age group is accidents. "Adolescent Health," Centers for Disease Control and Prevention, last reviewed June 11, 2021, https://www.cdc.gov/nchs/fastats/adolescent-health.htm. See also Gretchen Frazee and Patty Gorena Morales, "Suicide Among Teens and Young Adults Reaches Highest Level Since 2000," PBS News Hour, June 18, 2019, https://www.pbs.org/newshour/nation/suicide-among-teens-and-young-adults-reaches-highest-level-since-2000; Alia E. Dastagir, "More Young People Are Dying by Suicide, and Experts Aren't Sure Why," *USA Today*, September 11, 2020, https://www.usatoday.com/story/news/health/2020/09/11/youth-suicide-rate-increases-cdc-report-finds/3463549001/.
8. William Wan, "Teen Suicides Increasing at an Alarming Pace, Outstripping All Other Age Groups, a New Report Says" *Washington Post*, October 17, 2019, https://www.washingtonpost.com/health/

teen-suicides-increasing-at-alarming-pace-outstripping-all-other-age-groups/2019/10/16/e24194c6-f04a-11e9-8693-f487e46784aa_story.html.

9. David M. Cutler, Edward L. Glaeser, and Karen E. Norberg, "Explaining the Rise in Youth Suicide," in *Risky Behavior Among Youths: An Economic Analysis*, ed. Jonathan Gruber (Chicago: University of Chicago Press, 2001), 219–220.
10. Centers for Disease Control and Prevention, "Surveillance Summary Youth Suicide—United States, 1970–1980," *Morbidity and Mortality Weekly Report* 36, no. 6 (February 20, 1987): 87–89, https://www.cdc.gov/mmwr/preview/mmwrhtml/00000871.htm.
11. Amy Morin, "The Truth About Troubled Teens," Verywell Mind, April 4, 2021, https://www.verywellmind.com/what-is-happening-to-our-children-2606269.
12. "Child Sexual Abuse Statistics," National Center for Victims of Crime, accessed November 2, 2021, https://victimsofcrime.org/child-sexual-abuse-statistics/.
13. "Child Sexual Abuse Statistics," National Center for Victims of Crime.
14. Adrian Mojica, "FBI Issues Sobering Statistics on Child Pornography in the United States, Dark Web," Fox 17, April 26, 2017, https://fox17.com/news/local/fbi-issues-sobering-statistics-on-child-pornography-in-the-united-states-dark-web.
15. Barna Group, *The Porn Phenomenon: The Impact of Pornography in the Digital Age* (Plano, TX: Josh McDowell Ministry, 2016), 41, https://www.amazon.com/Porn-Phenomenon-Impact-Pornography-Digital/dp/0996584366.
16. "20 Mind-Blowing Stats About the Porn Industry and Its Underage Consumers," Fight the New Drug, December 4, 2020, https://web.archive.org/web/20210130132542/https://fightthenewdrug.org/10-porn-stats-that-will-blow-your-mind/.
17. "20 Mind-Blowing Stats About the Porn Industry and Its Underage Consumers," December 4, 2020.
18. KC, "20 Mind-Blowing Stats About the Porn Industry and Its Underage Consumers," Fight the New Drug, May 19, 2020, https://web.archive.org/web/20201101002259/https://fightthenewdrug.org/10-porn-stats-that-will-blow-your-mind/.
19. Nicholas Kristof, "Opinion: The Children of Pornhub," *New York Times*, December 4, 2020, https://www.nytimes.com/2020/12/04/opinion/sunday/pornhub-rape-trafficking.html.
20. Kristof, "Opinion: The Children of Pornhub."

21. "Top Websites Ranking," SimilarWeb, updated October 1, 2020, https://web.archive.org/web/20201202235546/https://www.similarweb.com/top-websites/.
22. Kristof, "Opinion: The Children of Pornhub."
23. Benedict Carey, "Getting a Handle on Self-Harm," *New York Times*, updated November 22, 2019, https://www.nytimes.com/2019/11/11/health/self-harm-injury-cutting-psychology.html.
24. Sherri Gordon, "5 Ways Social Media Affects Teen Mental Health," Verywell Family, July 13, 2020, https://www.verywellfamily.com/ways-social-media-affects-teen-mental-health-4144769.
25. Mayo Clinic Staff, "Teens and Social Media Use: What's the Impact?," Mayo Clinic, December 21, 2019, https://www.mayoclinic.org/healthy-lifestyle/tween-and-teen-health/in-depth/teens-and-social-media-use/art-20474437.
26. Randy Engel, *Sex Education: The Final Plague* (Charlotte, NC: TAN Books, 1993).
27. Engel, *Sex Education*, 4.
28. Engel, *Sex Education*, 109.
29. Michael Brown, "Please Stop Sexualizing Our Children," Townhall, August 14, 2011, https://townhall.com/columnists/michaelbrown/2011/08/14/please-stop-sexualizing-our-children-n1263279. See also Michael Brown, "Please Stop Sexualizing Our Children (Part II)," Townhall, August 16, 2011, https://townhall.com/columnists/michaelbrown/2011/08/16/please-stop-sexualizing-our-children-part-ii-n806457.
30. Michael Brown, "Outrage for the Children," *The Stream*, August 21, 2020, https://stream.org/outrage-for-the-children/.
31. Brown, "Outrage for the Children."
32. Michael Brown, "The Depravity of a Culture That Celebrates the Sexploitation of Young Girls," *The Stream*, September 11, 2020, https://stream.org/the-depravity-of-a-culture-that-celebrates-the-sexploitation-of-young-girls/.
33. Michael Brown, "You Do Not Exploit Children to Teach That Exploiting Children Is Wrong," *The Stream*, September 18, 2020, https://stream.org/you-do-not-exploit-children-to-teach-that-exploiting-children-is-wrong/.
34. Martin Dale, "French Producer Zangro on Sundance Entry 'Cuties,' and Upcoming Project," *Variety*, January 14, 2020, https://variety.com/2020/film/global/zangro-sundance-cuties-1203467120/.
35. Michael Brown, "Sorry Netflix, but You Don't Get to Lecture Americans on Moral Understanding," *The Stream*, October 15, 2020,

https://stream.org/sorry-netflix-but-you-dont-get-to-lecture-americans-on-moral-understanding/.

36. Brown, "Sorry Netflix, but You Don't Get to Lecture Americans on Moral Understanding."

CHAPTER 7

1. Marisa Linton, "Ten Myths About the French Revolution," *Oxford University Press's Academic Insights for the Thinking World*, July 26, 2015, https://blog.oup.com/2015/07/ten-myths-french-revolution/; Editors of *Encyclopaedia Britannica*, "Reign of Terror," *Britannica*, August 29, 2020, https://www.britannica.com/event/Reign-of-Terror.
2. Al Perrotta, "CHOP…As in Madam Guillotine: We're Watching the Reboot of the French Revolution," *The Stream*, June 24, 2020, https://stream.org/chop-as-in-madam-guillotine-were-watching-the-reboot-of-the-french-revolution/.
3. Michael Brown, "What Are You Going to Do When They Come for You?," *The Stream*, June 30, 2020, https://stream.org/what-are-you-going-to-do-when-they-come-for-you.
4. Brown, "What Are You Going to Do When They Come for You?"
5. Michael Brown, "Then They Burned the Bibles," *The Stream*, August 4, 2020, https://stream.org/then-they-burned-the-bibles/.
6. Ian Miles Cheong (@stillgray), Twitter, August 1, 2020, 6:50 a.m., https://twitter.com/stillgray/status/1289513913856352256.
7. Brown, "Then They Burned the Bibles."
8. Krystina Skurk, "4 French Revolution Trends That Have Started in the United States," *The Federalist*, July 31, 2020, https://thefederalist.com/2020/07/31/4-french-revolution-trends-that-have-started-in-the-united-states/.
9. Michael Brown (@DrMichaelLBrown), "First they burned the federal buildings, then they burned the churches, now they're burning Bibles," Twitter, August 1, 2020, 3:14 p.m., https://twitter.com/DrMichaelLBrown/status/1289640617597952007.
10. "Mayor Wheeler on Rioters Setting Fire at Portland Police Building: 'You Are Attempting to Commit Murder,'" Fox 12, August 6, 2020, https://www.kptv.com/news/mayor-wheeler-on-rioters-setting-fire-at-portland-police-building-you-are-attempting-to-commit/article_8e01541e-d839-11ea-8736-4b746b521476.html.
11. Brown, "Then They Burned the Bibles."

12. For one example, see my interview with Steve Uggen: "Setting the Captives Free," June 2, 2020, in *The Line of Fire*, podcast, MP3 audio, http://thelineoffire.org/2020/06/02/setting-the-captives-free/.
13. Jenkins, "Introduction," 15.
14. Keith Ablow, "The Dark, Destructive, Murderous Psychological Forces of Cancel Culture," PJ Media, February 24, 2021, https://pjmedia.com/columns/keithablow/2021/02/24/the-dark-destructive-murderous-psychological-forces-of-cancel-culture-n1427981.
15. "The World Watch List," Open Doors, accessed November 2, 2021, https://www.opendoorsusa.org/christian-persecution/world-watch-list/.
16. She linked this article: "We'll Starve Schoolboys to Death—Niger Abductors," Punch, February 25, 2021, https://punchng.com/well-starve-schoolboys-to-death-niger-abductors/.
17. Joseph Parker, "Commentary on Matthew 3: Verses 1–6," *The People's Bible*, 1885–1895, https://www.studylight.org/commentaries/eng/jpb/matthew-3.html.
18. Keith Green, "Pledge My Head to Heaven," *So You Wanna Go Back to Egypt*, Sparrow Records, 1980, https://www.lyrics.com/lyric/2654996/Keith+Green/Pledge+My+Head+to+Heaven.
19. "The Persecution of Christians in the Middle East, and Jewish Updates," June 11, 2015, in *The Line of Fire*, podcast, http://thelineoffire.org/2015/06/11/the-persecution-of-christians-in-the-middle-east-and-jewish-updates/; see also Tom Doyle, *Killing Christians: Living the Faith Where It's Not Safe to Believe, with Greg Webster* (Nashville: W Publishing Group, 2015).
20. For a free English edition online, see Richard Wurmbrand, *Tortured for Christ* (London: Hodder & Stoughton, 2005), https://www.richardwurmbrandfoundation.com/pdfs/tfc-english-original.pdf.
21. George Yancey and David A. Williamson, *So Many Christians, So Few Lions: Is There Christianophobia in the United States?* (Lanham, MD: Rowman & Littlefield, 2015), 12; see also George Yancey, *Compromising Scholarship: Religious and Political Bias in American Higher Education* (Waco, TX: Baylor University Press, 2017).
22. George Yancey, *Hostile Environment: Understanding and Responding to Anti-Christian Bias* (Downers Grove, IL: InterVarsity Press, 2015), 9–10.
23. Yancey, *Hostile Environment*, 10.
24. Yancey, *Hostile Environment*, 19–20.
25. Yancey, *Hostile Environment*, 21.
26. I received an email from a colleague who was present at the Sacramento rally and documented this information; none of the gay activists with whom I shared the email denied the report. For a

sustained (and, quite frankly, laughable) attempt to justify the "Taliban" and "jihadist" rhetoric, see Markos Moulitsas, *American Taliban: How War, Sex, Sin, and Power Bind Jihadists and the Radical Right* (Sausalito, CA: PoliPoint Press, 2010).

27. Michael Brown, "When Committed Christians Are Compared to ISIS," *The Stream*, September 13, 2015, https://stream.org/committed-christians-compared-isis/.
28. "Olbermann vs. Trump #2: Trump's Plan to Nullify the Election," Keith Olbermann, October 8, 2020, video, 8:40–9:15, https://www.youtube.com/watch?v=nzFtT4yKiZY.
29. Richard Deitsch, "Craig James Out at Fox Sports Southwest After One Appearance," *Sports Illustrated*, September 2, 2013, https://www.si.com/college/2013/09/02/craig-james-will-not-return-fox-sports-southwest.
30. Tony Perkins, "Fox Sports Sacks Outspoken Christian," Charisma News, September 11, 2013, https://www.charismanews.com/opinion/40945-fox-sports-sacks-outspoken-christian.
31. Perkins, "Fox Sports Sacks Outspoken Christian."
32. Deitsch, "Craig James Out at Fox Sports Southwest After One Appearance."
33. Perkins, "Fox Sports Sacks Outspoken Christian."
34. Michael Brown, "Keith Olbermann, Craig James and a Shocking Example of Double Standards," Townhall, September 12, 2013, https://townhall.com/columnists/michaelbrown/2013/09/12/keith-olbermann-craig-james-and-a-shocking-example-of-double-standards-n1698037.
35. Jase Peeples, "WATCH: Keith Olbermann Sochi Olympics Rant," *Advocate*, September 10, 2013, https://www.advocate.com/politics/2013/09/10/keith-olbermann-sochi-olympics-rant. See further Michael Brown, "Will Christians Be Prosecuted and Removed from Society?," *The Stream*, November 10, 2020, https://stream.org/will-christians-be-prosecuted-and-removed-from-society/.
36. Perkins, "Fox Sports Sacks Outspoken Christian."
37. Stella Morabito, "7 Open Leftist Threats That Political Terror Is Coming to America Whether Trump Wins or Not," *The Federalist*, October 26, 2020, https://thefederalist.com/2020/10/26/7-open-leftist-threats-that-political-terror-is-coming-to-america-whether-trump-wins-or-not/.
38. Morabito, "7 Open Leftist Threats That Political Terror Is Coming to America Whether Trump Wins or Not."
39. Morabito, "7 Open Leftist Threats That Political Terror Is Coming to America Whether Trump Wins or Not." For this guillotine event, see James Crowley, "Protesters Put Life-Size Donald Trump Doll in

Guillotine Outside White House," *Newsweek*, August 28, 2020, https://www.newsweek.com/protest-trump-doll-guillotine-outside-white-house-rnc-1528381.
40. Morabito, "7 Open Leftist Threats That Political Terror Is Coming to America Whether Trump Wins or Not."
41. Joe Biden (@JoeBiden), "After a year of pain and loss, it's time to unite, heal, and rebuild," Twitter, December 26, 2020, 7:45 p.m., https://twitter.com/JoeBiden/status/1342994857023983616.
42. David Cross (@davidcrosss), "[Expletive] that. I want blood," Twitter, December 26, 2020, 11:38 p.m., https://twitter.com/davidcrosss/status/1343053684347908097. In a follow-up, and in an apparent attempt at humor, he said, "I was referring to menstrual blood." (David Cross [@davidcrosss], Twitter, December 27, 2020, 5:17 p.m., https://twitter.com/davidcrosss/status/1343320092491313162.)
43. Justin Caruso, "David Cross Jokes About Beating Trump 'to a Bloody Pulp,'" Breitbart, August 24, 2018, https://www.breitbart.com/entertainment/2018/08/24/david-cross-jokes-beating-trump-bloody-pulp/.
44. David Ng, "Debra Messing Confirms She Wished 'Violence' on Trump, Hopes He Becomes Rape 'Victim,'" Breitbart, December 14, 2020, https://www.breitbart.com/entertainment/2020/12/14/debra-messing-defends-saying-she-hopes-trump-is-the-most-popular-boyfriend-in-prison/.
45. Bob Price, "WATCH: Antifa Forces Portland Bookstore Closure Over Journalist's Forthcoming Book," Breitbart, January 12, 2021, https://www.breitbart.com/law-and-order/2021/01/12/watch-antifa-forces-portland-bookstore-closure-over-journalists-forthcoming-book/.
46. Victoria Taft, "Seattle Antifa Hate Group Threatens to Burn Down Church Over Event With Charlie Kirk," PJ Media, April 24, 2021, https://pjmedia.com/news-and-politics/victoria-taft/2021/04/24/seattle-antifa-hate-group-threatens-to-burn-down-church-over-event-with-charlie-kirk-n1442372.

CHAPTER 8

1. See also Matthew 16:25; Mark 8:35; Luke 9:24; 14:26–27; John 12:24–25.
2. Quoted in Takim Williams, "InContext: Martin Luther King Jr.," Human Trafficking Institute, January 16, 2017, https://www.traffickinginstitute.org/incontext-martin-luther-king-jr/.

3. Robert Kraychik, "Exclusive—Ben Carson: 'Child Abuse' to Prey on Children's Curiosity With Transgender Ideology," Breitbart, February 26, 2021, https://www.breitbart.com/radio/2021/02/26/exclusive-ben-carson-child-abuse-prey-childrens-curiosity-transgender-ideology/.
4. Kraychik, "Exclusive—Ben Carson: 'Child Abuse' to Prey on Children's Curiosity With Transgender Ideology."
5. Kraychik, "Exclusive—Ben Carson: 'Child Abuse' to Prey on Children's Curiosity With Transgender Ideology."
6. Richard Menger, "A Neurosurgeon's View on Cancel Culture and Virtue Signaling," Foundation for Economic Education, February 7, 2021, https://fee.org/articles/a-neurosurgeons-view-on-cancel-culture-and-virtue-signaling/.

CHAPTER 9

1. "John Bunyan," *Christian History*, accessed November 2, 2021, https://www.christianitytoday.com/history/people/musiciansartistsandwriters/john-bunyan.html.
2. "John Bunyan," *Christian History*.
3. "Act of Uniformity 1662," UK Parliament, accessed November 2, 2021, https://www.parliament.uk/about/living-heritage/transformingsociety/private-lives/religion/collections/common-prayer/act-of-uniformity-1662/.
4. "The Clarendon Code Facts and Worksheets," School History, accessed November 2, 2021, https://schoolhistory.co.uk/notes/clarendon-code/.
5. Bunyan was actually imprisoned on two or three different occasions, and there is debate as to how much of *The Pilgrim's Progress* was written during which specific imprisonments.
6. Leland Ryken, "10 Things You Should Know About *The Pilgrim's Progress*," Crossway, October 1, 2019, https://www.crossway.org/articles/10-things-you-should-know-about-pilgrims-progress/.
7. "John Bunyan," *Christian History*.
8. "John Bunyan," *Christian History*.
9. D. L. Jeffrey, "Bunyan, John," in *Biographical Dictionary of Evangelicals*, ed. Timothy Larsen et al. (Downers Grove, IL: InterVarsity Press, 2003), 101.
10. Jeffrey, "Bunyan, John," 99.
11. Jeff Robinson, "Romanian Josef Tson Recounts God's Grace Amid Suffering," Baptist Press, July 19, 2004, https://www.baptistpress.com/

resource-library/news/romanian-josef-tson-recounts-gods-grace-amid-suffering/.
12. Robinson, "Romanian Josef Tson Recounts God's Grace Amid Suffering."

CHAPTER 10

1. Printed with his permission.
2. Muehlenberg, "Criminalising Christianity, Prayer, and the Bible."
3. Bill Muehlenberg, "The Trans War on Everything," Culture Watch, March 3, 2021, https://billmuehlenberg.com/2021/03/03/the-trans-war-on-everything/.
4. Acevedo, "From John David to David Acevedo."
5. For an excellent summary, see Lawrence S. Mayer and Paul R. McHugh, *Sexuality and Gender: Findings From the Biological, Psychological, and Social Sciences* (Washington, DC: The New Atlantis, 2016), https://www.thenewatlantis.com/wp-content/uploads/legacy-pdfs/20160819_TNA50SexualityandGender.pdf.
6. See, for example, "About Us," Brothers Road, accessed November 2, 2021, https://brothersroad.org/our-choice/.
7. Changed Movement, website, accessed November 2, 2021, https://changedmovement.com/.
8. "Stories," Changed Movement, accessed November 2, 2021, https://changedmovement.com/stories/.
9. *CHANGED: #OnceGay Stories*, accessed November 2, 2021, https://changedmovement.com/changed-book.
10. Gwen Aviles, "Ex-Gays Descend Upon D. C. to Lobby Against LGBTQ Rights," NBC News, October 30, 2019, https://www.nbcnews.com/feature/nbc-out/ex-gays-descend-upon-d-c-lobby-against-lgbtq-rights-n1074211.
11. Amanda Casanova, "Former Lesbian Rallies Against Bill That Would Ban 'Conversion Therapy,'" 99.5 KKLA, June 14, 2018, https://kkla.com/articles/blogs/religion-today-blog/former-lesbian-rallies-against-bill-that-would-ban-conversion-therapy.

CHAPTER 11

1. Mckenna Dallmeyer, "Harvard Business School Club of NY Cancels Speaker From…Cancel Culture Talk: Report," Campus Reform, February 26, 2021, https://campusreform.org/article?id=16920.

2. Ben Zeisloft, "Math Education Prof: 2 + 2 = 4 'Trope' 'Reeks of White Supremacy Patriarchy,'" Campus Reform, August 8, 2020, https://campusreform.org/article?id=15409.
3. Ben Zeisloft, "Academics Called Breastfeeding 'Ethically Problematic' Because It Endorses 'Gender Roles.' Their View Is Gaining Traction," Campus Reform, February 16, 2021, https://campusreform.org/article?id=16833.
4. Dion J. Pierre, "Cancel Culture Comes for Thomas Jefferson… and Fails Miserably," Campus Reform, February 24, 2021, https://campusreform.org/article?id=16809.
5. Angela Morabito, "UW Profs Attempt to Explain Away Devastating Free Speech Survey Results," Campus Reform, February 24, 2021, https://campusreform.org/article?id=16804.
6. James Delingpole, "Only 'Kamikaze Academics' Can Save Our Universities From Cancel Culture," Breitbart, August 15, 2020, https://www.breitbart.com/europe/2020/08/15/delingpole-only-kamikaze-academics-can-save-our-universities-cancel-culture/.
7. Delingpole, "Only 'Kamikaze Academics' Can Save Our Universities From Cancel Culture."
8. Daniel B. Ravicher, "As a Conservative UM Professor, I'm Fighting the Campus Cancel Culture," *Miami Herald*, December 13, 2020, https://www.miamiherald.com/article247812580.html.
9. Ravicher, "As a Conservative UM Professor, I'm Fighting the Campus Cancel Culture."
10. "'Unashamed Conservative' Professor Refuses to Back Down Against Cancel Culture Mob," The College Fix, December 14, 2020, https://www.thecollegefix.com/bulletin-board/unashamed-conservative-professor-refuses-to-back-down-against-cancel-culture-mob/.
11. "'Unashamed Conservative' Professor Refuses to Back Down Against Cancel Culture Mob," The College Fix.
12. John McWhorter, "Academics Are Really, Really Worried About Their Freedom," *The Atlantic*, September 1, 2020, https://www.theatlantic.com/ideas/archive/2020/09/academics-are-really-really-worried-about-their-freedom/615724/.
13. McWhorter, "Academics Are Really, Really Worried About Their Freedom."
14. McWhorter, "Academics Are Really, Really Worried About Their Freedom."
15. McWhorter, "Academics Are Really, Really Worried About Their Freedom."

16. Elisabeth Elliot, ed., *The Journals of Jim Elliot* (Grand Rapids, MI: Fleming H. Revell, 2002), 174, https://www.amazon.com/exec/obidos/ASIN/0800758250/.
17. Elliot, *The Journals of Jim Elliot, 50.*
18. Elliot, *The Journals of Jim Elliot, 18. For a* discussion of these quotes, see Michael L. Brown, *Revolution: An Urgent Call to a Holy Uprising*, 2nd ed. (Lake Mary, FL: Charisma House, 2020), 57.
19. Brown, *Revolution*, 205–228.
20. "How Japan's Youth See the Kamikaze Pilots of WW2," BBC, November 3, 2017, https://www.bbc.com/news/world-asia-39351262.

CHAPTER 12

1. Susan Berry, "Joe Biden Day 1: Order on Transgender Rights in Sports and Bathrooms," Breitbart, January 15, 2021, https://www.breitbart.com/politics/2021/01/15/joe-biden-day-1-order-on-transgender-rights-in-sports-and-bathrooms/.
2. Casey Chalk, "Virginia Plans for All Public Schools to Allow Boys in Girls' Bathrooms and Sleepovers," *The Federalist*, January 14, 2021, https://thefederalist.com/2021/01/14/virginia-plans-for-all-public-schools-to-allow-boys-in-girls-bathrooms-and-sleepovers/.
3. Ashe Schow, "Virginia's New Transgender Rules for Public Schools: Use Preferred Pronouns, Don't Question Bathroom Choices," *Daily Wire*, January 16, 2021, https://www.dailywire.com/news/virginias-new-transgender-rules-for-public-schools-use-preferred-pronouns-dont-question-bathroom-choices.
4. Samantha Schmidt, "Boy Scouts Must Settle 95,000 Abuse Claims by Next Summer—or Risk Running Out of Cash," *Washington Post*, November 19, 2020, https://www.washingtonpost.com/dc-md-va/2020/11/19/boy-scouts-bankruptcy-abuse/.
5. Mary Kay Linge and Susan Edelman, "NY Lawmaker Wants Sex Ed for Kindergartners," *New York Post*, March 6, 2021, https://nypost.com/2021/03/06/ny-lawmaker-wants-sex-ed-for-kindergartners/.
6. Alex Parker, "New York Democrat Pushes for Sex Ed That Would School 11-Year-Olds in Pansexuality and Anal Sex," March 7, 2021, https://redstate.com/alexparker/2021/03/07/new-york-democrat-pushes-for-sex-ed-that-would-school-11-year-olds-in-pansexuality-and-anal-sex-n339217.
7. Faith Karimi, "Three Dads, a Baby and the Legal Battle to Get Their Names Added to a Birth Certificate," CNN, updated March 6, 2021,

https://www.cnn.com/2021/03/06/us/throuple-three-dads-and-baby-trnd/index.html.

8. Elizabeth Elizalde, "NYC School Encourages Kids to Stop Using Words Like 'Mom,' 'Dad' in 'Inclusive Language' Guide," *New York Post*, March 10, 2021, https://nypost.com/2021/03/10/nyc-school-encourages-kids-to-stop-using-words-mom-dad/.
9. Robbie Pennoyer (@Robbie_Pennoyer), Twitter, accessed November 2, 2021, https://twitter.com/robbie_pennoyer?lang=en.
10. M. L. Webb, *The GayBCs* (Philadelphia: Quirk Books, 2019), https://www.amazon.com/GayBCs-M-L-Webb/dp/1683691628/.
11. Dave Urbanski, "VIDEO: Woman Has Little Boy Read 'The GayBCs'—a Children's Book With Terms Like 'Bi,' 'Coming Out,' and 'Queer.' And the Reaction Is Swift," *The Blaze*, March 2, 2021, https://www.theblaze.com/news/video-little-boy-reads-the-gaybcs.
12. See the comment from *But Why Tho?*, "Editorial Reviews," *The GayBCs*, accessed November 2, 2021, https://www.amazon.com/GayBCs-M-L-Webb/dp/1683691628/.
13. See, for example, the David Parker story, recounted in Brown, *A Queer Thing Happened to America*, 102–106.
14. For this broader subject, see Michael L. Brown, *Has God Failed You? Finding Faith When You're Not Even Sure God Is Real* (Bloomington, MN: Chosen Books, 2021); for specific guidelines on LGBTQ issues, see Tom Gilson, *Critical Conversations: A Christian Parents' Guide to Discussing Homosexuality With Teens* (Grand Rapids, MI: Kregel, 2016).

CHAPTER 13

1. Jonathan Andersen, "John Wesley's 12 Rules for Preachers," Seedbed, October 20, 2015, https://www.seedbed.com/john-wesleys-12-rules-for-preachers/.
2. "The Best 18 Quotes From William Booth," *Caring Magazine*, July 2, 2020, https://caringmagazine.org/the-best-18-quotes-from-william-booth/.
3. "The Best 18 Quotes From William Booth," *Caring Magazine*.
4. "The Best 18 Quotes From William Booth," *Caring Magazine*.
5. "Evangelism Bootcamp," Christ for All Nations, accessed November 2, 2021, https://www.cfan.eu/bootcamp/.
6. Joe Oden, "*Empowered to Share* Bundle," Joe Oden Ministries, accessed November 2, 2021, https://joeodenministries.com/product/empowered-to-share-bundle/. Both Daniel and Joe are graduates

of our ministry school, the Brownsville Revival School of Ministry, which was birthed out of the Brownsville Revival.

7. O. Hallesby, *Prayer*, trans. Clarence J. Carlsen (Minneapolis: Augsburg, 1931), 36, https://christlifemin.org/assets/pdf/Prayer_O_Hallesby.pdf.

CHAPTER 14

1. A. T. Robertson, *Word Pictures in the New Testament* (Nashville: Broadman Press, 1933), 4:253, https://www.studylight.org/commentaries/eng/rwp/2-corinthians-10.html.
2. Colin G. Kruse, *The Second Epistle of Paul to the Corinthians: An Introduction and Commentary*, Tyndale New Testament Commentaries (Grand Rapids, MI: Eerdmans, 1987), 174–75, https://www.google.com/books/edition/The_Second_Epistle_of_Paul_to_the_Corint/8zRnGtL8HC4C.
3. Martin Luther King Jr., "Loving Your Enemies" (sermon, Dexter Avenue Baptist Church, Montgomery, AL, November 17, 1957), https://kinginstitute.stanford.edu/king-papers/documents/loving-your-enemies-sermon-delivered-dexter-avenue-baptist-church.
4. King, "Loving Your Enemies."
5. King, "Loving Your Enemies."
6. King, "Loving Your Enemies."
7. King, "Loving Your Enemies."
8. King, "Loving Your Enemies."
9. King, "Loving Your Enemies."
10. Martin Luther King Jr., *Strength to Love* (Minneapolis: Fortress Press, 2010), 47, https://www.amazon.com/Strength-Love-Martin-Luther-King/dp/0800697405/.
11. Martin Luther King Jr., "The Meaning of Forgiveness" (sermon, 1948–1954), https://kinginstitute.stanford.edu/king-papers/documents/meaning-forgiveness.

CHAPTER 15

1. Amanda Prestigiacomo, "SiriusXM, Pandora, CMT, iHeartRadio Pull Morgan Wallen Music Following N-Word Video Recorded by Neighbor," *Daily Wire*, February 4, 2021, https://www.dailywire.com/news/siriusxm-pandora-cmt-iheartradio-pull-morgan-wallen-music-following-n-word-video-recorded-by-neighbor.

2. Francesca Bacardi, "Morgan Wallen Apologizes for Using N-Word," Page Six, February 3, 2021, https://pagesix.com/2021/02/03/morgan-wallen-apologizes-for-using-n-word/.
3. Brown, "There Is No Mercy and No Redemption in Today's Cancel Culture."
4. Ashlyn E. Wallen, Instagram, February 5, 2021, https://www.instagram.com/p/CK74VsygS9i/.
5. For textual questions on this verse, see Bruce M. Metzger, *A Textual Commentary on the Greek New Testament* (London: United Bible Societies, 1975), 180.
6. For more on Pastor Wurmbrand, best known for his book *Tortured for Christ*, see chapter 17.
7. The Richard Wurmbrand Foundation offers free copies of some of their titles, including these: Richard Wurmbrand, *Christ in the Communist Prisons,* ed. Charles Foley (New York: Coward-McCann, Inc., 1968), https://www.richardwurmbrandfoundation.com/pdfs/IGU-english.pdf and Sabina Wurmbrand, *The Pastor's Wife*, ed. Charles Foley (n.p.; printed by the author, 1970), https://www.richardwurmbrandfoundation.com/pdfs/pw-english.pdf.
8. "Richard and Sabina Wurmbrand Interview in 1989," Promotions, February 10, 2014, video, 12:07, https://www.youtube.com/watch?v=helKvd5ymeE.
9. Corrie ten Boom, "Guideposts Classics: Corrie ten Boom on Forgiveness," *Guideposts*, November 1972, https://www.guideposts.org/better-living/positive-living/guideposts-classics-corrie-ten-boom-on-forgiveness.
10. Ten Boom, "Guideposts Classics: Corrie ten Boom on Forgiveness."
11. Ten Boom, "Guideposts Classics: Corrie ten Boom on Forgiveness."

CHAPTER 16

1. Joseph A. Wulfsohn, "Bill Maher's Warning to the Left: Cancel Culture Is 'Real' and 'Coming to a Neighborhood Near You,'" Fox News, February 27, 2021, https://www.foxnews.com/entertainment/bill-maher-cancel-culture-gina-carano-chris-harrison.
2. Wulfsohn, "Bill Maher's Warning to the Left."
3. Ian Hanchett, "Maher: Cancel Culture Is 'a Purge' With 'Mentality That Belongs in Stalin's Russia,'" July 30, 2021, https://www.breitbart.com/clips/2021/07/30/maher-cancel-culture-is-a-purge-with-mentality-that-belongs-in-stalins-russia/.

4. Tyler Stone, "Nicki Minaj: You Can't Speak for the Fear of the Mob Attacking You," RealClear Politics, September 17, 2021, https://www.realclearpolitics.com/video/2021/09/17/nicki_minaj_you_cant_speak_for_the_fear_of_the_mob_attacking_you.html.
5. Jeff Charles, "Maybe Conservatives Shouldn't Be All That Worried About Cancel Culture," RedState, March 21, 2021, https://redstate.com/jeffc/2021/03/21/maybe-conservatives-shouldnt-be-all-that-worried-about-cancel-culture-n347647.
6. Christian Toto, "Exclusive: The Anti-Woke Rapper Topping the Charts and Shocking the Music Industry," *Daily Wire*, accessed November 2, 2021, https://www.dailywire.com/news/exclusive-the-anti-woke-rapper-topping-the-charts-and-shocking-the-music-industry. For the lyrics to his song "Cancelled," see https://www.google.com/search?q=lyrics+tom+macdonald+cancelled.
7. For a summary, see Michael L. Brown, *Playing With Holy Fire: A Wake-Up Call to the Pentecostal-Charismatic Church* (Lake Mary, FL: Charisma House, 2018), 1–7, with references.
8. Lactantius, *The Divine Institutes*, Book V, trans. William Fletcher, in *Ante-Nicene Fathers*, vol. 7, ed. Alexander Roberts, James Donaldson, and A. Cleveland Coxe (Buffalo, NY: Christian Literature Publishing Co., 1886); rev. and ed. for New Advent by Kevin Knight, https://www.newadvent.org/fathers/07015.htm.
9. "William Tyndale: Did You Know?," *Christian History*, no. 16, *William Tyndale: Early Reformer & Bible Translator* (1987), https://www.christianitytoday.com/history/issues/issue-16/william-tyndale-did-you-know.html.
10. "A Letter From Prison, in Tyndale's Own Hand," *Christian History*, no. 16, *William Tyndale: Early Reformer & Bible Translator* (1987), https://www.christianitytoday.com/history/issues/issue-16/from-archives-letter-from-prison-in-tyndales-own-hand.html.
11. "William Tyndale: Did You Know?," *Christian History*.
12. "William Tyndale: Did You Know?," *Christian History*.
13. "John Wycliffe," *Christian History*, accessed November 2, 2021, https://www.christianitytoday.com/history/people/moversandshakers/john-wycliffe.html.
14. "John Wycliffe"; Mark Galli and Ted Olsen, ed., *131 Christians Everyone Should Know: From the Editors of* Christian History *Magazine* (Nashville: Broadman & Holman, 2000), 211.
15. *Apologeticus*, L.13. For convenient discussion, see Wikipedia, s.v. "*Apologeticus*," last modified August 11, 2021, 17:36, https://en.wikipedia.org/wiki/Apologeticus.

16. Philip Schaff, *The Creeds of Christendom, With a History and Critical Notes, vol. 1., The History of Creeds* (New York: Harper & Brothers, 1877), 1:703.
17. Philip Schaff, *History of the Christian Church, vol. 7, Modern Christianity: The German Reformation, 2nd ed.* (New York: Charles Scribner's Sons, 1910; Oak Harbor, WA: Logos Research Systems, 1997), https://ccel.org/ccel/schaff/hcc7/hcc7.ii.vi.x.html.
18. Sarah Kramer, "Victory! Supreme Court Rules for College Student Silenced From Sharing the Gospel," Alliance Defending Freedom, March 8, 2021, https://adflegal.org/blog/victory-supreme-court-rules-college-student-silenced-sharing-gospel.
19. Kramer, "Victory! Supreme Court Rules for College Student Silenced From Sharing the Gospel."
20. Kramer, "Victory! Supreme Court Rules for College Student Silenced From Sharing the Gospel."
21. Only Justice Roberts dissented. See Michael Gryboski, "Supreme Court Sides With Christian Student Barred From Preaching on Ga. College Campus," *Christian Post*, March 8, 2021, https://www.christianpost.com/news/scotus-sides-with-christian-student-prohibited-from-preaching.html.
22. Kramer, "Victory! Supreme Court Rules for College Student Silenced From Sharing the Gospel."
23. For another secular perspective, this time from the famed attorney and law professor Alan Dershowitz, see Jack Phillips, "Alan Dershowitz: All Americans Need to Fight Cancel Culture," *Epoch Times*, March 5, 2021, https://www.theepochtimes.com/alan-dershowitz-all-americans-need-to-fight-cancel-culture_3722191.html.

CHAPTER 17

1. Leziga Barikor, "Compelling Story of Joy Through Despair," *Northern Iowan*, March 22, 2018, https://www.northerniowan.com/8168/showcase/compelling-story-of-joy-through-despair/.
2. Merv Knight, "Tortured for Christ," Christian History Institute, *Christian History* 109 (2014), https://christianhistoryinstitute.org/magazine/article/tortured-for-christ.
3. Knight, "Tortured for Christ."
4. Knight, "Tortured for Christ."
5. Richard Wurmbrand, *Tortured for Christ* (London: Hodder & Stoughton, 1967), 116, https://www.richardwurmbrandfoundation.com/pdfs/tfc-english-original.pdf.

6. Richard Wurmbrand, *Christ in the Communist Prisons*, ed. Charles Foley (New York: Coward-McCann, 1968), 76, https://www.richardwurmbrandfoundation.com/pdfs/IGU-english.pdf.
7. Graham Hill, "No Kneed: Lyle Taylor Claims BLM Support Is 'Scandalous' and Reveals He Won't 'Blindly' Take Knee as Gesture Has Been 'Diluted,'" *The Sun (US)*, January 11, 2021, https://www.the-sun.com/sport/premier-league/2117115/lyle-taylor-blm-scandalous-knee/.
8. Patrick Grafton-Green, "Footballer Lyle Taylor Says BLM Is 'Marxist' and That He Will No Longer Take the Knee," LBC, February 19, 2021, https://www.lbc.co.uk/news/footballer-lyle-taylor-says-blm-is-marxist-and-that-he-will-no-longer-take-the-k/; see further Jack Montgomery, "Footballer to Stop Taking Knee, Brands BLM 'Marxist Group' Pushing 'Racial Unrest,'" Breitbart, February 20, 2021, https://www.breitbart.com/europe/2021/02/20/footballer-stop-taking-knee-brands-blm-marxist-group-pushing-racial-unrest/.
9. "A Statement From the Brentford FC Dressing Room," Brentford Football Club, February 13, 2021, https://www.brentfordfc.com/news/2021/february/a-statement-from-the-brentford-fc-dressing-room/.
10. Grafton-Green, "Footballer Lyle Taylor Says BLM Is 'Marxist' and That He Will No Longer Take the Knee."
11. Tristi Rodriguez, "'I'm a Christian': Giants Pitcher Sam Coonrod Won't Kneel for BLM Moment of Unity," KRON 4, July 24, 2020, https://www.kron4.com/news/bay-area/im-a-christian-giants-pitcher-sam-coonrod-wont-kneel-for-blm-moment-of-unity/. For another example of an athlete pushing back, see Daniel Canova, "Ex-Virginia Tech Soccer Star Sues Coach, Claims He Forced Her off Team Because She Wouldn't Kneel," Fox News, April 22, 2021, https://www.foxnews.com/sports/ex-virginia-tech-soccer-star-sues-coach-claims-forced-her-off-team-she-wouldnt-kneel.
12. Michael Brown, "An Appeal to Bethany Christian Services to Reconsider Their Decision Regarding Gay Adoption," *The Stream*, March 3, 2021, https://stream.org/an-appeal-to-bethany-christian-services-to-reconsider-their-decision-regarding-gay-adoption/.
13. Albert Mohler, *The Briefing*, transcript, March 2, 2021, https://albertmohler.com/2021/03/02/briefing-3-2-21.

CHAPTER 18

1. Jordan B. Peterson, *Maps of Meaning: The Architecture of Belief* (New York: Routledge, 1999).
2. Zack Beauchamp, "Jordan Peterson, the Obscure Canadian Psychologist Turned Right-Wing Celebrity, Explained," *Vox*, May 21, 2018, https://www.vox.com/world/2018/3/26/17144166/jordan-peterson-12-rules-for-life.
3. Wikipedia, s.v. "Jordan Peterson," last edited October 29, 2021, 2:26, https://en.wikipedia.org/wiki/Jordan_Peterson. See further Izzy Kalman, "The Meteoric Rise of Professor Jordan Peterson," *Psychology Today*, February 4, 2018, https://www.psychologytoday.com/us/blog/resilience-bullying/201802/the-meteoric-rise-professor-jordan-peterson, where it is noted: "Amazingly, he has skyrocketed from relative obscurity to international celebrity in a couple of weeks!" And what was the key? "The massive support he gets from young adults—especially males—is an indication of their hunger for truth and responsibility. Feeding them with good science and the wisdom of the ages, he dispels the irrational, counterproductive beliefs with which they have been inculcated and provides them with instructions for taking charge of their lives. His teachings offer salvation not only for individuals, but also for society as a whole."
4. "Prof. Jordan Peterson Hunger Strike If Jailed Over Trans Bill: 'I'm NOT Doing This & That's That,'" LGBT Canada in the Media, video, 1:23, October 27, 2016, https://www.youtube.com/watch?v=WQ-M5MgqVOo.
5. "Dr. Jordan B. Peterson Announces the Follow-Up to His Global Bestseller *12 Rules of Life*," Penguin Random House, November 24, 2020, https://global.penguinrandomhouse.com/announcements/dr-jordan-b-peterson-announces-the-follow-up-to-his-global-bestseller-12-rules-of-life.
6. Jordan B. Peterson (@jordanbpeterson), Twitter, accessed November 2, 2021, https://twitter.com/jordanbpeterson.
7. Jordan B. Peterson, YouTube, accessed November 2, 2021, https://www.youtube.com/user/JordanPetersonVideos.
8. Brown, "Can You Be Gay and Christian?"
9. Michael Brown, "YouTube-Google Accused of Homophobia for Promoting My Video on LGBTQ Channels," *The Stream*, June 4, 2018, https://stream.org/youtube-google-accused-homophobia-promoting-video-lgbtq-channels/.
10. Brown, "How LGBT Activism Works, Illustrated in Front of Our Eyes."

11. Andrews Liptak, "YouTube Apologizes to LGBTQ Creators Over Issues With Its Ad and Monetization Policies," *The Verge*, July 1, 2018, https://www.theverge.com/2018/7/1/17522830/youtube-apology-lgbtq-creators-ads-demonitization-policies; Michael Brown, "YouTube Gets Flack for Advertising Our Video," *Line of Fire*, June 5, 2018, https://www.truthnetwork.com/show/line-of-fire-dr-michael-brown/4641/.
12. Michael Brown, "Google vs. God's Word," *The Stream*, March 19, 2019, https://stream.org/google-vs-gods-word/.
13. We had to delete hundreds of comments because of profanity and other violations of our own guidelines. As for the ratio between thumbs up and thumbs down, we are normally better than 95 percent to 5 percent. But because this video has been viewed by so many who differ with us, there are many more negative responses than normal. For our part, we are glad that people are watching.
14. Brown, "How LGBT Activism Works, Illustrated in Front of Our Eyes." I am not sure why, but YouTube has purged some of these LGBT videos of the great majority of their views, reducing some from millions to less than one hundred thousand. The count of a cumulative total of more 35 million views between all the videos bashing "Can You Be Gay and Christian?" was accurate as of early 2019.
15. Sen. Josh Hawley Writing Book: 'The Tyranny of Big Tech,'" AP News, October 16, 2020, https://apnews.com/article/entertainment-josh-hawley-media-social-media-f40a7667bef5af155397bc2004775b0b.
16. Rebecca Klar, "GOP Senator Writing Book Criticizing Big Tech for 'Tyranny,'" The Hill, October 16, 2020, https://thehill.com/homenews/senate/521425-gop-senator-writing-book-criticizing-big-tech-for-tyranny.
17. "Simon & Schuster Statement Regarding the Tyranny of Big Tech by Josh Hawley," Simon & Schuster, January 7, 2021, http://about.simonandschuster.biz/news/josh-hawley/.
18. Mollie Hemingway, "Josh Hawley Book on Big Tech Tyranny to Be Published Despite Cancellation Attempt," *The Federalist*, January 18, 2021, https://thefederalist.com/2021/01/18/josh-hawley-book-on-big-tech-tyranny-to-be-published-despite-cancellation-attempt/.
19. Alison Durkee, "Josh Hawley's Controversial Book Becomes a Bestseller—With Help From His 'Big Tech' Foes and Bulk Buys," *Forbes*, updated May 15, 2021, https://www.forbes.com/sites/alisondurkee/2021/05/14/josh-hawley-controversial-book-tyranny-of-big-tech-becomes-a-bestseller-with-help-from-his-big-tech-foes-and-bulk-buys/?sh=c76680e1b914.

20. Tim Pearce, "Fans Carry Morgan Wallen to 3 Billboard Music Awards After Ban, Deplatforming Over Leaked N-Word Video," *Daily Wire*, May 24, 2021, https://www.dailywire.com/news/fans-carry-morgan-wallen-to-3-billboard-music-awards-after-ban-deplatforming-over-leaked-n-word-video.
21. For the full letter, see Derek Sloan, letter to Rob Hoogland, https://www.massresistance.org/docs/gen4/21b/Rob-Hoogland-freed-from-prison/images/Derek-Sloan-letter.pdf; for further background, see "Rob Hoogland Is Freed From Prison! Powerful New Attorney Takes Over His Case and Successfully Files for Appeal," Mass Resistance, May 7, 2021, https://www.massresistance.org/docs/gen4/21b/Rob-Hoogland-freed-from-prison/index.html.
22. Gwendolyn Sims, "Look What Happened When a Professor Questioned His University's Diversity/Equity/Inclusion Efforts," PJ Media, October 6, 2021, https://pjmedia.com/culture/gwendolynsims/2021/10/06/look-what-happened-when-a-professor-questioned-his-universitys-diversity-equity-inclusion-efforts-n1522219.
23. Gwendolyn Sims, "UPDATE: Professor Canceled by Woke Outrage Mob Has Last Laugh," PJ Media, October 12, 2021, https://pjmedia.com/news-and-politics/gwendolynsims/2021/10/12/update-professor-canceled-by-woke-outrage-mob-has-last-laugh-n1523199.

CHAPTER 19

1. "April 14: Holidays and Observances (Alphabetical Order)," Holidays-and-Observances.com, accessed November 2, 2021, http://www.holidays-and-observances.com/april-14.html.
2. "April 14: Holidays and Observances (Alphabetical Order)."
3. "International LGBTQA Dates to Know," LGBTQA Center, Wright State University, accessed November 2, 2021, https://www.wright.edu/inclusive-excellence/culture-and-identity-centers/lgbtqa-affairs/international-lgbtqa-dates-to-know; Wikipedia, s.v. "National Coming Out Day," last edited October 11, 2021, 20:25, https://en.wikipedia.org/wiki/National_Coming_Out_Day.
4. "The Reverend Dr. Martin Luther King, Jr. at Oberlin," Electronic Oberlin Group, accessed November 2, 2021, https://www2.oberlin.edu/external/EOG/BlackHistoryMonth/MLK/MLKmainpage.html.

My FREE GIFT to You

Thank you for reading my book. I hope it has empowered you to tear off and shred the muzzle that has been placed on conservative Christians and to take a stance of boldness in our generation.

As my way of saying thank you, I am offering you the e-book for *Jezebel's War With America*...for **FREE!**

Jezebel was the wickedest woman in the Bible. She killed the prophets, led Israel into idolatry and immorality, and emasculated men. She was seductive and determined to snuff out the voices coming against her, because these voices were calling out for repentance.

This book will show you how the spirit of Jezebel is active in America today and teach you how to protect the church.

To get this **FREE** gift, scan the code below with your smartphone or go to **BooksByDrBrown.com/freegift**.

God bless,

Dr. Michael L. Brown

SCAN FOR FREE GIFT